THE HAKKAS OF SARAWAK

Sacrificial Gifts in Cold War Era Malaysia

This book tells the story of the Hakka Chinese in Sarawak, Malaysia, who were targeted as communists or communist sympathizers because of their Chinese ethnicity in the 1960s and 1970s. Thousands of these rural Hakkas were relocated into "new villages" surrounded by barbed wire or detained at correction centres, where incarcerated people were understood to be "sacrificial gifts" to the war on communism and to the rule of Malaysia's judicial-administrative regime.

In this study, Kee Howe Yong looks at how these incarcerated people struggled for survival and dealt with their defeat over the course of a generation. Through extensive ethnographic fieldwork and archival research, *The Hakkas of Sarawak* provides a powerful account of the ongoing legacies of Cold War oppression and its impact on the lives of people who were victimized.

(Anthropological Horizons)

KEE HOWE YONG is an assistant professor in the Department of Anthropology at McMaster University.

Anthropological Horizons

Editor: Michael Lambek, University of Toronto

This series, begun in 1991, focuses on theoretically informed ethnographic works addressing issues of mind and body, knowledge and power, equality and inequality, the individual and the collective. Interdisciplinary in its perspective, the series makes a unique contribution in several other academic disciplines: women's studies, history, philosophy, psychology, political science, and sociology.

For a list of the books published in this series see page 243.

KEE HOWE YONG

The Hakkas of Sarawak

Sacrificial Gifts in Cold War Era Malaysia

UNIVERSITY OF TORONTO PRESS
Toronto Buffalo London

ISBN 978-1-4426-4735-0 (cloth)
ISBN 978-1-4426-1546-5 (paper)

Publication cataloguing information
is available from Library and Archives Canada.

This book has been published with the help of a grant from the
Canadian Federation for the Humanities and Social Sciences, through
the Awards to Scholarly Publications Program, using funds provided by
the Social Sciences and Humanities Research Council of Canada.

University of Toronto Press acknowledges the financial assistance
to its publishing program of the Canada Council for the Arts and the
Ontario Arts Council.

Canada Council   Conseil des Arts
for the Arts   du Canada

ONTARIO ARTS COUNCIL
CONSEIL DES ARTS DE L'ONTARIO
50 YEARS OF ONTARIO GOVERNMENT SUPPORT OF THE ARTS
50 ANS DE SOUTIEN DU GOUVERNEMENT DE L'ONTARIO AUX ARTS

University of Toronto Press acknowledges the financial support of
the Government of Canada through the Canada Book Fund for its
publishing activities.

Contents

Acknowledgments

Summarizing the seeds that sustain a manuscript is an incredibly overwhelming experience. Indeed, I can only hope to make a few gestures of appreciation and acknowledgment towards the most pressing gratitude for those I am indebted to. If I left out some individuals, allow me to offer my apologies in advance. First, thanks are due to my dissertation committee for being a constant source of encouragement and guidance that in turn enabled bolder forays and critique. Vincent Crapanzano's incisive questions profoundly changed and deeply instructed how I think through the many issues of this project and beyond. Michael Blim not only knew when and how to nudge me along but also left me enough of my own space that I seem to require. Miki Makihara was especially insightful with the linguistic aspects of the data I amassed. Anna Tsing was and continues to be, from my first encounter with her work, a model for the possibilities of a reflexive and politically engaged research. But most of all, I am grateful to all of them for their confidence in me, even when my own was weak, and the enthusiasm they sustained for this project. I hope this work in some way reflects well on their teaching.

I would also like to thank Louise Lennihan and the late May Ebihara for guidance and support through graduate school. I am indebted to Nilajana Chatterjee for her tireless effort in thinking through the early phase of the proposal for this project. The same goes to Talal Asad for being such a careful interlocutor. I would also like to acknowledge Nancy Peluso who opened many doors for me to do fieldwork in Sarawak. Similar gratitude is due to Christine Padoch. In addition, I would like to thank former cohorts Molly Doane, Aseel Sawalha, Hugo Benavides, Murphy Halliburton, Yizhou Jiang, Banu Karaca, Ceren Ozgul, aRman aRtuc, and Raja Abillama who, at different junctures, offered much-needed sources of intellectual support as well as entertainment. I can't imagine how I could have survived graduate school without our program assistant, Ellen DeRiso. Her generosity and support can never be repaid. Similar gratitude is due to Heather Clarke, Janet Kaplan, and the late Charlotte Ann Frick. This manuscript would not have been possible without the financial support I received for my research. I am grateful for the Fulbright-Hays Doctoral Dissertation Research Abroad Grant, United Nations Ralph Bunche Fellowship, and a CUNY Writing Fellowship.

Of those who took time to work with me during my fieldwork, I would like to record my gratitude to Michael Leigh, Daniel Chew, Jayl Langub, and Kevin Egay. I would also like to thank the staff at the Sarawak Museum Library for their hospitality and assistance, especially to Puan Rokiah and Mrs. Chan. For fear of reprisals against those concerned, I deeply regret that I am unable to reveal the names of my interlocutors in Sarawak who worked with me, often at no little risk to themselves. I trust that they will recognize who they are and understand the depth of my gratitude to each of them should any of them ever happen to read this volume.

I am grateful to McMaster University, its Department of Anthropology – especially Petra Rethmann and Harvey Feit – who supported this project and helped to steer it through the final passage of this voyage. To my undergraduate students who took my "Reflections on the Gift Economy" classes, thanks so much. I also thank the editors of *Anthropological Quarterly* and *Critique of Anthropology* for permission to use versions of articles published with them in certain chapters of this work.

I am grateful and have learned a lot from the three anonymous reviewers' comments and engaged criticism. Thanks to the staff at the University of Toronto Press, especially to acquisitions editor Douglas Hildebrand and managing editor Anne Laughlin for so seamlessly bringing it to closure. Beth McAuley and Nina Hoeschele earned my gratitude for their careful copy-editing.

My deepest gratitude goes to the people in Sarawak, some mentioned in this book, some not, who received me in their homes, talked to me, and let me talk to them. I am forever grateful to them for their stories, their hospitality. I hope the book manages to convey my debt to them and much more. Naturally, none of those whom I have named above bear any responsibility for any aspects of the contents of this book, the onus of which rests on me alone.

THE HAKKAS OF SARAWAK

Sacrificial Gifts in Cold War Era Malaysia

Introduction

For the *three heroes* Wang Yong-zen, Loh Lian-chen, and Chong Yung-hwa, for we are also what we lost.

I have never met the *three heroes,* or the guerrillas who died in the jungles of Borneo, or those who were detained at correction centres or relocated into barbed-wire *new villages* in Sarawak during the Cold War. But through my journey of fieldwork over the course of twelve months, I learned about their sacrifices, their demise, and, equally important, the survivors who live to reluctantly talk about the ambiguities of the battles that they fought. In fact, the first time I heard of the *three heroes* was at a coffee shop by the Sarawak Omnibus Company (SOC) bus station in Kuching, Sarawak.[1] This was the morning I heard about the death of Ong Kee Hui, the former president of the Sarawak United People's Party (SUPP).

Interestingly enough, the topic that was immediately raised by some bus drivers and conductors at the coffee shop was whether there would be a funeral procession for Ong through certain streets of Kuching, as was traditionally the case for past Chinese leaders, including Ong's father and grandfather. But it was not to be. Ong's body would lie in state at the SUPP headquarter for two days and from there it would proceed to the Saint Thomas Cathedral for a memorial service before heading straight to the Kuching Hokkien cemetery.[2] There would be no procession, signifying perhaps that a certain landscape of memory associated with funeral processions for Chinese leaders through particular streets of Kuching was already on the brink of being lost – or of becoming history. The potentiality of this loss triggered those at the coffee shop to recall a funeral procession that took place in the early 1960s – one that was not only extremely grandiose, at least in the way they talked about it, but that defied the power of the State.

This was the funeral procession for the *three heroes* – two males and one female communist guerrilla – who were killed by the government. I was told that they symbolized the "never-give-up" mentality of the communist movements in Sarawak. There was a massive turnout for the funeral procession, with people coming from all over Sarawak – from Serian and Simanggang and as far away as Sibu and Miri, journeys that took an entire day. Some twenty or more busloads of people made it to the funeral procession. As a bus driver affirmed, "They were an angry lot! Yelling and swearing at the police, venting their anger at the violence unleashed by the government on the rural Chinese populations. Ibans and Bidayuhs were [at the funeral procession] as well, including some Malays."[3]

Today, there is a monument for the *three heroes* at the 7th Mile Hakka Association cemetery located next to the Kuching-Serian Road. The fact that it is located on a Hakka cemetery ground would suggest some sort of connection between the Hakkas in Sarawak and things that might be interpreted as communist, a violent inscription that will be addressed in this book.[4] I bring up this episode at the coffee shop to shed some light on the undesirable state of affairs that most, if not all, of my subjects experienced as hyphenated citizens of Malaysia. From what I was witnessing that morning, it seemed as if everyone had become something of a "historian with an axe to grind … [They were advancing] a claim, to levy praise and blame, and to … condemn the existing state of affairs" (Scott 1985, 178). They were *context statements* about a certain event which provided a frame for discussing specific episodes of violence in Sarawak.[5] Their comments on both funeral processions materialized out of a complex set of narratives that were affected by a certain collective memory.[6]

French sociologist Maurice Halbwachs ([1950] 1980) claims that the collective memory of any society is determined by the interplay of both its historical as well as its contemporaneous frame of reference. In other words, it is our social environment – the circumstances and conditions of our remembering – that shape our capacity to remember or, in the case of Sarawak, the will to forget. Influenced by Halbwachs's work, Pierre Nora (1996) and several French historians came up with the notion of *lieux de memoire* (sites of memory). These are basically external props "that help incite our remembering … tangible reminders of that which no longer exists except *qua* memory" (7–8). Borrowing the term of "loci memoriae" from classical mnemotechnique, Nora labels those places and events – artefacts, monuments, rituals, festivities, and funerals – as "sites of memory" that are capable of stimulating acts of recollection. Although Nora and his colleagues focus on the investigation of French history and society, one can discover similar trends and processes in other societies. This process is already visible in Sarawak. The inscription of (neo)liberal economic integration with its uneven economic development and new patterns of working relations are dissolving traditional structures and modes of living memory. In their stead we are witnessing the creation of archives, museums, and monuments – historical storehouses – that are imbued with all sorts of commemorative, even sentimental, value.[7]

As what happened that morning at the coffee shop, the signs and grandiosity of a previous funeral procession through a certain landscape of memory were the standard against which the funeral for Ong Kee Hui was assessed – along with the fact that he was not given the privilege of having a funeral procession through certain streets of Kuching. It was this absence that provided the stimulus for their remembering of an earlier event. As Paul Antze and Michael Lambeck (1996) remind us, "memories are never simply records of the past, but are interpretive reconstructions that bear the imprint of local narrative conventions, cultural assumptions, discursive formations and practices, and contexts of recall and commemoration" (vii). Narratives of the funeral procession and others that I have collected are useful for excavating certain Sarawak residents' pasts from being lost and, at the same time, offer a commentary on the contemporary conditions in Sarawak for certain communities.

Bumi Kenyalang

Known as *Bumi Kenyalang* (Land of the Hornbills), Sarawak is the largest state in the Federated States of Malaysia. It is located on the island of Borneo, which it shares with the Malaysian state of Sabah, the country of Brunei, and the Indonesian province of Kalimantan. Like other areas in Borneo under the Brunei Sultanate during the early part of the nineteenth century, Sarawak was in a state of constant battle among its different indigenous groups. However, Sarawak has a unique colonial history in that it was ruled not by a European empire but by a British family, the Brookes. When James Brooke, then a young English officer with the East India Company, arrived in Borneo in 1839, the sultan of Brunei sought his help to subjugate a local rebellion. For that, James was not only awarded the title of White Rajah but a sizable territory in what was to become known as Sarawak (Runciman 1960; Walker 2002). This sizable territory is called Kuching today. Thus, when one talks about Sarawak in the historical sense, one is really talking about Kuching. Looking at the size of Sarawak today in contrast to that of Brunei will give one an idea of the relentless pressure the Brookes exerted on the Brunei Sultanate in pursuit of land and resources.

The Brookes dynasty lasted about a century. During this time the infrastructure of Sarawak flourished, especially in Kuching, its administrative capital. Kuching was a trading centre with settlers coming from far away. Over time, Chinese, Malays, South Asians, Europeans, and others joined with the many indigenous groups to create a vibrant and rich cultural heritage that is uniquely Sarawak. The Brookes dynasty, which started with James Brooke, lead to his nephew Charles, and finally to Charles's son, Vyner, ended when Japan invaded Sarawak in 1941.

Sarawak suffered much during the Japanese Occupation. Its economy was devastated and starvation was widespread due to the Allied blockage of the shipping lanes for the distribution of goods, especially rice. But what the Occupation did was send shock waves across the region as British protectorates and the Netherlands Indies fell almost without a fight. Southeast Asian specialist Harry Benda (1972) even went so far as to suggest that "history" was fundamentally changed by the Occupation, especially in the Netherland Indies "since the destruction of the colonial *status quo* directly led to the subsequent, and still contemporary, era of revolution, liberation, and modern nationhood" (148, cited in Reid 2005, 180). Others took a more detached view of the importance of the Occupation, arguing for the continuities between European and Japanese colonial policies and the subsequent development of Southeast Asian nationalism.[8] Regardless of the debate, all parties to the war in the Pacific understood it as a race war (Daws 1994, 17, cited in Reid 2005, 178).[9]

To be sure, it was not just a race war between Imperial Japan and various European empires. With a growing Chinese nationalist consciousness that had been spawned by modern education, which inculcated a uniform "Mandarin Chinese" identity, and buoyed by Sun Yat-sen's republican movement in China and the atrocities of the Rape of Nanjing, the Japanese Occupation was received differently by the Chinese in Southeast Asia.[10] The Japanese military knew that many Chinese organizations were involved in anti-Japanese mobilization and boycotts, thus they were the main victims of Japanese military brutalities.[11] By contrast, nascent Malay nationalists in British Malaya and the Netherland Indies were given unprecedented opportunities through Japanese propaganda organizations, something that "widened and embittered the gap between Chinese nationalism and its local equivalents" (Reid 2010, 67).

When Japan surrendered in 1945, Sarawak was placed under the Australian Military Administration, and it was ceded to Britain in 1946. Sarawakians were divided on the cession, as witnessed by massive resignations of government officers and teachers as well as growing anti-cessionist movements. Eventually these anti-cession movements subsided and on September 16, 1963, Sarawak *became* part of the Federated States of Malaysia under the Greater Malaysia Plan that included the territories of Malaya, Singapore, Sarawak, and North Borneo (Sabah), a move that haunts the majority of the population of Sarawak and Sabah to this day.

Less than a year after Malaysia was formed, ethnic riots hit Singapore in opposition to it. A year later, Singapore was expelled from the Federation by the leaders of the United Malays National Organization (UMNO), the main proponent of the Alliance government in West Malaysia, and with it the delicate political and communal ethnic balance was drastically altered, arousing plenty of anxiety in Sarawak and Sabah.[12] Not only were their political leaders not consulted over the expulsion, the financial assistance for Sarawak and Sabah coming from Singapore was now curtailed. At the same time, there were calls within UMNO for more stringent citizenship laws for non-Malays and a speedier implementation of Malay as the sole official language of the Federation. The threat of increasing domination by UMNO became more alarming when the East Malaysian states were featured less and less in the political balance of Malaysia's communal equation, essentially becoming the perennial backwaters of Malaysia.

Many of the Sarawakians I met were aware of their backwater position and it affected their relationship with West Malaysians. But, backwater or not, the Sarawakians I met were extremely proud that Sarawak is unique from the rest of Malaysia in that not one identifiable ethnic or religious group makes up more than a third of the population. They were also proud of the region's abundance of natural resources – even as many of them were concerned about the plundering of these resources due to rapid deforestation (massive concession of logging activities), the proliferation of oil palm plantations encroaching upon Native Customary Rights (NCR) land, the construction of close to a dozen hydroelectric dams (especially the controversial Bakun Dam that has no benefit for Sarawakians, not to mention the displacement of hundreds of local communities that goes along with it). Regardless, even in the face of all the plundering that has turned Sarawak into one of the poorest states in the Federation of Malaysia, Sarawakians remain proud of the broad swathe of their cultural and linguistic heterogeneity.

One of my favourite pastimes in Kuching was to walk along the riverfront of the Sarawak River. The river cuts right into the heart of Kuching. The areas north of the river are predominantly Malay *kampungs* (villages) while the Chinese occupy areas south of it. The common form of transportation to cross the river is the *sampan* – small, long, colourful wooden boats with hot tin roofs that crisscross the river. Riding on them is also a splendid way to catch a spectacular view of Kuching, with nineteenth-century Chinese shop houses along the Main Bazaar,[13] colourful Taoist temples, the Brookes-era buildings, the mosque, and the waterfront park on the south side of the river. On the northern side of the river you have Fort Margherita (originally built to monitor the river against pirates), the *Istana* (palace), and the Malay *kampungs*.

The population of Sarawak was around two million in 1999, with slightly more than half a million residing in Kuching. The Chinese are the predominant group in Kuching, followed by the Malays. In addition, there are more than twenty other indigenous groups – the Ibans, Bidayuhs, Melanaus, Kenyahs, Kayans, Kelabits, and others. There is also a small population of European expatriates. Sarawakians were also extremely friendly, whether I met them on the streets, at bus stations, in coffee shops, at food markets, in their homes, or, of course, at pubs. Although Sarawak is relatively peaceful today, it did have a violent past. It is this violent past that this book will focus on.

The Cold War and Development Discourse

Many studies of violent conflicts have pointed out that remembering and forgetting do change under different socio-political circumstances (Amadiume and An-Na'im 2000; Crapanzano 2004; Young 1990). Because of the need for social healing, there are times when there is a greater need for forgetting than remembering. This can be witnessed, for example, in the case of Japan, where the Japanese government has been very reluctant to face the darker sides of its recent past (Yoneyama 1994), and in the construction of the two Germanys, in which war was treated as an aberration (Buruma 1995; La Capra 1994). Ethnographies dealing with the Hutus and Tutsis (Malkki 1995), Algerian Jews (Bahloul 1996), or Crimean Tartars (Uehling 2004) have also explored what happens when communities whose memory has long been suppressed suddenly gain a licence to remember. The recent outpouring of memories in Indonesia of the violence in 1965 not only magnifies the contrast between a pre- and post-Suharto era and points to the degree of self-censorship that most Indonesians went through (Zurbuchen 2005; Mrazek 2010), but also provokes us to think of more inclusive ways of embodying the experience of human memory within particular socio-political frames of reference (Radtke 1999). In fact, the collective memory of the Holocaust did not come into popular circulation until more than a decade after Israel was firmly established (Gillis 1994; Meister 2011).

But what about situations in which the political, social, and economic atmospheres remained relatively unchanged, situations that are less publicized but no less bloody? Despite gaining independence from British colonial rule more than fifty years ago, Malaysians have only known one ruling regime. The United Malay National Organization (UMNO)-led government has won twelve consecutive general elections, a feat that would be considered preposterous in any democratic country, or to any *managed democracy*. Under the realm of this regime, using the pretext of fighting communism during the Cold War, thousands of Chinese were targeted in Malaya and, later on, in Sarawak as communists or communist sympathizers and detained at correction centres or relocated into barbed-wire *new villages*, one of the modern state-inscribed spatialities. But the Cold War is more than just fighting communism.

In *The Accursed Share* (1991), Georges Bataille offers an important and alternative perspective on the Cold War. According to Bataille, the Cold War "is not essentially the struggle of two military powers for hegemony; it is the struggle of two economic methods. The Marshall Plan offers an organization of surplus against the accumulation of the Stalin plans" (173).[14] In 1949, during his inaugural speech, President Truman launched his famous Point Four Program, a technical-assistance project for underdeveloped countries as part of the American's anti-communist strategy. The project aimed at curbing communist nationalistic tendencies and applying similar "Marshall Plans" to the rest of the world, in essence, by coming up with plans to rebuild upon ruins (Haugerud and Edelman 2004).[15] Immediately after that, the United Nations insisted on economic growth based on the expansion of international trade, free access to raw materials, and the return to monetary stability to bring about an improvement in the living conditions of the Third World – which meant, in fact, establishing an environment to "shape and re-shape the spaces of capital accumulation and commodity exchange, subjecting them, simultaneously, to processes of fragmentation, hierar-chization and homogenization" (Brenner and Elden 2009, 359). By the late 1950s, President Kennedy had launched the Alliance for Progress project in Latin America, which was soon reinforced by the Peace Corps to develop the Third World through the export of its natural resources as well as adopting measures that would stimulate the flow of private investment capital (de Senarclens 1997).

On the whole, this development project was well received by the governments of the Third World, for it corresponded to the image that the ruling classes had the attributes of state power and vision to mobi-lize all of its resources to stimulate growth. In other words, it created an environment to facilitate capital accumulation and to enhance po-litical domination. As Henry Lefebvre (1976; 1991) points out, what we have witnessed is the increasing role of the state in the production of space on local, regional, national, and global scales for the survival of capitalism since the second half of the twentieth century – in managing the crisis tendencies of modern capitalism through the production of capitalist spatiality.

In *The Production of Space* (1991), Lefebvre characterizes this new spa-tiality as "abstract space" and suggests that it represents a qualitatively new matrix of sociospatial organization that is at once produced and regulated by the modern state in compliance with the World Bank, In-ternational Monetary Fund, and regional development banks. A key characteristic of abstract space is that it appears to be homogenous, or an "appearance" of homogeneity in a way that is instrumental for both capital and the modern state – "it serves those forces which make a *ta-bula rasa* of whatever stands in their way, of whatever threatens them – in short, of differences." Abstract space "destroys its (historical) condi-tions, its own (internal) differences, and any (emergent) differences, in order to impose an abstract homogeneity" (Lefebvre 1991, 370).[16] In other words, abstract space is the political product of state spatial strat-egies – of administration, repression, and domination. One can think of the construction of ports and highways, the proliferations of free trade zones and the production of a so-called homogenized cheap labour within these spaces, and, in the case of Malaysia, the production of *new villages* and their supposedly homogenized Chinese victims. These are inherently violent spaces.

Almost everywhere the correlation was made between processes of economic growth and political development that include a range of political actions concerning the mobilization of nationalism as an ideology, but also a whole range of state projects designed to shape and reshape territorial spaces into nationalized, nationalizing unities within a broader context defined by the world market, imperialism and its strategies, and the operational spheres of multinational corporations (Lefebvre 1991, 112).

Paradoxically, the enlargement of the United Nations coincided with the triumph of this development ideology, and since the early 1960s the United Nations Development Program has been the agent of this policy, insisting on its "moral" (if not colonial) mission to educate, train, advise, and give meaning to development plans. Meanwhile, no conceptual or operational linkages were made between its economic objectives and the social aspects of development.

To be sure, the Marshall Plan and the other developmental plans were/are not about aid, welfare (re)distribution, or growth – not when the Cold War and nuclear proliferation turned out to be the preferred examples of reckless waste (Bataille 1991, 188), and not after millions of casualties from the war on Asian communism (in China, Korea, Vietnam, Cambodia, Indonesia, and Malaysia), to be followed by the War on Terror combined with a war on drugs in South America and elsewhere, and a war on immigration disguised as a security concern. Similarly, the gestures of the Soros and the Gates in establishing charity "foundations" is not just a matter of philanthropy, it is also a necessary gambit of containment as they export their cyber-evangelism to the markets of Eastern Europe, South Asia, and East Asia (Hutnyk 2004). Or, as Zizek (2008, 22) puts it, "In liberal communist ethics, the ruthless pursuit of profit is counteracted by charity. Charity is the humanitarian mask hiding in the face of economic exploitation."

Since the fall of the Berlin Wall, leaders of the Western world have been making gestures at conferences and summits regarding the need to address poverty, equality, and the latest buzzwords: sustainability and human rights (Meister 2011). Let us not forget that these conference junkets are also attended by multinational CEOs that are hardly known for their desire to redistribute the global share of surplus expenditure for the welfare of all. As John Hutnyk (2004) points out, the liberal rhetoric of charity and the militant drums of war are basically the carrot and stick of capitalist hegemony. It is not about generosity when a gift is not a gift but a debt of time. Perhaps the same can be said about war – it is not war but profit. Indeed, back in 1933 Bataille had written of the bourgeois tendency to declare "equality" and make it their watchword. Written in the context of rising fascism in Germany, Carl Schmitt's ([1932] 1996) philosophical reflections deserve our full attention:

> When a state fights its political enemy in the name of humanity, it is not a war for the sake of humanity, but a war wherein a particular state seeks to usurp a universal concept against its military opponent. At the expense of its opponent, it tries to identify itself with humanity in the same way as one can misuse peace, justice, progress, and civilization in order to claim these as one's own and to deny the same to the enemy ... The concept of humanity is an especially useful ideological instrument of imperialist expansion, and in its ethical-humanitarian form it is a specific vehicle of economic imperialism ... It would be more exact to say that politics continues to remain the destiny, but what has occurred is that economics has become political and thereby the destiny. (54–78)

In a much more contemporary sense, Mike Davis (1984) also reminded us of the political economy of the Cold War: "it was multi-national military integration under the slogan of collective security against the USSR which preceded and quickened the interpenetration of the major capitalist economies, making possible the new era of commercial liberalism which flowered between 1958 and 1973" (9). Closer to Sarawak, Bradley Simpson's (2008) analysis of the political and economic aid that lay the foundations for the mid-1960s emergence of a military-led regime in Indonesia – a regime which was committed to the violence of modernization – deserves to be quoted at length:

> These forces included the U.S. and other Western governments, which provided military and economic assistance; philanthropic foundations, which trained economists and military officers in management and administrations; international financial institutions such as the International Fund (IMF) and the World Bank, which promoted early variants of what would later be called structural adjustment; and social scientists, who deployed theory to account for and legitimize the growing political and economic role of the military in the development process, not just in Indonesia but throughout the so-called third world. (3–4)

Critiques of the modernization theory, dependency theory, world system theory, and the corresponding violence of developmental discourse are well documented and to rehash them would be superfluous.[17] Simply put, an entry point for an analysis of the role of development as a violent discourse is the belief that modernization is the only force capable of eradicating poverty in Third World countries, despite any social, cultural, and political costs. The ingredient for modernization (i.e., exporting agricultural cash crops, industrialization, and urbanization) is capital, and capital has to come from somewhere. It has to come from abroad – and local governments and international organizations need to take an active mediating role in establishing a set of capital relations. To understand development as a discourse, one must look not at the elements themselves but at the system of relations established among them. It is this system that allows the systematic creation of state-inscribed spatiality/territories, objects, concepts, and strategies. In other words, the system of relations establishes a set of rules on who can speak, from what points of view, with what authority, and according to what criteria of expertise, and through these rules the discourse moves across the cultural, economic, and political geography of the Third World. Yet, despite these critiques, the processes that encouraged the development of authoritative regimes that have bred corruption, weak civil societies, nepotism, and a military culture of violence and impunity have not gone away.

A Violent *Gift* Economy

Among anthropologists, the idea of looking at military aid and development discourse not as a gift or generosity but as a violent exchange was adopted by Alan Klima (2002) on Thailand. But the idea goes back to Michael Taussig (1977) when he discussed the uneven and unholy penetration of capitalism into a Colombian peasantry. Both of these scholars owe much of their critique of "the gift" of military aid and development to Bataille, Derrida, and Deleuze, who in turn were indebted to Nietzsche. Without doubt, Mauss's *The Gift* is the text that initiates the modern reflections of gifts and gift giving, especially his thesis that although the gift might appear free and disinterested, it is in fact both constrained and quite interested. In the archaic societies he examines, Mauss finds that the gift is given in a context in which both its reception and its reciprocal return are obligated in terms of well-articulated social rules. In anthropology and related disciplines, the well-worked theme of the *kula* finds the Trobrianders engaged in a series of gift exchanges – of shells and necklaces – which bind trading partners together in a circle of reciprocal gift relations, establishing (inherently asymmetrical) social ties and securing trading relations (Malinowski 1922). Whether it was the *kula* ring exchange or the festivals of destruction in North American indigenous potlatch ceremonies, the gift is about ostensible generosity, in excess of utility, given beyond what would be a practical and reasoned calculation of value. As such, there is also a political agenda in *The Gift*, for Mauss was drawing on an analysis of these archaic societies in order to offer some moral conclusions concerning the organizational principles that grounded his own society, which was enmeshed in the violence of the First World War and rising inequality.

But as Derrida points out, if the gift is never only a gift but the exchange of gift and counter-gift within the logic of exchange and contract that Mauss himself has identified, then generosity is impossible. For Derrida (1992), the basic, irreducible idea of a gift is that it is something given, and that is that. But if we reflect on what would need to be the case for such a simple and incontestable example to occur, then it emerges as deeply paradoxical (7). As Laidlaw (2000) points out, for Derrida, the condition implicit in the idea of a gift is that there must be no reciprocity. To prevent reciprocity, the recipient must not recognize the gift as a gift, and thus no sense of debt of obligation. Similarly, the donor must not recognize the gift, since to do so is to praise and gratify oneself; and lastly, as a result of the foregoing, the thing cannot exist as a gift as such. Derrida (1992) writes: "The simple identification of the passage of a gift as such, that is, of an identifiable thing among some identifiable 'ones,' would be nothing other than the destruction of the gift" (14). In sum, then: "For there to be gift, it is necessary that the gift not even appear, that it not be perceived or received as gift" (16). As soon as it appears "as gift," it becomes part of a cycle and ceases to be a gift.

In other words, if a gift is to be a gift there must be no exchange, no debt to be repaid, no reciprocity, not even the idea of a payback. As such, the *kula* or the potlatch is more like a contest, and a destructive one. For Derrida (1992) the unreason of the gift is that it is always a debt that is invoked; this is the paradox of the gift, the aporia of the gift.[18] To further illustrate this paradox, Derrida argues that what the gift gives is time – the possibility of taking time before repayment, whether that be a return gift or an even more extravagant potlatch. As such, there could only be a gift on the condition that the flow of time is suspended. And until we can do that, a gift is impossible (Laidlaw 2000).

According to Deleuze and Guattari ([1972] 1983), who elaborated on the violence of the gift when writing on colonial economy, the centrality of the gift is not exchange and circulation but rather inscription: "The essential thing seemed to us to be, not exchange and circulation, which closely depend on the requirements of inscription, but inscription itself, with its imprint of fire, its alphabet inscribed in bodies, and on blocks of debts" (188). As for Georges Bataille, his economic reflections of the gift are much like those from Mauss, but he does so in order to overturn the "restrictive" economic principles of the utilitarian calculation that defines the rationality of contemporary society. This overturning will make possible a different economic logic – one based on unproductive expenditure of excess that defines the workings of a "general economy," of gift giving "without return." According to Bataille, this unproductive expenditure animates Mauss's potlatch analysis, and Bataille (1991) claims that modern economic forces of commodity accumulation obscure "the basic movement that tends to restore wealth to its function, to gift-giving, to squandering without reciprocation" (38). The gift and potlatch, argues Bataille, are part of a calculus which suggests the necessary expenditure of an organism that, generally, receives more energy "than is necessary to maintain life." Furthermore,

excess energy (wealth) can be used for growth of a system ... if the system can no longer grow, or if the excess cannot be completely absorbed in its growth, it must necessarily be lost without profit, it must be spent ... gloriously or catastrophically. (21)

In many ways, volume 1 of Bataille's *The Accursed Share* can be read as an attempt to provide a rationale for a political and economic policy of capitalist nations in the face of communism during the Cold War; and to explain how, in a master/slave dialectic with America playing the master, the country is willing to risk their wealth in the face of death (or nuclear destruction) in order to be recognized as having the superior economic system. As for the Marshall Plan, Bataille (1991) writes,

In a paradoxical way, the situation is governed by the fact that without the salutary fear of the Soviets (or some analogous threat), there would be no Marshall Plan. The truth is that the diplomacy of the Kremlin holds the key to the American coffers ... This truth dominates current developments. (183–4)

These philosophers' reflections on the gift are inspired by Nietzsche's philosophy of the self/other relation as a debtor/creditor relation, and on his concept of justice. As Deleuze points out, the second essay of the

Genealogy is an attempt to interpret the primitive economy not so much as a process of exchange and circulation, but as an economy of debts in the debtor-creditor relationship. In fact, Nietzsche explicates the *burden of the debt* as the central problem in any debtor-creditor relationship. For him, the most fundamental social relation is the creditor/debtor relation wherein debts can be repaid through the body via a contractual arrangement between creditor and debtor – he notes that inflicting pain on another was "originally" a way of recovering a debt (Nietzsche 1969, 62–70). Nietzsche echoed the same sentiment on the relationship established between the giver and the receiver in "Thus Spoke Zarathustra" (1978). When Zarathustra came down from his cave to rejoin humanity, he cautioned his followers against the dangers involved in gift giving and told them to practise reserve in accepting gifts; Zarathustra "knows that the gift is a *pharmakon* (medicine and poison),[19] for those who benefit from receiving the gifts often feel beholden to the one who gave to them" (Schrift 1997, 3).

As Rosalyn Diprose (2002, 29–30) points out, for justice to exist in a Nietzschen creditor/debtor exchange economy, exchange would have to be a reciprocal exchange – one that is without loss or without a debt being incurred by either party, and one that assumes "approximately equal power" between creditor and debtor (Nietzsche 1969, 70; 1984, 64). What Nietzsche exposes in his genealogy of justice and the creditor/debtor relation is this erroneous assumption of sameness, where one reduces the other to the self. On the level of society, this equates to a community of conformists wherein any expression of non-conformity is taken as a hostile act, a refusal to return the gift. It is here that a debt is incurred and "the disappointed creditor, will get what repayment it can" through punishment and expulsion (Nietzsche 1969, 71).

It is in such discursive logic of the gift that I find it meaningful to talk about the Cold War economy as a gift economy whereby the recipients (postcolonial national elites) were inscribed with a debt and thus the obligation to sacrifice certain victims as some form of payment. In the most contemporary sense, one of the ideal gifts is the loan made by the World Bank, IMF, and other regional development banks to the underdeveloped and developing countries, which then felt obligated to reciprocate by *agreeing* to the conditions of the structural adjustment packages. It is my hope that more scholars will take up such discursive logic of the gift in terms of development and military aid as one way to debunk one of the oldest maxim of modern economics – our natural "human propensity to truck, barter, and exchange" – and by extension, the notion of "free trade."[20]

In the case of Sarawak, while the Malaysian government lurched forward on its warpath against communism, it reassured its population of *justice* (i.e., politicized justice) with the watchwords of security, democracy, and development that really meant death and despair to those on the wrong side of the fence. The construction of *new villages* (i.e., asylum and "aid" programs) was the appeasers' gift, appeasers who acceded to the Cold War gift economy and its excesses – civilian deaths, curtailment of civil liberties, and so on. This was a kind of gift whereby social categories like the Hakka speech group, their marginal socio-economic statuses, and their diverse ideological affiliations were reduced (or made to appear as homogenous) to a single denominator – communists or communist sympathizers – and forcibly relocated to the *new villages*. To borrow from Stanley Tambiah (1996), who wrote in the context of Sri Lanka, such a discourse could be called a "levelling crowds" discourse, targeting the rural Hakkas with anti-communist rhetoric – in essence, treating *Hakka-ness* as an object of criminality.

To be sure, the aggression against the Hakkas in Sarawak – whether social, economic, or political – had roots in the imperialist mercantile tradition. After all, James Brooke was an officer of the British East India Company, and one of the main objectives throughout the Brookes regime was the imposition of *free* trade, which all along had been one of a paternalistic kind: the promotion of British commerce, and the monopoly to exploit mineral resources, among them gold and oil (Chew 1990; Ooi 1997).[21] The War on Communism in Sarawak – as in other "low intensity" counterinsurgencies – was clear and sustained. Under the pretext of the Cold War, not only did it turn Sarawak into a society of control and sacrifices, it was a war for profit – one that not only reassures the superior status of the gift givers but also unleashes a terror of its own. It was war and plunder in pursuit of resources in ostensibly resource- and oil-rich Sarawak.

We can gauge how excessive the anti-communist operations were by looking at logistics. Immediately after the formation of Malaysia, the beginning of a series of lethal gifts – so-called developmental aid – started pouring into Sarawak under the supervision of British expatriates (Grijpstra 1976). Expenditure on the armed services in Sarawak from 1963 to 1975 alone was estimated at RM 1,023 million, with another RM 816 million spent on development in Sarawak during that period (see Porrit 2004). According to official estimates, there were more than seven battalions of Allied soldiers (Malay soldiers, British Gurkha forces, and some senior British officers) against fewer than 700 guerrillas in Sarawak (Sri Aman: Peace Restored in Sarawak, 1974). Not counting those stationed in Indonesia or Brunei, by 1962 some 22,500 Malaysian and Commonwealth forces were deployed to protect Sarawak from Sukarno's *Konfrontasi* policy and the activities of the communist organizations within Sarawak.

This excessive spending – of both materials and manpower – was an ideal potlatch in that the debt could never be repaid. It obliged the receivers (state elites) to give more, with heavy interest, not to mention sacrifices. This was a potlatch of a very destructive kind that continues to this day under the aegis of neoliberal capitalism – massive appropriations of natural resources and labour, the building of dams, extensive deforestation through loggings, the Green Revolution and its massive appetite for *cash crops*, the construction of the world's biggest aluminum smelting plant by Rio Tinto – or, more appropriately, as destructions marketed as excessive spending go on in the name of development.[22] The effect of the Cold War and its accursed share in Sarawak – as in other Cold War counterinsurgencies – is a curse of a sacrificial expenditure going out of control.

Figurations of Collective Assembly

… societies are nothing other than figurations of interdependent people … and individuals within a figuration can be amicable as well as hostile to one another.

Norbert Elias ([1969] 1983, 18, 161)

To understand the complexity of the situation during the Cold War in Sarawak, I looked at materials touching on issues of communism during the 1960s and 1970s at the Sarawak Museum Library. In the archives I reviewed newspaper reports from 1946 to 1970 – English newspapers, translated versions of Chinese newspapers, and the Malay editions of the *Sarawak Vanguard* and *Utusan Sarawak*. I also looked at other kinds of documents I felt were important for my work: reports of enquiry commissions, journals, and, of course, books. Of these, the *Sarawak Gazette* is the most comprehensive, but contains a colonialist bias. Taken "archeologically," most of the written records reveal layered strata of colonial and nationalistic views of Sarawak. Some of the recent attempts at writing Sarawak histories seem to me as if they were creating new layers that mirror earlier reports (see, for example, Fidler 1972;

Lockard 1973). However, within their recurring images and for all their limitations, there is a certain stability in their interpretations of Sarawak and in what has been systematically omitted. It is in such stability and systematic omissions that a different Sarawak can be glimpsed, and this offers the possibility that a history from a perspective other than the victor's can be written.

In addition to archival research, I collected stories from a figuration of subjects: bus drivers, bus conductors, clothing vendors, and other individuals in Sarawak. The emphasis here is on their experience of a certain past. Most of the subjects I worked with were in some manner *related* to the *new villages*. All of them experienced some form of displacement. Some were complicit with such politics. But what is important within this figuration of individuals is that there are also differences, if not hidden animosity, among them. By paying close attention to how some of them talked about the recent past, or about being labelled as communists, I found that they not only offer important insights into the silent past that continues to haunt their present but also allow for a nuanced understanding of the meaning of "communism" – of what communism was to these individuals.

Bus Drivers and Conductors

In 1996 I spent five months at a longhouse close to Sematan where I researched property issues, particularly land and fruit tree tenure. I spent another four months in 1998 researching labour and national boundaries issues as seen by indigenous longhouse inhabitants.[23] During these field trips, I was fascinated at the level of interaction between the bus drivers and conductors and their passengers. Besides being a form of public transportation, there would often be groceries, newspapers, livestock (chicken, ducks, etc.), and sometimes even articles of furniture that were brought onto the bus to be dropped off at pathways leading to houses or villages scattered along the way. Working on the same route for more than thirty years, if not more, these bus drivers and conductors were extremely familiar with the social gossip of the various communities they served. I often saw them at festivals in the different villages. To play on Michel de Certeau (1984), in many ways the bus and its route would resemble the "long poems of walking" that he identified in his musings on big city life (91–102). I could just as easily contemplate these "long poems of walking" through the countryside as experiences of journeying, sharing, suspense, happiness, identification, and altruism that the bus drivers and conductors had with the inhabitants of the different villages.

But during those field trips, not once was I told that there was a history of communism in Sarawak. It wasn't until I started my dissertation fieldwork in 1999 that I found out not only that there was a history of communism in Sarawak, but that the company these bus drivers and conductors worked for, the Sarawak Omnibus Company (SOC), had a socialist bent to it. It was for this reason that I ended up working with its bus drivers and conductors as my primary source of information.[24] I not only used them as portable lenses to look into a certain past, but also examined their personal experiences during that period.[25] I also worked with bus drivers and conductors from other bus companies because some of them were former SOC employees who could offer added perspectives of their former company and colleagues. Following Benjamin's history in the present, the narratives I have compiled from working with these interlocutors not only provide a glimpse into their past, but also resonate with present circumstances that were affecting their daily lives and livelihoods within the structural hierarchies of the workplace and that of the larger political economy.

Besides being the first and the biggest bus company in Sarawak, the SOC was also uniquely connected with the Sarawak United People's Party (SUPP). Formed in 1959, SUPP was the largest and most active opposition party in Sarawak (Leigh 1974). In addition, its founder and former general manager, Hong Hee Siaw, was one of the most outspoken leaders of SUPP and had a good deal of influence over SOC policies and its employees, the majority of whom were rural Hakkas who "escaped" from the *new villages*. Also, in 1998 the management of SOC was reorganized following a partnership with a *bumiputra* company,[26] a development which brought about a radical change in the company's relations with its employees. I will address this in chapter 7.

In choosing which bus conductors and drivers to work with, I made a conscious effort to include individuals from different ethnicities to see if there were indeed communist activities, or representations of communist members, among the non-Hakkas. I also included those who were living marginally as retail operators at a hawker centre next to a bus station – retail operators that shared a certain socialist history. Obviously, I befriended others at the bus station because they had things to say and I enjoyed their gossip. Consequently, the selection of people I worked with was both random and by design. Within this figuration of collective assembly are networks that are formed according to Chinese speech groups, surnames, age groups, religion, occupations, and those who escaped from the *new villages* and other former *communist-influenced* areas. Such conceptualization of this collective assembly allows me to explore the latitude given to an individual by his/her position within a specific figuration, and in the "tactics" of his/her personal behaviour, instead of within the abstract ideas of the collective or of resistance. In other words, these are sets of personalities – bus drivers, bus conductors, clothing vendors, former communists, former communist sympathizers, or just simply rural Hakkas – that prefigure a set of constellations and each proffer potential flashes of illumination of a certain past. Ultimately the project that I am interested in is not the collection of individuals, but a collective assembly in which "the joins, the disagreements, are allowed to show" (Buse et al. 2005, 39).

It is from this experience of fieldwork and archival research that I have come to understand that the incorporation of Sarawak into the Federated States of Malaysia came out of a complex set of politics: colonialism and its racist ideology, the politics of decolonization and development and its elitist interests and manipulation, the ideological battle between so-called democracy and communism – or this war for profit – and its continued inscription under the regime of (neo)liberal capitalism. When I looked at what the larger political facts of this history seemed to be saying, it would seem that those periods are now over and done with, a thing of the past. But I see a different reality. Political parties in Malaysia are still divided along *bangsa* (racial) lines and the "brain-drain" phenomenon is on the rise, with an estimated one million Malaysians now living abroad. Malaysia was once one of the economic leaders in the region (from the 1960s to the 1980s). Since the 1997 region-wide financial and economic crisis, foreign direct investment into Malaysia continues to dwindle, with Malaysia now lagging behind the Philippines, Vietnam, and Indonesia. This sad state of affairs can only be attributed to the financial mismanagement and lack of accountability and transparency that have become so endemic over the last three decades. Despite all of this, the government is still using the attribution of race and religion to divide up its citizens and, lately, religious fundamentalism or terrorism as master narratives to secure its own legitimation.

While I was doing my fieldwork in 1999 and 2000, the federal government was actively promoting "nationalism" as part of a strategic response to their falling popularity in the aftermath of the 1997

region-wide financial and economic crisis. Malaysia was also witnessing, for the first time since independence, the emergence of an opposition coalition, *Reformasi*, which consisted of political parties across
bangsa lines. In the face of such disunity, the state launched a full-scale
ideological campaign to regain lost ground. The term "common enemy" resurfaced time and time again within the nationalist language
against so-called internal and external threats. Disunity within the Malays was considered "Un-Malay" and globalization and its new world
order was neocolonialism. What was apparent was that this "common
enemy" rhetorical gimmick was essentially a rephrasing of an old vocabulary used throughout Southeast Asia during the Cold War. Back
then, the "common enemy" was communism.[27]

For the past fifty years, the draconian Internal Security Act (ISA) – a
throwback from the days of British colonial rule that allows for indefinite detention without trial – has been consistently invoked for a wide
range of purposes: detaining ordinary citizens as well as opposition
leaders, trade unionists, academicians, and religious, social, environ-
mental, and women's rights activists. Drafted by colonial British lawyer R.H. Hickling at the end of the Malayan Emergency (1948–60), the
very basis of the ISA was founded upon the notion of protecting the
nation against the evil of communism. Subsequently, it was also used
against non-communist elements. For instance, during *Operasi Lalang*
(Weeding Operation) in 1987, the then–prime minister Dr. Mahathir
Mohammad used the ISA to detain more than a hundred civil society
activists, political opposition leaders, educationalists, and religious
converts. Four newspapers' publishing licences were also revoked.
Since September 11, 2001, the ISA has been used for terrorism.[28] All in
all, more than 10,000 people have been detained under the ISA.

Besides the ISA, the government has an impressive array of other
equally repressive laws aimed at curtailing freedom of expression, association, and thought. For example, to name only three, the Press and
Printing Act requires newspapers to apply for annual printing permit re-
newals; the University College and Colleges Act prevents students from
participating in politics; and the Sedition Act is frequently used to curtail
freedom of expression and public debate. In Malaysia, a police permit
is required for any gatherings of five or more people and peaceful civil
society protests are often met with water cannons, tear gas, and arrests.

After more than fifty years of independence, in the 2008 general elections the BN regime for the first time was denied its two-third majority,
in what many social critics termed "the political tsunami." Even though

there is still a lack of transparency and accountability, corruption is beginning to be reported by the alternative electronic media. These are indeed desperate times for the ruling regime to hold onto power and, at the same time, quicken their pace of plundering the nation as seen in the projected governmental mega-projects that will flow, as usual, to the tiny sliver of UMNOputras and their business partners.[29] In the recent UMNO general assembly on October 21, 2010, the current prime minister Najib Tun Razak warned of "crushed bodies," "lost lives," and "ethnic cleansing" if UMNO failed to hold on to *Putrajaya* (the new and costly federal administrative capital of Malaysia). Najib also told his party delegates that *"kewarganegaraan Malaysia pada dasarnya bukan lagi bersifat sama rata"* (Malaysia does not have equal citizenship). To be sure, this was not the first time these UMNOputras have resorted to such irresponsible scaremongering tactics.

Under such a culture of plunder and the manufacture of fear, I believe it is more crucial than ever to analyse the meaning of the Cold War gift economy in Malaysia and, by extension, that of Sarawak – an economy that gave birth to the current corrupted and repressive regime. Not to talk about them, not to illuminate them, is to continue with the same denial of reality that the state practises in relation to its politicized distinction between Malays and non-Malays, a set of economic relations that is imbued with violence and material greed for the elites. It is by talking about the omissions and silences that we can hope to transcend beyond a restricted economy in Malaysia, a *poverty* in the Bataillian sense that refuses to acknowledge its own genealogy – the debris of the Cold War. It is also by offering a critique of these omissions that I can give voice to the increasing Malaysian labour force, be they working legally or illegally, or even as foreign brides in Singapore, Hong Kong, Taiwan, and Japan.[30] Recently, many have also travelled to the United States, Canada, England, and beyond to work at restaurants, as nannies, or in sweatshops.

Forgetfulness

Even a happy life is possible without remembrance, as the beast shows; but life in any true sense is absolutely impossible without forgetfulness.

Nietzsche ([1874] 1983, 62)

To some of my Hakkas subjects, my initiative to write about their past was perceived as a chance to challenge the official history of communism in Sarawak, an official history that viewed episodes of communism as momentary interruptions in the normal progression of Malaysia's history of growth and democracy (see, for example, Asli 1993; Mahmud 1993). However, the majority of them claimed to have forgotten about that experience, or stated that it was pointless to remember. In fact, most of them make it a non-subject, just something that happened. Even though the Cold War is supposedly over,[31] why would it not have produced a set of perspectives that would encourage these Hakkas to remember the past outside of the official remembering? Given the passage of time, why were they so unwilling to talk about their past?

As Susan Slyomovics (2005) points out in her ethnography on the performance of reparation in Morocco, "As with other projects in which a state [staged a terror campaign] against [some] of its own citizens, the attempt to analyze such an historical past tests the limits of our ability" (2) to *rescue* such experiences from oblivion – especially, as in the case of Sarawak, when most of the victims are not speaking out, never mind the absence of governmental acknowledgement or apology.[32] The word "rescue" comes from Benjamin's dialectical image that calls for a recognition of history's forgotten and discarded issues and objects so that a history from a perspective other than the victor's can be written. The aim of such project is not about illuminating *what happened* "in the context of their time, but to bring to representation, in the time when they were produced, the time which recognizes them – that is, our time" (Benjamin 1999, 464).

What, some of my interlocutors would ask me, is the use of remembering or excavating memories they have put behind them? Essentially, they were arguing that "what is past is past." Many studies on history, memory, and violence have pointed out that there is often the need to forget about the past in order to continue to live (Casey 1987; LaCapra 1994; Butalia 2000). In the case of Sarawak, how does one interpret my subjects' reluctance, their silences? There is the moral question of whether the silence should or could be "penetrated" in order to give it a voice. The breaking of silences has to be done with a great level of sensitivity to what can be pursued and what is better left as "silence." Each time I was faced with such a question, I came up with a question of my own. Why, I wondered, were some of these people so reluctant to remember this experience? Surely this reluctance in itself pointed to something. Did it have to do with the horrific nature of their experience? Or, did it have to do with – at least for some of the participants – their own complicity and duplicity in this history? Furthermore, telling one's story in public or, in this case, to an anthropologist is not simply an act of self-expression and self-making but can be first and foremost a profoundly political act (Franklin and Lyons 2004). Similar to what Leslie Dwyer (2009) has observed among victims in post-1965 Bali, one of my observations from working with my interlocutors in Sarawak is that sharing a certain violent past "does not necessarily lead to solidarity, a collective memory, or a shared subjectivity or political position among those it affects" (122; see also Das 2000; 2007).

Indeed, what is it about these former communists and their reluctant stories of the Cold War that is compelling enough to warrant a book? One of the defining features of my fieldwork was that I had more questions (if not repetitive ones) than answers. I was interested in exposing one of the theatres of state violence. Yet, despite my pleas, for the most part these Hakkas were not interested. In the process of struggling with this conundrum, I began to realize that this was not necessarily a disappointing feature of my enterprise. Indeed, this reluctance is what defines the fields in which my fieldwork occurs and what gives my analysis of memory and history its unique character.[33] However, the important question here is whether it is possible to evoke the paths to knowledge that are "shot through with power relations and personal cross-purposes" (Clifford 1988, 25) and yet not disavow the strategically repressed silences of these Hakkas in the wake of a history of systematic state violence.

Walter Benjamin's (1968) historical materialism, a historiography arrested with the task of writing histories in the present, is helpful in reconciling the reciprocal relationship between the types of thinking an anthropologist employs and the animating forces of the life or the events an anthropologists confronts, a paradoxical gesture that pays recognition to an organized violent past that nevertheless remains an accessibly alive and accessible encounter. But it is never quite as easy as Benjamin has suggested to comprehend and appreciate the animating forces between what can be said and what is whispered inaudibly. It took a while in my struggles with this conundrum, "where thinking suddenly stops in a configuration pregnant with tensions" (Benjamin 1968, 262), before I began to recognize that my whole enterprise was weighted not entirely on my ability to collect stories of their past but also on acknowledging their silences – and seeing these silences as a force that haunts these Hakkas to the extent that they not only suppress their memories but also confront the ethical limits of representation for an anthropologist who is interested in rescuing a piece of their past from falling into oblivion. Silence here is understood not only as a complex system of repression but also as a thing in itself that shuts people up, including those it never directly silences. The silent, then, are not just dead communists or communist sympathizers but, rather, those who lived through enforced silence and complicity, and those who have no desire to sympathize.

To put it differently, my entire enterprise is less interested in "what actually happened" (in itself an impossibility) than in the influence of what happened on successive presents, "in memory not as remembrance but as the overall structure of the past within the present" (Nora 1996, xxiv). But there is more to it. As the precondition for establishing the humanistic knowledge of our subjects' troubled pasts and *out of a concern for justice*, my role here is to take cognizance of the production of these silences in order to recognize the notion of my subjects' forgetfulness as necessarily a force that sustained their happiness, pride, and ambivalence (Nietzsche [1967] 1989).[34]

Ultimately, this book is about the politics of telling history under the violence of the Cold War *gift* economy, an attempt to write about the anamnesis that calls the present into question. In Malaysia, allegedly communist cadavers are simultaneously censored and forgotten messages of this Cold War global story. The fusion of developmental tropes and violence – whether accomplished in the silent rhetoric of transition or in the imagery of *new village* relocation – offers a critique of the neoliberal economy we are forced to live in, an economy by which a new world order can appear to sever its connection to the old order that gave it life (Klima 2002) – the Cold War gift economy that remains the raison d'être, if not the main pretext, for its continued global dominance and its silences.[35]

The Hakkas of Sarawak: Sacrificial Gifts in Cold War Era Malaysia is divided into eight chapters. The first chapter touches on the political and economic relations of Malaya to Britain at the beginning of the Cold War, followed by the inscription of Sarawak and Sabah under the Greater Malaysia Plan. It will briefly touch on the Malayan Emergency (1948–60) and the colonial/postcolonial mechanism of dispossession whereby half a million so-called rural Chinese Hokkiens and Teuchius communist sympathizers were relocated into 400 *new villages*, something so successful (in an ironic sense of the word) that it was adopted for the Chinese Hakkas in Sarawak in the mid-1960s. To understand how race has been so politicized, the first chapter will touch upon the

New Economic Policy in order to highlight just how widespread discrimination has been and continues to be against non-Malays in the Malaysian landscape, particularly but not limited to those of the working class, in areas of employment, education, civil service, military, police, language policy, and so on.

Chapter 1 provides a historical background of the overseas Chinese. It is directed to those readers who are unfamiliar with the historical scapegoating of overseas Chinese, often labelled as "the Jews of the East." Other than my own readings of this literature, it offers little that will be new to readers who know that history. The chapter also touches on *bangsa* political economy to provide an understanding of how race is politicized in Malaysia and how it has affected the overall well-being of non-Malay Malaysians socially, economically, and politically to this day. Pertaining to the subjects I worked with in Sarawak, most if not all of their temporal orientation is to live in the present, with little interest in the past and little thought for the future.

Chapter 2 starts off with the racial politics and economics of the Greater Malaysia Plan that incorporated Sarawak (and Sabah) into the Federated State of Malaysia. It is also concerned with those who were dispossessed and relocated into *new villages* after Sarawak became part of Malaysia. The chapter is guided by the following questions: was there any logic for the suppression and relocation of the Hakkas? Was it because some of these rural Hakkas were supporters for a certain section of the Sarawak United People's Party? Or were they sacrificed because of politics that were external to them?

Chapter 3 seeks to interrupt the naturalness of Malaysia's claim to Sarawak and investigate the procedures of nationhood, history, and particular forms of sociality. If the history of communism is treated as an aberration in order to deny its eventfulness, have the events that transpired during the 1960s and 1970s been forgotten, erased from the consciousness of those who were affected by them? If not, how can we write the dimension of disdain and its messiness back into the fore of history? More importantly, in dealing with certain former guerillas, the chapter touches on the messiness and fuzziness of how one might be construed as communist or socialist inclined.

Chapter 4 deals with my daily interactions at the bus station. It also deals with the history of the bus company and why most of their employees during the 1960s and 1970s came from the *new villages*.

Chapter 5 touches on aspects of how dislocation and trauma shaped some of my subjects – how families were divided and how they coped with that dislocation and trauma. The chapter is also concerned with how they rebuilt their lives, what resources – both physical and mental – they drew upon, and how that shaped the *new villages* and towns they settled in.

Chapter 6 elaborates on the discussion that ended chapter 1, touching on the strategies and tactics some of my subjects deployed in relation to the power they were conscripted by – how the annexation of Sarawak into the Federated States of Malaysia in the context of the Cold War military gift economy and *bangsa* political economy, and the dominance of the *Barisan Nasional*, not merely altered the balance of forces during the 1960s but also affected their course of political practicalities.

Chapter 7 discusses how, after thirty years, SOC finally succumbed to the reality of *doing business* in Malaysia – where private non-Malay companies are forced to have *bumiputera* partnership(s) – which speaks volumes to the company's past leftist bent. This development had, for many of the bus conductors and drivers, severed all links with their past struggles and aspirations. I will talk about the kind of sensibilities and emotions that underpinned its once-loyal employees who stuck with the company throughout the tumultuous past, but who now found themselves, more than thirty to forty years later, on the wrong side of the fence once again. In many ways, the dispositions of SOC's old-timers would present themselves as part of the ongoing discrimination against the working-class non-Malays (as well as the working-class Malays) in Malaysia.

In the final chapter, I reflect on the many themes laid out throughout the book and attempt to emphasize the unstable relationship between memory and history, putting the relationship between memory and history under the sign of a question mark. Indeed, some of these Hakkas seemed to offer a few perspectives about memory and history: that they are not crucial; that they can be a burden; or that memory and history continue to haunt them. In fact, most of them made their involvement in past struggles a non-subject, just something that happened, while others fabricated glories where none probably existed. To be sure, none of them were at ease with this past. This is what the politics and economics of the Cold War meant to these Hakkas who have been sacrificed and must live with the overriding violence of the Cold War gift economy.

Chapter One

Overseas Chinese

For most of the subjects I worked with in Sarawak, the Cold War's personal meanings, its profound sense of rupture, and the differences it engendered or strengthened still lived on in their lives. It was also a division of properties, of assets and liabilities – or, as a bus conductor put it, "a division of feelings." It brought untold suffering and trauma. It is true that many of them managed to move on, developing a sense of indifference towards their community leaders, their employers, and the State. But for many of these rural Hakkas, their easy victimization did not start with the Cold War. It started earlier.

An overview of the history of the "overseas Chinese" of Southeast Asia is useful in developing an understanding of how the "Chinese" have been characterized historically and how this affected the Chinese communities in Southeast Asia during the Cold War and in the historical present.[1] The history of the "overseas Chinese" in Southeast Asia can be described as having passed through a number of phases. The first was when the *countries* in Southeast Asia were still ruled by their native princes. During this period the Chinese settlements were small, though on occasion isolated groups of Chinese were able to maintain a local independence of some sort, as in Palembang in the fifteenth century and in West Borneo during the late eighteenth and early nineteenth centuries (Purcell [1951] 1965; Bassett 1980; Chew 1990).

The second phase was when the European powers had established their colonies, and the expansion of trade opportunities as well as the protection provided by the colonial governments encouraged the Chinese from south China to emigrate in larger numbers (Purcell [1951] 1965; Skinner 1957; 1996; Wickberg 1965). In 1833, with the Act of Emancipation (the abolishment of slavery in Great Britain), cheap labourers for the colonies had to be sought from elsewhere. Labourers or what were then called coolies were "recruited" en mass from South Asia in 1838, and from south China to the Caribbean, the Americas, and Southeast Asia around 1845 (Campbell 1971; Breman 1989; Chew 1990). This is often called the *Age of Coolieism.*

As demand increased, heavy competition to ship coolies took place between syndicates consisting of brokers, junks, and European vessels. Chinese coolie brokers in Singapore and Penang were working in cooperation with "eating-house" keepers in Swatow and Amoy, China, as well as in Hong Kong and Macau. Often the coolies were subjected to fraudulent methods of recruitment and kidnapping, shortages of food and water, frequent riots, and murder. Extremely racist descriptions of the "subhuman" aspect of coolies and their social structure were common in the colonies. Many coolies, concubines, and both female and male prostitutes became victims of infectious diseases, including a virulent form of syphilis (Campbell 1971). The coolie labour systems of the nineteenth and twentieth centuries (1845–1911) were largely a veiled slave trade, with indentured labourers replacing earlier slaves.

To this day, millions of Chinese in Southeast Asia are street hawkers, trishaw drivers, shops assistants, squatters, and wage labourers of some sort (Soon 1962). Notwithstanding, there are many stories of coolies who became prosperous merchants over time (Chew 1990), and such "rags-to-riches" stories are written by historians, told in coffee shops, and retold inside the homes of ordinary people. These are common and yet important stories for those who did not "make it," providing inspiration in order to endure the harsh realities in the countries they had "adopted." But for those Chinese who were doing well in the colonies, the colonial governments had another weapon. It was racialism.

Racialism in Southeast Asia, as many have pointed out, was imported from Europe (Campbell 1971; Breman 1989). Hannah Arendt (1951) argued that there was a vital qualitative shift in European colonialism during the third quarter of the nineteenth century. Colonialism, which up to that period had been essentially a Crown project, became an enterprise for the new *bourgeoisie.* It was during this period that a full-scale racist (anti-Semitic) ideology was exported to the colonies to naturalize racial divisions.[2] Among the local elites, who were mostly educated in Western countries and learning the meaning of modern nationalism, many came to appreciate the political dimensions of ethnocentrism and the doctrine of anti-Semitism (see Skinner 1957; Soon 1962; Purcell [1951] 1965; Wickberg 1965). Anti-Semitic texts became the bible for anti-Sino discourse, and the Sinophobes spoke only of the rich Chinese, ignoring the thousands who died in shipwrecks during the Second Middle Passage as well as in mines, on the plantations, and in the overcrowded quarters of indentured coolies.[3]

In addition, racialism in one country helped to create an armory of racialism in another. For instance, as early as 1898, Warrington Smyth, the British Director of the Royal Department of Mines in Thailand, called the Chinese in Thailand the "Jews of Siam." Soon anti-Semitism and the "Yellow Peril" doctrines were circulating among the Western-educated Thai elites. In 1914 King Wachirawut launched several Sinophobic discourses, starting with a series of articles called "The Jews of the East" which equated the Chinese with the anti-Semitic caricatures of the Jews (Skinner 1957; Soon 1962). Under the Spanish Regime the Spaniards freely catalogued more than forty "evil cultural characteristics" of the Chinese communities in the Philippines. They were restricted to *parian* (quarters) and had to pay higher taxes because it was assumed that the Chinese (as they were essentialized) had the highest earning power and assets (Rizal 1997). When the Philippines entered into the second period of Western tutelage, this time under American control, the Americans immediately applied the same Chinese Exclusion Act that existed within the United States (Wickberg 1965).

Treatments of more or less similar natures were found in Indonesia, Burma, the former South Vietnam, and Malaya (see Furnivall 1967 for Netherlands India; Coppel 1983 and Mackie 1996 for Indonesia; Freedman 1979 and Purcell [1951] 1965 for Southeast Asia). The Chinese communities in Southeast Asia were variously depicted or used as "middlemen" between the Colonial governments and the native populations, and often became easy targets for various forms of "scapegoating"; they were commonly depicted as "uncivilized," generally loathed, and described in anti-Semitic vocabularies.

It is not incorrect to say that the "overseas Chinese" in Southeast Asia were, from their earliest arrivals, considered to be outsiders (for similar arguments, see Heidhues 1974; Freedman 1979; Bassett 1980; Milner 1986; Tejapira 1992). Integration theory and the concept of a "plural society" were to affect scholarship on the Chinese communities of Southeast Asia – these led to preoccupations with concepts such as assimilation and acculturation, and how these affected the socio-legal distinction between aliens and locals in the host countries (see, for example, Skinner 1957; Purcell [1951] 1965; Furnivall 1948; Lockard 1973; Anderson 1998). What preoccupied these analysts were issues concerning the allegedly unique "social cement" of Chinese communities, typically stressing elements of sworn brotherhoods, *kongsi, Kapitans*, and the role of the Chinese as the "middlemen minority" (see Cushman and Wang 1988).[4]

In addition, these studies were preoccupied with describing the manner in which Southeast Asian states imposed structural limitations on the labour, land, and property rights of its Chinese populations (see T'ien [1953] 1997; Lockard 1973 for Sarawak; for similar accounts in other parts of Southeast Asia, see Furnivall 1967; Skinner 1957; Wickberg 1965). In each country, the colonial administration passed land ordinances that dictated the specific settlement patterns of the various Chinese "dialect" groups. These ordinances – or, rather, restrictions – in turn shaped the occupational, socio-economic, and political dispositions of the Chinese as they competed amongst themselves as well as with other ethnic groups for resources and/or to overcome the civil restrictions placed upon them. Though speech group distinctions were often more important than ethnicity in defining their places in social and economic hierarchies, this literature often ignores the divisions and competitions within the Chinese communities. What is puzzling is that none other than John Furnivall (1948) argued (more than half a century ago) that relations within ethnically defined groups of the "plural society" merit no less scrutiny than relations between each group.[5] What is also puzzling in these studies is that the idea that heterogeneous societies existed in Southeast Asia prior to the European conquests seems to have escaped their imaginations. Furthermore, from my reading of this literature, including articles from the *Sarawak Gazette* and other older English newspapers in Sarawak, I detected a sense of aloofness in the scholars' attitudes towards the countries or the communities they studied.

According to Hannah Arendt, this aloofness had something to do with the idea of the commonwealth. The British Commonwealth, Arendt (1951) argued, was never a "Commonwealth of Nations" but was built on an assumption of one nation dispersed over the earth. British subjects believed that they had reached a comparatively high plane of civilization and therefore held positions of power by right of birth. They also saw it as their right to spread British law and culture; consequently, over the course of Empire, argued Arendt, there was a tremendous degree of aloofness exerted by the colonizers over their subjects. On top of that, colonization was perceived as a "free gift" – as seen in the context of Kipling's "The White Man's Burden" – as its purported goal was to cultivate the cultural development of the colonized, to eradicate

the *poverty* of the lazy native (Alatas 1977; Mbembe 2001).[6] Such aloofness, Arendt continued, can be seen in Hobbes's *Leviathan,* wherein a
new body politic was outlined to correspond to the new needs and interests of a new class – the *bourgeoisie.* Hobbes's insistence on power
as the motion of all things human and divine sprang from the theoretically indisputable proposition that a never-ending accumulation
of property must be based on a never-ending accumulation of power.
This determined the "progressive" ideology of late-nineteenth-century
Great Britain that foreshadowed the rise of imperialism. It is with such
aloofness that much of the literature surrounding issues of nationalism,
ethnicity, modernity, development, and progress in Southeast Asia
were written. Time and again, even when divisions by speech groups
were acknowledged, "Chineseness" became essentialized and transformed into an obstacle to the formation of a common "will" in the
colonies – the materialization of the colonies as one Commonwealth of
Great Britain.

Another observation is that much scholarship on the Chinese communities in Southeast Asia can be seen as part of an effort to draw
synthesis or antithesis with Weber's *Protestant Ethics* (see, for example,
Geertz 1963; Purcell [1951] 1965; for a similar argument, see Wertheim
1964; 1995). Depending on the scholars, the country, or the period studied, most of this scholarship was involved in debating the nature of
Chinese capitalism, whether to add salience or debunk Weber's thesis of pariah capitalism. For instance, in the two decades prior to 1997,
when most countries in Southeast Asia were not only registering high
GNPs and economic prosperity but also competing with Western nations in the global economy, we can see a proliferation of triumphalist
literature celebrating Chinese capitalism. Much like earlier scholarship
that focused on community leaders and their achievements, this literature concentrates on the industrialists, financiers, and conglomerates
of Chinese "transnational" entrepreneurs, invoking their "flexible citizenship" as agentive strategy to accumulate capital. "Citizens without
borders" and "holders of multiple passports" were often used to describe Chinese entrepreneurs as they jet-setted between the metropo-
lises of capitalism, of transcending national and regional boundaries.
Once again, stereotyped "cultural values" of the family, *quanxi,* and
Confucianism were invoked to talk about "Chinese" capitalism (see,
for example, Goldberg 1985; Berger and Hsiao 1988; Yoshihara 1988;
Tai 1989; Castells 1996; Nonini and Ong 1997). But, as Hui (2007) points
out, it was not the transcendence of boundaries by these triumphalist
subjects that was new, but the nature of the boundaries themselves that

were affected by colonial, national, regional, and, lately, global developments (340).

But by rendering them as Asians par excellence, this literature not only tends to disenfranchise other non-Chinese groups but also negates the class alliances between Chinese entrepreneurs and local political leaders (Blanc 1997). Moreover, "Chineseness" is transformed from an ethnic group into an upper-class elite category, obscuring a very essential feature of socio-economic development in capitalism: the sweat of working-class Chinese who began their sojourning as one of the "unsuccessful" reserve armies in the world economy (Dirlik 1993) whereby "boundaries" come in many different forms – passports, linguistic ability, culture, and cuisine, not forgetting bankbooks. As anthropologists we should be aware of some of the issues surrounding the usage of "culture." Maurice Freedman (1975) once pointed out that culture is not a homogeneous substance with the power to spread like butter, but that is how Chinese culture seems to be presented: as a pattern of seepage, of slow overspill. Freedman points out that there is a tendency to look for order and concurrence once we use the word "culture," blinding us to all its ambiguity, movement, and complexity; and, in the case of the triumphalist literature, focusing on a collection of stereotypical values and behaviours at the level of the nation state that have been made exotic by the latest form of capitalism.

The above outline indicates some of the preoccupations among scholars of Southeast Asia with the question of China and the Chinese living in Southeast Asia. In the West, and to a lesser extent in Southeast Asia, the concept of China remains that of a giant with an expanding population that will someday overflow beyond its frontiers. This of course is not a recent fear but in the maintenance of Western policy it is both politically and economically desirable that the nations of Asia be constantly reminded of the danger in which they stand from an imminent Chinese expansion. And, to the extent that the reality of this threat is accepted, it sways the attitudes of local Southeast Asian nationalists towards the Chinese communities in their midst. Propaganda and strife have fed one another, leading to a generalized construction of Chineseness. In all, they represent more of a vicious message – not a factual history.

Second Imperial World War

As I mentioned earlier, Chinese communities as a whole appear to have suffered more than any other group in Southeast Asia during

the Japanese Occupation (Soon 1962; Heidhues 1996; Wang 1981).[7]
With the Sino-Japanese conflict of the 1930s, there was an increase in
China-focused nationalism in Southeast Asia, and it was within this
context that the Anti-Fascist League was formed in Malaya and elsewhere in Southeast Asia. In Sarawak, collections for war funds, patriotic
entertainment, and the boycotting of Japanese goods played an ever-
increasing part in local Chinese lives. At the same time, more than half
of the Chinese population hid in the interior to avoid the Japanese soldiers, and those who remained behind to manage their shops did so at
high risk of endangering their lives (Liew 1956).

After Japan surrendered in 1945, Sarawak was ceded to England.
Most Chinese business leaders welcomed the new arrangement as they
saw the transfer to Crown colony status as promising in terms of im-
proving trade prospects and perhaps widening their role in local political affairs (Chew 1990). Indeed, Crown colony status brought closer
relations between British-ruled Malaya and Singapore, and large European and Chinese companies in these colonies began expanding their
operations to Kuching. By this time, however, another set of politics
was unfolding. Chinese communities throughout Southeast Asia found
themselves caught in the precarious position of choosing between Taiwan and Beijing, and, either way, they remained politically suspect
by their respective local nationalists (Cushman and Wang 1988; Wang
1996; Anderson 1998). In the case of Sarawak, China-focused nationalism was closely entwined with local speech groups and economic orientation. For instance, the Kuomintang branch in Kuching had a strong
attachment with the Cantonese, Teochiu, and Hokkien merchant class
(T'ien [1953] 1997). On the other hand, there was a nascent socialist
movement within the rural Hakkas.

From my reading of the *Sarawak Gazette* and various Chinese newspapers published within this period, there was an increasing interest
in "pan-dialect unity." Although the term is misleading in a linguistic
sense, "pan-dialect unity" denoted an emphasis on Mandarin as the
unifying language for the different speech groups in Sarawak at the
private Chinese Chung Hwa schools. But "pan-dialect unity" rhetoric
was unpopular with the colonial/postcolonial government, and many
graduates from these Chung Hwa schools who went for advanced
study in China and Taiwan were not allowed to return. In fact, the first
student society at one of these Chung Hwa schools was outlawed by
the government as a "subversive" organization.

On another level, the rise of Mandarin education at these Chung
Hwa schools had the effect of accentuating differences with those

English-educated students at the Anglican and Catholic mission schools. The rise of Mandarin education and the simultaneous growth of English-medium schools were significant developments, suggesting a situation in which the language of education and cultural orientation (Eastern versus Western) might eventually supplant speech groups as the major division among the Chinese, at least among those who were literate. However, despite all these developments, speech group differences remain dominant in economic and commercial life and livelihood to this day, as seen in the rivalries in many different trade organizations.

The potential for conflict became even stronger during the post-war period when you consider that the Malays were increasingly distrustful of Chinese nationalism during this time, particularly since the traditional "favouritism" for the Malays was weakened under the new colonial administration. Furthermore, the Malays were concerned with communism, especially since the ideology was interpreted as being anti-religion (Said 1976). For the Chinese, especially the merchants, the increasingly well-organized Malay political organizations and nationalism constituted a threat to the favourable economic position to which they believed they were entitled due to their numerical superiority throughout Sarawak.

Another important development that spurred the consciousness of the educated Chinese population in Sarawak was the proliferation of Chinese newspapers. Following the end of the Second World War, nine Chinese newspapers were established in Sarawak within a span of ten years. By the late 1950s these newspapers were also instrumental in affecting their Chinese-educated readers' attitudes towards Malaysia. News of arrests, hunger strikes of political detainees, last-minute cancellations by the police of permits for anti-political events, and any other political issues that could be deemed as anti-Malaysia were covered daily in these newspapers. It was no coincidence that all of these Chinese newspapers were deregistered or banned at one point or another, only to resurface under different names (Lim 1970).[8]

Because of the growing anti-Malaysia sentiments among most of the Chinese-educated population in Sarawak, especially the rural Chinese, a political outlet was found in 1959 through the formation of an anti-Malaysia political party, the Sarawak United People's Party. According to Michael Leigh (1974), it provided a focal point for the rural "angry young Chinese" (15), the majority of which were Hakkas. Barely a year after its formation, the legislative council of the British colonial government in Sarawak promulgated the "Restricted Residence Ordinance," giving the Attorney General arbitrary power over any political activity in the state. This reminds me of Nietzsche when he says that the justice system depends upon the methods it criminalizes.[9] To express its disgust over the ordinance, the SUPP organized rallies to "mourn the death of democracy" at its party headquarters in Kuching. About 5,000 people attended, wearing black armbands as a sign of mourning. A black paper coffin with the word "democracy" written on it was placed onstage and party leaders made fiery speeches condemning the ordinance. Similar rallies were held in Sibu, Miri, Simanggang, and Engkilili (Teng and Ngieng 1990).[10]

To counter the SUPP's demonstrations and growing popularity, the colonial government responded with accusations of communist infiltration into the party and made many arrests. These arrests could not be timelier, since they served to deprive many SUPP candidates of a chance to run in the local and regional elections. When Sarawak became part of the Federated States of Malaysia, the Chinese communities throughout the rural areas of Sarawak were conveniently labelled as a "Fifth Column" and, by extension, socialist inclined. Under a series of state and federal bills and ordinances, many rural Chinese, predominantly the Hakkas, were detained as communists or communist sympathizers at various correction centres. Many were also forcibly relocated into barbed-wire-fenced *new villages*.

Readers of the Chinese newspapers were also exposed to "unofficial" or alternative indicators, like the standard cost of living in Sarawak. Besides reporting on the dire situations in Sarawak, they were also the source of information about world events, in particular events that were unfolding in the former Indo-China. They were aware of the roles that China (and other communist regimes) played in their lives and livelihoods as a major provider of rice and other foodstuffs to Sarawak, as well as a major importer of rubber from Sarawak.[11]

In addition to economic and livelihood concerns, news of the People's Republic of China was captivating the imagination of these Chinese readers in Sarawak. China's successful launch of its atomic bomb in 1964 was widely advertised and celebrated among the Chinese populations in Sarawak (*Sarawak Vanguard*, October 17, 1964), with every local Chinese newspaper dedicating its front page to the event. A few years later, news of China's launch of its first satellite on April 24, 1970, created much joy among the Chinese population in Sarawak. Again, *The International Times, See Hua Daily*, and all the other Chinese newspapers in Sarawak dedicated their entire front pages to this. At the same time, the *Chinese Daily News* went on to criticize the international committee by stating, "Now that China has emerged as a nuclear power, it is really unreasonable that she is still kept outside the door of the United Nations" (April 27, 1970).

The situations I have described had tremendous implications for the Chinese communities in Sarawak. They stemmed from the inherent contradictions of living under the politics and economics of the Cold War that had little consideration for local conditions in Sarawak. As one newspaper put it, "Confrontation between East and West is not fought there, but on the Third World's turf. This will never be beneficial to the Third World" (*See Hua Daily News*, February 14, 1968). Indeed, how were the rural Chinese in Sarawak, and the Hakkas in particular, affected by the Cold War? To be sure, the particulars are harder to discover; they exist privately in the stories told and retold inside many households.

Bangsa Political Economy

An overview of the construction of *bangsa* political economy, *Ketuanan Melayu*, and the New Economic Policy is useful in developing an understanding of how race is politicized in Malaysia. *Bangsa* is a Malay word for race but it also has a religious connotation in Malaysia, for most Malays are also Muslims; and being Malay and Muslim comes with certain privileges (real or imagined) over non-Malays and non-Muslims. *Ketuanan Melayu* (Malay lordship or supremacy) is the claim that the Malay people are the *tuan* (masters) of Malaysia. Malaysian Chinese and Malaysian Indians, who form a significant minority, are considered beholden to the Malays for granting them *citizenship* in return for special privileges as set out in Article 153 of the Constitution of Malaysia. This quid pro quo arrangement is usually referred to as the Malaysian social contract, an unwritten contract that had effectively institutionalized communalism as the state ideology.

Politicians from the United Malays National Organization (UMNO) usually reference the concept of "Malay Right and Entitlement," which is the cornerstone of *Ketuanan Melayu*, to *naturalize* the asymmetrical balance of power within the Alliance government. However, it must be noted that "Malay Right and Entitlement" is an ideological design instead of a legal and constitutional construct, and Article 153 only mentions the "Special Position" and not the "Special Right" of the Malays. Moreover, according to the Reid Commission that drafted the constitution, Article 153 was intended as a temporary resolution to the search for racial parity, subject to review by the Parliament after fifteen years of independence. It was supposed to be reviewed in 1972 but unfortunately was preceded by the 1969 racial riots – commonly known as the May 13 Incident – and the subsequent introduction of the 1971 Sedition Act which made it illegal to even discuss Article 153 in Parliament. It was under this context that the ideological "Malay Right and Entitlement" was institutionalized into the New Economic Policy (NEP) two years after the riot on May 13, 1969.

The May 13 Incident came immediately after the third general election when the Alliance Party realized it had failed to retain its two-third majority, thereby jeopardizing its power to amend the Constitution at will.[12] On the night of May 11 and early morning of May 12, when supporters of the opposition parties (the Democratic Action Party and Gerakan) were celebrating their victory in Kuala Lumpur, UMNO youth from all over the state of Selangor were seen assembling at the residence of its chief minister. The events that followed would suggest that certain plans were laid down to teach those who dared to challenge UMNO supremacy. On May 13, the carnage that started at Kampung Baru and Batu Road quickly spread elsewhere in the capital. A curfew was immediately imposed and foreign correspondents have alleged that the army fired indiscriminately at Chinese shop houses. There were also reports of looting on Chinese shops, including by military personnel. To this day, the actual figures surrounding the fatalities, including ethnic distribution of casualties, have been a matter of dispute. According to the official figures, the event claimed 196 lives and left 459 injured by firearms and other weapons. More than 200 vehicles and 753 houses were gutted, rendering 6,000 persons homeless. The overwhelming majority of the victims were ethnic Chinese. International correspondents gave a much higher number of fatalities.

Contrary to the official version that blamed supporters of the opposition for provoking the spontaneity of the riot – or alternatively blamed it on the communists, who were discounted as a cause by officials at the British High Commission – recent evidence coming from declassified documents would indicate that it was the work of certain Malay groups orchestrated by certain politicians. They also suggested that this had all along been part of the plan to oust the then–prime minister, Tunku Abdul Rahman, for failing to secure the two-third majority and to justify a total change in Malaysian politics and economy. Incidentally, for alleged national security reasons, the riot was used to suspend

the anticipated state elections in Sarawak. On May 15 the local press
was suspended and two days later the National Operations Council
(NOC) was formed. With that, Tunku had effectively lost his power to
the new regime, headed by his deputy, Tun Razak. With the formulation of a "national ideology," the NOC laid down the ground rules for
what could and could not be raised in the new post-1969s Malaysia. At
the same time, the electoral boundaries were redrawn, ten more seats
were added to the advantage of the Alliance regime, and UMNO dominance was once again restored.

Indeed, the May 13 Incident of 1969 gave the UMNO-controlled government the pretext to launch the National Economic Policy (NEP). The
NEP was announced in 1970 and launched in 1971 as the government's
(read: UMNO's) *gift* to a section of its population. Incidentally, in less
than a week after the May 13 racial riots, when the Malaysian Ministry
of Home Affairs and Internal Security proposed to expand the scope of
the Internal Security Act beyond elements of communism, the World
Bank announced its first series of loans to Malaysia (*Financial Times*,
May 23, 1969). Coming out at the tail end of the Bretton Woods policy
of development, the NEP was supposed to be a plan to provide an engine of growth and a source of employment. The aims of the NEP, as
embodied in the Second Malaysia Plan (1971–5), were (1) to correct the
economic imbalance between the races and (2) to eradicate poverty.
That was the theory. The proposed method to correct the economic imbalance was to increase Malay participation and ownership in private
companies from 1.5 per cent in 1970 to 30 per cent by 1990, and the onus
of achieving this goal was given to a group of ascending Malay state
capitalists.

According to Kia Soong Kua (2007), the ascendancy of the state capitalist class can be seen in the politics and practices of the various Malaysian developmental plans, beginning in the First Malaysian Plan
(1966–70) with the creation of various federal and state institutions.
The enlarged bureaucracy that had been created for the management
of these institutions to provide credit, marketing, and distribution services to the Malay sector provided the contexts for the creation of a
Malay middle class and the new state capitalists.[13] By the Second Bumiputra Economic Congress in 1968, it became evident that the Malay
state capitalists were not content with the position adopted by the aris-
tocratic, English-educated Malay ruling class of "sitting" on the boards
of directorship in non-Malay and foreign companies. Taking the cue
from Suharto's calling for a greater *Maphilindo* – this alleged solidarity

among ethnic Malays across the Malay Archipelago – the appetite of these ultra-communalistic UMNO Malays for a united Malay race across the Malay Archipelago became even more ravenous.[14] During the same year, the expulsion of Singapore from Malaysia also ensured the Malays' position as the largest ethnic community in the Federation. The predominance of UMNO within the Alliance was thus guaranteed, and the communal bargaining within it had to be on terms favourable to these Malay state capitalists. Using the communalist rhetoric of *Ketuanan Melayu*, the inclusion of these UMNO state capitalists into the economy was a *fait accompli*.

The interests of these state capitalists were further boosted in the latter half of the 1960s by the *gift* of the Green Revolution – the World Bank–inspired scheme for increasing agricultural productivity. Not only were the two largest padi schemes in Malaysia – the Muda scheme in Kedah and the Kemubu scheme in Kelantan – funded by the World Bank, but all the necessary nutrients, fertilizer, pesticides, and herbicides as well as the HYVs (high-yielding varieties of padi) that are part and parcel of the Green Revolution were supplied by multinational agribusinesses. For example, all the fertilizer in Malaysia was supplied by a subsidiary of Imperial Chemical Industries (ICI), Chemical Company of Malaysia. The nitrogen fertilizer plant was linked to Esso. British agency houses, like Harrison and Crosfield as well as Guthrie, were responsible for marketing and distributing these products. And, as a way to ensure the loyalty of the Malay peasantry, a guaranteed minimum price for rice was enforced by the *Lembaga Padi Negara* (National Padi Authority) to encourage wet-rice cultivation even though it was the consumer who actually bore the cost of these subsidies.[15]

Using the rhetoric of "catching up with the Chinese," the NEP was an expression of the Malay state capitalists' communalist ideology and a violent marriage of liberal economics and *bangsa* politics. To correct the economic imbalance among the races, the federal government (i.e., the Malay state capitalists) designated itself to the role of achieving about three-quarters of the target of 30 per cent Malay share ownership in the national economy. Under the NEP, public development expenditure increased sharply, as evidenced by the proliferation of government and semi-government agencies.[16] Preference and financial assistance in government contracts, business licences, grants, land, national stocks and bonds, tertiary education and scholarships, access to civil service jobs, and all sorts of state and federal benefits and incentives were reserved for the connected private Malay individuals. All the shares in

profitable government and semi-government corporations – Bank Bumiputra, Malaysia Mining Corporation, Amanah Saham Nasional, and
so on – were channelled into a national unit trust for *bumiputras*, or
more accurately, certain privileged UMNOputras. These UMNOputras
were usually the first to take advantage of the new business opportunities that they themselves had created. Besides their corporate interests,
these Malay state capitalists also benefited from the large salaries and
perks that went with being in command of the state apparatus. The opportunity for gain from bribery and corruption in the hugely enlarged
bureaucracy that came to be following the implementation of the NEP
was notoriously widespread.

Studies that seemed to argue that the NEP had led to a decline in
poverty within the Malays nonetheless revealed that income inequality
and wealth differences within the Malays had also increased substan-
tially (Mehmet 1986). There were those who suggested that the NEP
had promoted, at least psychologically, a sense of well-being among
the Malay populations, as witnessed by the increase in Malay family
sizes; they noted that with its "Money Politics," the NEP has created a
class of "New Rich" through what they coined "rentier opportunities"
(Gomez and Jomo 1997). Because of the ways government contracts
were awarded under the NEP and the official stipulation of 30 per cent
Malay participation in new enterprises, it became imperative for private non-Malay businesses to have Malay partnerships, or "Ali Baba"
business arrangements. An "Ali Baba" business arrangement is when a
Chinese *"Baba"* invites a *bumiputra "Ali"* to be a sleeping business partner to help secure government contracts (cf. Nonini 1997). To be sure,
there were plenty of jokes about the deceptions of "Ali Baba" business
arrangements, jokes that usually affirmed an interpersonal ethnic victory of the Chinese over the *bumiputras*.

From an economic standpoint, the NEP was a non-negotiable race-
based resource distribution. While UMNO dictated, the rest of the
political parties within the BN, especially the Malaysia Chinese Association (MCA), complied and navigated the lopsided terms and conditions using money as the medium of cooperation with the UMNO
shining stars. Working in this system, well-connected wheelers and
dealers, regardless of race or religion, obtained rewarding outcomes for
themselves via the "Ali Baba" arrangement. One could say that racial
muhibah (amicable racial cooperation) materialized under the NEP, albeit only in high society.[17] The NEP, which came about in the aftermath
of a racial riot in 1969, is an extension of that violence and its excesses,

serving to create an effective organization of unequal plundering of the nation's wealth in its allocation of utilities and the creation of allegiances – this holy trinity of violence, allocations, and allegiances.[18]

On the whole, for non-Malays, the sense of being Malaysian continues to be questioned by the State. Since the inception of the NEP, more and more non-Malay families have begun sending their children to New Zealand, Australia, Britain, and North America, hoping that this might be a way out of Malaysia for their children and, subsequently, for themselves – a phenomenon that is reserved only for the very rich. One could argue that the brain-drain phenomenon did not start with the NEP but with the ascendency of the Malay state capitalists. Since then, discrimination against non-Malays has been quite widespread in the form of unequal opportunities for the working class in areas of employment, education, civil service, military, police, language policy, and so on.[19] But the root of the continued discrimination started during the colonial/early postcolonial economy, and in particular the Emergency (1948–60) that gave shape to the communalist politics of the "Alliance Formula" that ensured political power for the Malay ruling class. To be sure, forms of differences existed along ethnic lines before the European encounter, but the colonial politics of divide and rule politicized the Malay/non-Malay differences, giving rise to race-based political identities and systems of law.[20]

In 1990, after thirty years of the NEP, the government launched *Wawasan* 2020 (Vision 2020) in the hope of achieving a self-sufficient, Malaysian-centric industrial economy by the year 2020 – bringing with it many rhetorical gimmicks and varied economic jargon. For example, the NEP became the New Development Policy (NDP 1990–2000), followed by the 3rd Outline Perspective Plan (OPP3 2000–10), which also includes the National Vision Policy (NVP) that will soon be replaced by the yet-to-be defined NEM (New Economic Model) under the slogan of 1Malaysia, each piling on top of one another in the ruin of governmental institutions that virtually forced out any competition from the nonelites. Even though the details of the NEM have yet to be announced, the current prime minister Najib Razak has unleashed a barrage of incomprehensible acronyms to reform the Malaysian economy. According to its department's website, the economic driver in charge of the task is called *PEMANDU* (*pemandu is* the Malay word for driver) and it is charged with formulating and implementing NKRAs (National Key Result Areas), MKRAs (Ministerial Key Result Areas), and getting "Big Results Fast."[21] PEMANDU is part of the GTP, the Government

Transformation Programme, which also involves the SITF (Special Implementation Task Force). Even if you add in the EPU (Economic Planning Unit) and the NKEAs (National Key Economic Areas), you would not even come close to the end of the list of economic acronyms invented by its economic technocrats.

Meanwhile, the global investors – and Malaysians, in my opinion, to a lesser extent – are waiting for another barrage of economic acronyms when the details of the NEM are unveiled. To be fair, the Malaysia government is not the only regime in love with economic acronyms. But it is fair to ask what ordinary Malaysians have gotten from the NEP and the billions spent. *Bangsa* politics continue to serve as smokescreens in order to obscure the accumulation of gift networks of the politically well-connected that produced cronyism and corruption, especially with privatization and other policies that have been associated with economic liberalization since the mid-1980s. To borrow from John Hutnyk (2004), who writes in a different context, it is here that the hypocrisy of the NEP and other developmental *gifts* are most explicitly revealed – these are agendas "mouthed by those whose privilege to speak rests upon an inequality they will not admit" (174).

The NEP and a series of other developmental policies have forced a switch in self-identity among most non-Malays (and some Malays), including myself, from the "we" (active agents) to the "us" (dominated subjectivity), denoting the passive subjectivity that seems to cloud our existence – so much so that one could ask: how different is the history of the *bangsa Melayu* (the Malays), whose position is so natural that they are not even aware of their privileges as citizens (I acknowledge that I am generalizing here), whereas for non-Malays the phrase "privileges of citizenship" sounds almost ironic? Meanwhile, hundreds of thousands of *Malaysians* living abroad are denied their voting rights, as the Malaysian's Election Commission only allows four categories of citizens residing overseas to cast their votes as postal voters: military personnel, public servants, their spouses at Malaysian high commissions or consulates, and full-time government scholarship students – the overwhelming majority of whom, of course, are *bumiputra* recipients.

After having been *legally* discriminated against, the stories of the Japanese Occupation, the Emergency, and the War on Communism no longer seemed so remote to me. I began to realize that the past was not a closed chapter of history. Policies from the past continued to divide us Malaysians. I could no longer pretend that these were histories that belonged to another time, to someone else. I began, like any other researcher, by looking at what had been written about the Cold War in Sarawak. Yet, as I read, I found myself becoming increasingly dissatisfied. If the materials I was reading were to be believed, the actions taken by the government to sacrifice the rural Hakkas in Sarawak in the 1960s and 1970s were justified. They were not.

Moreover, I find no discussion of the violence at the *correction centres* and *new villages* in Malaya and Sarawak. The idea of the *new villages* was one of those ideal gifts invented by English advisors in British Malaya. Such spatialities were essentially modern state concentration camps that were, in the words of former Special Branch officer, Leon Comber (2008), first "successfully" tried out during the Malaya Emergency (1948–60) and later implemented in Sarawak, where the Hakkas were later allowed to "suffer peacefully" within its fences – an experience that seems to have an invisible status in the Malaysian consciousness. As Gyanendra Pandey (2005) points out, history proceeds on the assumptions of a fixed subject – community, nation, state – and a predominantly predetermined course of human development or transformation whereby silences and omissions are an essential part of an ideological discourse (see also Duby [1974] 1985; Trouillot 1995).[22] The violence that accompanies "progress" and "civilization" finds little place in the historical narratives, unless it is extreme – such as insurrection, uprising, revolution, or war. The "less extreme" forms of violence are often reduced to a set of statistics that find no expression of agency or contestations even though they remain one of the central features of modernity.

Refractory Tropes

Since one of the concerns of this ethnography is about the life and livelihoods of a figuration of individuals I can call my subjects, I need to address what was central to them in their daily lives. My subjects had to deal not only with memories (real or rehearsed), but also with the will to forget about events of the past in order to live on, something that was momentarily interrupted when they met the anthropologist. And why shouldn't they forget when one considers that their living conditions at the time were just as bleak as they had been during the Cold War? Even though the killings and tortures had stopped, their social, economic, and political situation had not improved a bit. What preoccupied them most were their survival techniques – today, this week, this month, this year – within an entire complex of a social, economic, and political system that remained indifferent to their plights. To most of them, the past was history and the future was quite gloomy. Many of the bus conductors and drivers had been doing the same job for over three or four decades, day in and day out, and with low salaries. Most of them were already in their late fifties to mid-sixties. What preoccupied them was an effort to live in the present, with little interest in the past and little thought for the future.[23]

I prefer the term "refractory" to describe how they dealt with the structure of power – whether it came from the State, their local community, or, in the case of the bus drivers and conductors, their workplace. According to *Webster's Third New International Dictionary*, refractory means, among other things, resisting control or authority, stubborn, unmanageable, and perverse. In many ways, the word refractory has a lesser tendency to obscure practices of competition, cooperation, co-optation, collaboration, or alliance with existing power structures that affect people's daily lives – or, in better words, that structure their way of living sanely, albeit at times tragically, in accordance with their experiences, situations, and limitations. In short, following Marcel Mauss's (1979) discussion of *habitus*, an agent's actions are not so much read as rejections or acceptances of discourse, but rather come out of a set of cultivated sensibilities that are affected by both historical forces as well as contemporary conditions. It would be better, then, to treat them as "learned capabilities ... that are linked to authoritative standards and regular practice" (noted by Asad 1993, 74–5; see also Asad 2000).

To refract also captures the notion of being indifferent towards the wielders of power. They were fully aware that the government they were subjected to governed not on the principle of legitimacy or the "right" to govern. The NEP and the subsequent policies under different names were essentially a string of austere affirmative action packages that had produced such a degree of structural limitation for my subjects that they considered themselves as hyphenated second-class, even third-class citizens. On top of this, the lower-class non-Malays – a group to whom most, if not all, of my subjects belong – often felt that their past and current dispositions were considered to be insignificant not only by the federal and state governments, but even by the other sectors of the Chinese communities that did not share what they went through. Let me elaborate.

I had the opportunity to meet a few Hokkien and Teochiu merchants along the Main Bazaar, a busy street I frequently passed by as I made my way to the SOC and KTC bus stations located at the furthest west end of this street. The Main Bazaar was the oldest and busiest street in Kuching, situated parallel to the Kuching River. This was where most of the long-established Hokkien and Teochiu merchants had their shops. Apart from doing my occasional grocery shopping there, I also checked out the daily pepper prices so I could start up conversations with some rural Hakka pepper farmers who came from the *new villages*, something I will touch on in chapter 5. Over time, as I became familiar with some of these merchants, they would often ask if I knew whether this or that pepper farmer was using some other buyers since they had not seen them for quite some time. For my part, I pretended to have no knowledge of it.

From the few conversations I had with these merchants, I was somewhat dismayed to find that many of them seemed puzzled as to why I was interested in the history of those living at a few *new villages*. One of the merchants once remarked to me, "The leaders are the ones who can tell you about the history of the Chinese in Sarawak, not those ordinary folks." These Teochiu and Hokkien merchants had many contacts among the Hakka pepper farmers. After all, they did buy peppers from them. But even as these merchants might have been told stories of the curfews and deaths that occurred within the *new villages*, they meant little to them. The history of displacement remains very much within the boundaries of those that were sacrificed. This degree of specificity, as I have indicated earlier, has to do with the long-established divisions that existed between the different sectors of the Chinese population in Sarawak along the contours of speech groups, classes, languages of education, occupations, religions, and geography.

Indeed, the specificity of which history is worth writing (or narrating) has to do with the degree of complexity and complicity within the general Chinese population. The displaced Hakkas from rural areas have no camaraderie with the urban Teochius and Hokkiens, and vice versa. This intense feeling of betrayal and competition among some of the Chinese population in Sarawak has to do with their particular history. During the 1960s and 1970s, Kuching was predominantly a Hokkien and Teochiu area. Some of my Hakka subjects recalled how hostile Kuching could be, especially along the Main Bazaar or the Padungan areas. They would tell me that these were Hokkien and Teochiu areas, and that these groups did not like the Hakkas on their turf.

The degree of contact that the Hakka farmers had with these Hokkien and Teochiu merchants was in most cases a strategic consideration based on economics. They needed to sell their peppers or vegetables to

these merchants and they did their grocery shopping with them as well
(see T'ien [1953] 1997). Beyond that, the merchants were not concerned
with the violence that had occurred in the rural areas or in the *new villages*. Some of these merchants even looked down on the Hakkas, as
expressed by comments such as, "Those are the *san-sang* [mountain/
rural] people, the *sancun swa ngiau chee* [the village jungle rats]."

I suspect there were reasons behind their derogatory comments.
Since the mid-1960s, there has been an increase in the number of Hakkas living in Kuching due to the massive migration of young Hakkas
from the *new villages* and as well as from the traditional Hakka stronghold in Bau. While there, I heard comments from Hokkiens and Teochius in coffee shops, food markets, or even pubs about how they now
have to learn the Hakka language because of the increasing presence
of the Hakkas in Kuching. Another factor that contributed to the increasing number of Hakkas in Kuching came about in the mid-1980s
when the pepper prices were extremely favourable to Hakka pepper
farmers. With significant capital, many of these farmers from the Serian
District started to venture into all sorts of businesses in Kuching. Many
Hokkiens and Teochius would agree, albeit reluctantly, that Hakka was
becoming the lingua franca of Kuching and that was not sitting too well
with them. In many ways, I suspect their disinterested attitude towards
the Hakkas reflected their refusal to acknowledge the growing presence
of the Hakkas in Kuching; and, in retrospect, that it provided them with
a discourse to hold on to the conceptual facade of their past majority
and business monopoly in Kuching.

It is my opinion that the past and the present inevitably laid down
the limits of my Hakka interlocutors' existence in Sarawak. It was these
concrete experiences – both from the discourse of dislocation as well
as their current dispositions as low-income, working-class bus conductors, drivers, and clothing vendors – that shaped, to a degree, their
outlook. Most of their daily manoeuverings, as will become clearer in
the ethnography, were pragmatic in spirit, even ironic, humorous, and
most of all, had the capacity of hardened stubbornness that allowed
them to remain indifferent to the institutional circuits of symbolic
powers. These activities or behaviours should not, and must not, be
identified as their form of alienating themselves from or resisting the
normative consensus. At best, these routines of theirs can be seen as
their attempts to reduce the degree of their subjugation by "working
the system to their minimum disadvantage" (Hobsbawm 1973, 7). Being indifferent was a big part of the survival tactics that sprung from

their experience of their past as well as the quotidian material they had to negotiate. Make no mistake about it, they were fully aware of the political system in Malaysia: a system founded on Malay dominance, particularly by a small, elite group within the Malay population. If it is even possible to talk about the goal of these individuals, if they had any, it was to survive. Their intention was always survival. They were, after all, pragmatic individuals.

Chapter Two

The Greater Malaysia Plan

Prior to the formation of Malaysia, Britain's principle concern in its protectorates of Malaya, Singapore, Brunei, Sarawak, and Sabah was how to maintain its political and economic influence in the region with less police, military, and administrative forces – and without increasing their costs (Subritzky 1999). It was hoped that under a gradual decolonization policy that would promote political liberalization and trade, these protectorates would become quasi-independent and yet remain a pro-British federation. Only then would the idea of Greater Malaysia be considered. Unfortunately, developments in the region forced Britain to abandon its so-called benign federation plan and pursue more coercive measures to safeguard its economic interests.

In fact, the idea of a Greater Malaysia has been circulating among British officials since the mid-1950s. The initial formula was only meant for a merger between a Malay-majority Malaya and a Chinese-dominated Singapore, an idea that was rejected by Malaya's Chief Minister Tunku Abdul Rahman (commonly known as Tunku) and other Malay conservative leaders (Easter 2004). As Malaya was the most prosperous country in Southeast Asia following the end of the Second World War – being the major exporter of rubber and tin, and with a per-capita income more than double that of Indonesia – the British Foreign Office strategically worked to appease Tunku and the Malay conservatives by suggesting that Sabah, Sarawak, and Brunei be added to the federation, thereby ensuring a Chinese minority in the federation (Simpson 2008, 115).

Besides Malaya, one of Britain's primary interests in the region was maintaining unrestrained access to Brunei's vast oil reserves, something vital to its postwar economy (Poulgrain 1998). The British Malayan

Petroleum Company would manage Brunei's oil industry, and would reciprocate handsomely by giving the Brunei sultan not only huge sums of oil capital but also political and military support to keep the sultanate in power. Unfortunately, this cosy relationship was at risk of being upset in 1956 by the rapid rise of Sheik A.M. Azahari and his populist People's Party of Brunei (PRB). Native to Brunei, Azahari was a veteran of the Indonesian Revolution, and upon his return in 1951 he publicly condemned royal corruption and called for democratic reforms in the hope of uniting all three English Borneo protectorates (Brunei, Sarawak, and Sabah) into a single entity, North Kalimantan (Mackie 1974).

When the PRB won all the contested seats in the Brunei's 1962 legislative council elections, the British colonial government not only denied it legitimacy, they arrested PRB members in Sarawak. Fearing their imminent arrests, despite Azahari being away in Manila, the PRB leaders and its armed wing, consisting of 2,000 to 3,000 poorly trained and ill-equipped members of the *Tentera Nasional Kalimantan Utara* (North Kalimantan National Army, or TNKU), launched a revolt. Within hours, local police in Brunei and Sarawak, along with British and Gurkha soldiers arriving from Singapore, crushed the revolt.[1] Having reinstated the sultan to the throne, Britain had to revisit the idea of the Greater Malaysia Plan (Simpson 2008).

As for Sarawak, although oil had not yet been discovered in the early 1960s, it was home to an allegedly pro-China and resilient Chinese population – backed by the Sarawak United People's Party (SUPP) – that was opposed to the Greater Malaysia Plan. At the beginning of the 1960s, SUPP claimed a membership of 47,000 – more than half of which were of Chinese descent. Because of their virulent anti-Malaysia position, the British authorities together with the Alliance government in Malaya and its counterparts in Sarawak announced that communist field workers had infiltrated a large part of the SUPP.[2] The main concern of the British authorities was not the pro-British moderates within the SUPP but some 2,500 allegedly communist core members, as well as its base supporters of students and teachers from the Chinese Chung Hwa schools, members of Chinese Associations, trade unionists, and peasants.[3] Consequently, many of the SUPP members were charged with having communist connections and were detained at various correction centres (Teng and Ngieng 1990).

Sarawak government intelligent sources also believed that communist core members within the SUPP were in alliance with Azahari's PRB in Brunei. A Sarawak that was aligned with Azahari would not only threaten British access to Brunei's oil reserves but, in the context of Indonesia's *Konfrontasi*, it might also create a pro-leftist stronghold in the region.[4] Within a year after the Brunei Revolt, the infamous slogan *Ganyang Malaysia* (Crush Malaysia) became one of Indonesian President Soekarno's political catchphrases in the nation-building process – a daunting task, considering this was a heterogeneous country spanning thousands of islands with diverse cultural, religious, and linguistic affiliations (Davidson 2008).[5]

Meanwhile, despite evidence of widespread local opposition to the Greater Malaysia Plan in Sarawak and Sabah, as part of a strategic move to contain the expansionary vision of President Soekarno – and, by extension, that of the USSR and the People's Republic of China – the plan was supported by Britain and the United Nations (Thant 1963).[6] Considering the United States' strategic relations with Indonesia, and with its hands already tied down by the widening and costly war in Vietnam, it offered somewhat muted support, calling the plan a positive arrangement for sustaining British influence and military presence in the region (Sodhy 1988).[7] In other words, with the war in Vietnam and Laos dragging on, the Johnson and Nixon administrations could not entertain another potential scenario in Southeast Asia whereby the United States was pinned down by the USSR and China via an Asian proxy (Khalidi 2009).[8]

Right from the beginning, the Greater Malaysian Plan was a plan that was orchestrated by interests external to Sarawakians (and Sabahans), which explains why the "official" state government journal, the *Sarawak Gazette*, gave a contrasting (if not lukewarm) reception on the day Sarawak became part of the Federated States of Malaysia: it "was a day of contrast: on the one hand you have the official celebrations, on the other hand ostentatious absence of many municipal officials, community leaders, and other persons of position, whose presence upon such occasions was normally presumed obligatory" (*Sarawak Gazette*, December 31, 1963). This lack of a sense of "sentimental" sovereignty was not surprising. Frantz Fanon (1963) has explained this aptly: "for 95 percent of the population of underdeveloped countries, independence brings no immediate change" (95).

The Danger Within

Just a few months after Sarawak *became* part of the Federated States of Malaysia, Tim Hardy, the head of the Sarawak Special Branch (the intelligence arm of the Sarawak Constabulary), published a white paper entitled *The Danger Within* (1963), which claimed that there were enemies within the state in the form of communist-inspired organizations.[9] Like the doctrine of "national securities" discussed by Avery Gordon (1997), the doctrine of the "internal enemies" is highly flexible in that it allows the State to conjure up any ghosts to then justify its exorcising rites. In the context of the Cold War, and with Indonesia as its immediate neighbour (and its *external enemy*), the Malaysian state conjured up a malevolent spectre under the looming international communist conspiracy. But in the process of exorcising the ghosts that the government believed were ruining the nation, it created another set of ghosts.

The Danger Within asserted that the existence of a communist-inspired organization in Sarawak went as far back as 1941 (Hardy 1963, 2, 45), referring to the Sarawak Anti-Fascist League (SAFL), an anti-Japanese organization that fought alongside the Allied forces against the Japanese Imperial Army during the Second World War. One cannot help but question the basis of such an assertion.[10] Was it because the majority of the members of the Sarawak Anti-Fascist League were Chinese and allegedly had sympathy and support for China? But the most intriguing question is this: why was the SAFL not invoked as a threat to the Malayan Union when they were fighting alongside the Allied forces against Imperial Japan during the Second World War, but only during the Malayan Emergency and, in the case of Sarawak, almost twenty years later when Malaya and Britain were formulating a strategy to annex Sarawak and Sabah under the Greater Malaysia Plan?

By asserting the communist problem in Sarawak as a Chinese problem, *The Danger Within* essentially started a sacrificial frenzy towards those on the wrong side of the wire. In itself, *The Danger Within* was an assertion of necessary state policies and actions; it described an internal problem that was dangerous and explained the need for sacrifices to be made to solve the problem. It also provided the state with a claim to moral legitimacy as knower, arbiter, and protector of "the people." By the time *The Danger Within* was published, most, if not all, of the anti-imperial and anti-Malaysia organizations had been outlawed, many of them metamorphosing into a number of guerrilla organizations in the jungles of Borneo that were subsequently glossed over by the authorities with the description "Clandestine Communist Organizations" (CCOs). By 1965, all the constituent elements of state abuse were in place: forced relocation, arrest without warrant, arrest without any charges, detention incommunicado, and so on – something the authority had learned from the Malayan Emergency, and which thrust Sarawak into an episode of Cold War violence using the politics and mechanisms of dispossession.

Allow me to briefly touch on the Malayan Emergency for those who are not familiar with this dark episode of Malaysian history. The Malayan Emergency (1948–60) was the euphemistic term adopted by the British colonial government to describe the uprising of the Communist Party of Malaya (CPM).[11] Instead of calling it a war, the term "Emergency" was adopted in order not to disrupt the London commercial insurance rates, which were relied upon by Malayan commerce and industry. Malaya's abundant supplies of rubber and tin were compelling economic reasons for Britain to ensure that Malaya did not fall into communist hands.[12] Besides economic reasons, with the event coming so soon after the Second World War, the colonial government had to downplay the seriousness of the situation so as not to affect public morale. The High Commissioner of Malaya even gave the directive that emotive terms such as "war," "enemy," and "rebellion" should be avoided, and words such as "banditry," "thugs," "terrorism," and so on be used instead (Comber 2008, 13). In all but name, the Emergency was a fiercely fought low-intensity war waged in the Malayan jungle between the government security forces and the CPM's guerrillas, the Malayan National Liberation Army. In fact, no one realized at the time that the Emergency would drag on for twelve long years.[13]

During the Emergency, the colonial government applied a three-pronged offensive that combined the police, army, and civil government, and that was waged concurrently with a political and psychological campaign to win the hearts and minds of the Malayan people. Suspending the writ of habeas corpus, the Emergency Regulations were proclaimed to confer on the Special Branch and the police's extralegal power of arrest and detention without trial. The Special Branch was also given the authority to search persons and premises without warrant, impose curfews, control movement of foodstuffs, and so on (Short 1975).

But the major offensive that proved to be the communists' Achilles heel was ironically something the authorities had learned from Mao Zedong's often-quoted dictum regarding the relationship between the masses and the guerrillas: the masses were likened to water and the guerrillas to the fishes who inhabit it (Mao Zedong 1962).[14] And so, two years into the Emergency, the British colonial government adopted the clichéd anti-guerrilla tactic of "draining the water so the fish can't swim" (*he ze er yu*). Under Lieutenant General Sir Harold Briggs's resettlement plan, some half a million people – 85 per cent of whom were Chinese living along the fringes of the jungle (and the majority of whom happened to be Hokkiens and Teochius)[15] – were forcibly relocated into close to 400 barbed-wire-fenced *new villages*.[16] This was where the Special Branch played a huge role by planting spies and recruiting informers in the *new villages* to intercept the guerilla courier system, and then by arresting these couriers or turning them into progovernment undercover agents (Comber 2008, 82).[17] The Emergency and its "spatial articulations of state power," to invoke Henri Lefebvre's (1991) insights on the territorialization of modern state power, have wide-reaching effects on everyday life in Malayan society. As Chin and Hack (2004) point out, we are talking about the compulsory uprooting of over 10 per cent of Malaya's population who referred to the *new villages* as concentration camps.

The lessons learned from the Emergency in supposedly winning the hearts and minds of the population were deemed to be so successful that the British adopted a similar three-pronged offensive approach in Kenya, Rhodesia, and Cyprus. The British Advisory Mission also tried them out in Vietnam upon invitation by the South Vietnamese government and its ally, the United States (Kua 2007; Comber 2008). Needless to say, the lessons learned from the Emergency were also applied to Sarawak.

In regards to Sarawak, what is so blatantly silent in *The Danger Within* is its hasty abdication of any forms of dissident feelings among the indigenous population against the inclusion of Sarawak as part of Greater Malaysia. According to a once-classified/controlled paper of the United States Information Agency (USIA) (1963), entitled "Sarawak and North Borneo Insurgency: Racial and Ethnic Factors" – a mere fourteen-page report published on June 17, 1963 – dissident groups in Sarawak and West Kalimantan, most of them of indigenous makeup, had been active since the early 1950s in promoting possible reunification between the Dayaks of Indonesia's West Kalimantan and their brothers in the British protectorates of Sarawak, North Borneo (Sabah), and Brunei.[18] A substantial number of them had received training in guerilla warfare and were being morally supported by the Indonesian Communist Party (PKI) (4). In December of 1962, the governor of Indonesian West Kalimantan, Oeray, who was also a paramount Dayak leader, threatened to launch Dayak "volunteers" in "*kajau anak*" (jungle warfare) to reunite them with their brothers in Sarawak. Many Dayak leaders shared Oeray's assertion that "[g]eographically, ethnologically, and from the standpoint of traditional bonds, the entire Dayak people consider themselves one and united" (2) and were against the idea of a Greater Malaysia. In fact, Dayak leaders have on occasion asserted that the very name of "Malaysia" (the land of the Malays) sounds odd to their ears, since they consider themselves to be the true indigenes of Borneo (2).[19]

The same report also mentions that in 1963 a radio station of the North Borneo Rebel Government, calling itself the "Voice of Kalimantan Utara (North Borneo) Freedom Fighters," made its debut in Borneo in the Malay, English, Indonesian, and Iban languages. Its leader, Azahari, and commandant, Zulkifi, were demanding the overthrow of Malaya's Tunku Abdul Rahman, Singapore's Lee Kuan Yew, and the British imperialists (5). In addition, as early as 1963, the Indonesian press and news services carried periodic reports of Dayak mobilization in response to the North Borneo liberation struggle. For example, the Djakarta Domestic Service announced that thousands of Punan Dayaks employed as miners in West and East Kalimantan provinces intended to join their oppressed fellow tribesmen in their struggle to liberate themselves from any form of colonialism (3). Colonialism, as one Dayak spokesmen charged, "has split the island into pieces" (4).

Regardless of these *noises*, the strategy of the British authorities, the federal government of Malaysia, and its alliance counterparts in Sarawak were to treat them as isolated instances and to put their concerted efforts into the purported main issue of the early 1960s: the War against Communism – a war against the rural Chinese population that was purportedly feeding the communists (literally with food as well as information), and which, in this case, happened to be made up of the Hakkas. As far as the state was concerned, the gravest danger in the Borneo territories of Malaysia during that time consisted of the possibility of a revolt in Sarawak engineered by the CCOs and the discontented members of Sarawak's anti-Malaysia political parties, in particular the Sarawak United People's Party (SUPP). It is my opinion that by constructing the communist problem as a Chinese issue, the government did manage to prevent any types of alliances that the Chinese communities in Sarawak might have had with indigenous groups, which could have threatened the wielders of power.

Operation Hammer

One of the hallmarks of the state's pedagogical discourse is its ability to camouflage violence and disorder underneath the construction of its glorified pasts and intended destiny. In other words, the official claims (and denials) by nationalist leaders and official historians lie at the heart of the "aestheticizing impulse" of the nation state (see Anderson 1991; Daniel 1996; Redfield 1999; Reid 2010). After becoming part of Malaysia, in an effort to fashion an identity for themselves, the Alliance government in Sarawak – with aid from the federal government in Kuala Lumpur – set about sifting through its population for convenient scapegoats to be *saved* (i.e., sacrificed), subjects that allegedly embodied this persisting threat of Evil (i.e., communism). Indeed, the conclusion of who needed to be *saved* was an afterthought as judgments had already been reached behind closed doors at official meetings and security councils – the Oedipal theatres that cared little about preserving or affirming life.

On June 29, 1965, less than two years after Sarawak became part of Malaysia, key personnel in the defence and internal security departments met at the state capital, Kuching, to discuss the situation in so-called communist-influenced areas. At some point during the meeting, the inspector general of the Royal Malaysian Police Force, Sir Claude Fenner, pounded the table with his fist and said, "we'll hammer them – let the operation be called Operation Hammer" (Porrit 2004, 122). Once again, adopting the clichéd anti-guerrilla tactic of "draining the water so the fish can't swim" (*he ze er yu*), Deputy Prime Minister Tun Abdul Razak announced the immediate resettlement of people living in some rural areas (Lee 1970). By this he was referring to the rural areas along the Kuching-Serian Road that were predominantly populated by Chinese Hakka farmers, who provided fresh fruits and vegetables to Kuching, Serian, and other smaller townships.[20] Under Operation Hammer, the police and military forces sealed off an eighty-square-mile area, extending from the fifteenth to the twenty-fourth mile along the Kuching-Serian Road. Within a three-day period, some 1,200 families, amounting to close to 8,000 rural Hakkas living in the area, were forcibly relocated into three newly constructed barbed-wire-fenced *new villages* equipped with floodlit security fences and a twenty-four-hour curfew, with the explanation that this was the government's *gift* to protect them from the communists.

Just like the Emergency in Malaya (with the construction of 400 *new villages*), this was a historically specific form of modern state power – "as a politico-spatial organization and as a strategic dimension of modern politics" (Brenner and Elden 2009, 356).[21] To invoke Deleuze and Guattari ([1972] 1983), these rural Hakkas were not given time to consider the *risk* of accepting the *gift*. It was too late – and they remain violently *inscribed* by the gift to this day. A local newspaper described the operation as the day "thousands of Chinese [Hakkas] began their long period of suffering" (*The Vanguard* 1965, 1). An editorial in the *Far Eastern Economic Review* (1965), as well as representatives of the Sarawak United People's Party (SUPP), described them as "concentration camps" (12). Not surprisingly, two days after these remarks, the Sarawak Police banned SUPP representatives from visiting these *new villages* or any other controlled areas (*Sarawak Gazette* 1965).

The original plan of Operation Hammer was to relocate not 8,000 but 60,000 Chinese, but it was abandoned because it was thought that relocating 60,000 people would antagonize the entire Chinese community along the Kuching-Serian Road and would exacerbate the situation (see Porrit 2004, 122).[22] Perhaps they had learned from the Malayan Emergency that this strategy was not that *cheap* after all – and that attempt had lasted twelve years. It is important to note that the relocation of rural Hakkas into *new villages* in Sarawak occurred less than two years after it became part of Malaysia. If anything else, the launching of these operations and relocation schemes would seem to go against the "neutral" finding of the United Nations observers in 1963: that the majority of Sarawakians supported the Greater Malaysia proposal.

Moreover, even though there were scattered Iban and Bidayuh communities living in these *communist-influenced* areas along the Kuching-Serian Road, in its intention to sacrifice certain communities, only the Hakkas were forcibly "saved" by the *new villages* (Porrit 1991). If any indigenous subject was suspected of being a communist or communist sympathizer, the usual course of action was to place the individual under house arrest, restricting him to the confines of his longhouse or village. Normally, these house arrests would last no longer than a month.[23] Furthermore, when reading the newspaper archive, I find it interesting that reports of indigenous subjects held under house arrest could only be found in Chinese newspapers.[24] Writing in a different context, Sally Falk Moore (1998) notes that a *politicized* legal system is extremely useful because it can "limit that of which it will take official cognizance" (132), recognizing some and excluding others as legally relevant. Similarly, some legal scholars have suggested that law is a "specialized discourse" with the capacity to construct its own reality (Luhmann 1982; Teubner 1989).

To say that communism is a Chinese problem not only ignores non-Chinese involvement in communist activities but at the same time homogenizes the diversity of, if not the rivalries that have always existed between and within each Chinese speech group in Sarawak. As Sino anthropologist Ju-Kang T'ien ([1953] 1997) pointed out, there have always been tremendous conflicts among the different Chinese speech groups in Sarawak. The "old guards," the Teochiu and Hokkien merchants in Kuching, have always been wary of possible inroads by the rural Hakkas into their business realms. Indeed, one can trace Chinese speech group conflicts back to the Brookes era. During the Bau Revolt in 1857, local Hokkien and Teochiu merchants in Kuching were instrumental in helping the Brookes defeat the Hakka *Kongsi* miners from Bau (Chew 1990).[25] In fact, throughout the 1960s and 1970s, some parts of the Chinese population in the urban sectors were fully supportive of the government's War on Communism. The Teochiu Association in Kuching, for example, even carried out a full-page advertisement in the *Sarawak Gazette* announcing their full support for Operation Hammer the day after the operation was launched (July 8, 1965).

Some critics contend that the actions taken by the authorities were an extreme form of communalism stemming from the fears of the elite about a potentially powerful and dissident rural Hakka population (Asli 1993; Pusat Arakib Negara 1994). I would not contest that there were possible grounds for such fear. As T'ien (1997) has pointed out, "historically the Hakka speaking people have a long history not only as farmers and sojourners in China, but also as reformists" (14; see also Hsu 1983). But there are other interpretations of the Hakkas both in China and elsewhere, depending on whom one asks. Although some have argued that the various operations and resettlement schemes succeeded in preventing a certain section of the Chinese population from contributing to covert activities (Asli 1993; Pusat Arakib Negara 1994), the most obvious (or serious) consequence of the relocation campaign was to legitimize the hyphenated status of the Chinese in Sarawak. It was this backdrop of local politics and the possibility of ethnic and language group manipulation that allowed the State to stereotype and encapsulate certain Chinese speech groups.

Beginning with the three *new villages* along the Kuching-Serian Road, the designation of "communist-influenced areas" spread to other parts of Sarawak, which were mainly determined by the presence of significant Hakka populations. Coastal areas around Kuching (in Hakka:

Hai Wai) were zoned as such areas. Similarly, *Batu Kawa, Matang, Bau, Lundu, Simanggang, Engkilili,* and most border towns and outposts were classified as "sensitive areas." Military personnel from West Malaysia, many of whom were Malays, were called in to patrol these areas, and their arrival almost immediately became a source of contempt for many Sarawakians, even the local Malays.[26]

In less than two years after Sarawak was annexed by Malaysia, the lives of thousands of rural Hakkas living in the *new villages,* coastal areas, and "sensitive areas" and at border outposts along the Malaysian–Indonesian border were to be changed forever. The inspector general's reference to "hammering" his victims takes up the lexicon of the military's paradigmatic working vocabulary, as seen in the names of a series of relocation operations like Operation White Terror, Operation Freedom, Operation Spearhead, Operation *Hangat* (Hot), Operation *Paku* (Nail), Operation *Kilong* (Fish Trap), Operation *Jala Raya* (Royal Net), Operation *Lada Pedas* (Hot Pepper), Operation *Hentam* (Assault), Operation *Ngayau* (an Iban word for "Total War"),[27] and so on.

Looking at the series of operations and relocation schemes that were enthusiastically enforced by the state in the War on Communism, one wonders if the government of Malaysia shared the legal fetishism so characteristic of countries ruled by authoritative regimes.[28] A Hakka bus driver once remarked ruefully to me, "The law in this county is the government. It has nothing to do with what is right or wrong." After a slight pause, he added, "Actually, it is not the law we are scared of, it's the police." His characterization of "the law" – in essence, the blurring between legalization and legitimization – was shared by most of the Hakkas I met. To invoke Michael Taussig (2004), the rural Hakkas seemed to be living in a situation "when law's lawlessness becomes law seeking out dramatic displays," as when the names of the *new villages* and its inhabitants "were display pieces, sacrificial victims to the grim reality of a phantom justice system" (274).

The Theatre of Language

Language shows clearly that memory is not an instrument for exploring the past, but rather its theatre. It is the medium of past experience, as the ground is the medium in which dead cities lie inferred.

Benjamin (1978, 25–6).

Even though the episodes of dislocation and displacement during the Cold War in Sarawak cannot be compared to those of the Jewish

Holocaust – the "extremest of extreme" events, as it has been characterized (Diner 1992, 128) – some of the scholarship written on the Holocaust is helpful for providing both questions on and understandings
of the notions of violence, memory, history, and state power. James
Young (1990), writing on Holocaust memories and testimonies, poses
the question: how can we know the Holocaust except through the many
ways in which it is handed down to us? Young answers by suggesting
that, as much as through its "history," we know the Holocaust through
its literary, fictional, historical, and political representations, as well as
through its personal, testimonial representations. Equally important as
the "facts" of any event are the ways people remember those facts and
how they represent them.

The question might be extended to the Cold War in Sarawak. Memories of the violence during the 1960s and 1970s in Sarawak are very
much alive among a certain population. We can attempt to reconstruct
the events through their memories, through the divisions it has unleashed, and through the silences and reluctant stories it has produced.
This collection of narratives – individual and collective, familiar, messy,
or contradictory – and the motions and textures of silences is what
makes up part of the reality, the eventfulness of the Cold War. They
are part of that history, part of its theatre. Together, these have made
for a narrative in which my presence, as an author, as a friend and ac-
quaintance of my interlocutors, as a mediator, interpreter, translator,
and even as an adversary, is quite visible. I make no apologies for this.
I have always had a deep suspicion of histories that are written as if the
author were but a mere vehicle, histories that, to paraphrase Roland
Barthes ([1957] 1972), seem to write themselves, as if the absence of
the "I" in such histories helped to achieve the illusion of objectivity, to
establish factuality.

One might even say that the "histories" I am writing are an attempt
to reconcile the needs of academia with the demands of conscience, and
ones that proceed cautiously with the ethics and politics surrounding
silence. To quote Leslie Dwyer (2009), it is not just an attempt to rescue
a certain past, since "[s]peaking memories of violence does not simply
place one in relation to a distant past but also engages with a complex
politics of the present and its articulation and concealment in social
practice" (138–9). It is also a response to the needs of the moment –
however remote such a possibility exists – for the Sarawak Hakkas to
rethink what it means to speak truth to power.

As Pandey (2005) points out, decolonization or the *independence* of
"new nations" has, in many ways, roused our consciousness about the

rape of colonization. Independence has, in most cases, been succeeded by another kind of colonization. Some of us call it "the gifts of development," with similar or worse effects on the general population of the planet; the continued adverse effect on minorities, communities that had abundant reserves of memory, but little in the way of history. On another level, I seek to identify both the local contexts as well as the conceptual frameworks that construct "Chineseness" historically and in the contemporary setting. This can provide invaluable insights into the way that being "Chinese" has come to be an inescapable, if perhaps incoherent social ascription, in contrast with the stereotyped conception of overseas Chinese as merely a collection of merchants, community leaders, or "middlemen minorities."

In using the narratives of my subjects (as well as my own) to talk about the politics of telling history under the shadows of the Cold War in Sarawak, I am emphasizing the performative aspect of language that treats utterances as speech acts (Austin 1962). The emphasis here is not on whether statements (or utterances) are facts of truth or falsity but, instead, on what such utterances accomplish or do not accomplish. It is not so much what was said or could be said, but what was happening or taking effect between speaking bodies (my subjects and I) during the course of our interlocution. In other words, the emphasis here is both on the sign (signifier/signified) as well as the utterance, a combination of what is actually verbalized and what is non-verbalized but assumed by all the interlocutors in conversation. As Bakhtin ([1965] 1984) puts it, "The simultaneity of the said and unsaid is apparent in the effects of intonation (how a thing is said) on language (what is said)" (207). This is especially important when one considers how communism is still a sensitive topic in Malaysia.[29]

However, I am aware that the employment of narratives to excavate a certain past is a deeply contested method in ethnography (Crapanzano 1984). There is no way of knowing if the stories people choose to tell are accurate or not, nor of knowing what they choose to suppress. How can we know, four or five decades after the events took place, that the stories are not rehearsed performances? How can we know whether they are told differently for different people, perhaps tailored to suit what the storytellers think the researcher wishes to hear? Also, working with memory is always problematic. Memory is never pure, unmediated, or stable (Antze and Lambeck 1996). So much depends on who remembers, when, with whom, to whom, why, and how. In essence, new experiences and revised expectations continually reshape memory. This poses an epistemological question: how should we consider feelings, memories, silences, pauses, and discontinuity in the concept of history?

All told, my analytic process is interpretive and inferential. I could only talk with my interlocutors and live for a time with them, and so I must rely on my reading into the dialogic "telling" of their lives and livelihoods, and into their words for traces of meaning along with other non-verbal actions – bodily gestures, silences, hesitation, pauses, jokes, laughter, and so on – all of which are "riddled with cultural assumptions, political tensions, pragmatic moves, rhetorical pitches, and subjective vicissitudes" (Desjarlais 1997, 10). In other words, the ethnographic writing I present here is pregnant with a multifaceted reflexivity in which the voices of the Others have been incorporated into my own (Fabian 1983), producing what Bakhtin (1981) describes as "a plurilinguistic poetics," an overlapping of voices and exchanging status, of subject and object.

Hammer Villages

When we name, we freeze reality, as with facing the Gorgon. In naming ... we make it protuberant in the vortex that is history. This naming not only petrifies but awakens life, no matter how spectral, in congealed things.

Michael Taussig (2004, 277)

Until that late morning in November 1999 when I arrived by bus to Siburan, one of the three *new villages* that materialized out of Operation Hammer, this particular *new village* was little more than a name to me, and a particular kind of modern state-inscribed territory.[30] After I had visited Siburan as well as Tapah and Beratok – the other two *new villages* – several times, I became curious as to how the residents might feel about the names of their villages. After all, in Malay, Siburan means "New Life Village" or *Xin Shen cun* in Hakka. Beratok translates as "Come and Develop Village" or *Lai Tuo cun*, and Tapah is "Great Wealth and Prosperity Village" or *Da Fu cun*.[31]

It might help to think along the lines set out by Keith Basso (1983; 1996), who points out how the usage of place-names among the Western Apache can serve as important indicators towards certain historical events and their geographical locations, as well as pointing towards the systems of rules and values that organize and regulate the lives of individuals within a community. But in the case of these *new villages* in Sarawak, what if the names of places do not sit well with the individuals who were forcibly relocated into them, into these modern form of spatiality that were mediated through state power that organized, regulated, and dominated their lives and livelihoods? It is unmistakable that the names of these *new villages* were used to establish precedents and convey an "authorized" inscription of reality in advance of the reality within them. Considering Taussig's (2004) provocative illumination of the law-like (if not lawless) entity of a prison, one may ask how the naming of these prison-like *new villages* might provide "what is named with a special quality of being, a personality, we might say, and in that sense brings life to what it boxes in" (277). I was curious as to how the names of their *new villages*, combined with the policing of their movements and the danger these residents experienced from the mid-1960s until 1980, might have impregnated their sensibilities, their bodily behaviour, and their overall well-being.

One Sunday afternoon, I asked a group of men who were playing mah-jong on the second floor of a coffee shop at Tapah what they thought about their village's name. Immediately, I could tell they were slightly irritated, judging from the sudden quiet in the room. It took a while before a young man responded, "Why are you nagging us?" This made others in the room somewhat embarrassed, and they remained silent. Eventually, as if the silence was becoming unbearable, the middle-aged man next to him asked, "Do you know what *Da Fu* means? Do you see a lot of wealth and prosperity here?" I nodded.

When I went over my field notes I realized that not once did any of these village residents adopt the Hakka place-names of their *new villages*. Instead it was always Siburan. The same was true for the Hakka residents at Beratok and Tapah. With that in mind, whenever I met up with these residents, or when I chatted with the bus conductors and bus drivers who had fled from these villages, I would be especially alert as to how they would address their villages. And sure enough, all of them adopted the Malay place-names. A barber at Siburan and his regulars once told me that *Da Fu cun*, *Xin Shen cun*, and *Lai Tuo cun* were merely literal translations of the official Malay place-names. But still, that did not explain why they would not utter the Hakka equivalents.

Following Frege's (1960) theory of Sinn (meaning), it would appear that the Malay place-names they uttered, even as they carried the same reference as their Hakka equivalents, had different Sinn (or meanings). Taking speech context and speaker purpose (Evans 1973) into consideration, their utterances of the Malay place-names of the *new villages*, especially among fellow residents with a certain biographical history, can be read as part of their acquiescence, consciously or otherwise, to alleviate the degree of injury of not only being forcibly relocated but also of being inscribed by the *gift* of these place-names, which were supposed to signify their acceptance of state ideology that purportedly adhered to the *peace* and *prosperity* of the nation.

As it turned out, only "outsiders" would use the Hakka equivalent place-names and whenever that happened, they would endure taunting for their usage. I remember one afternoon at a particular *warong* at the SOC bus station in Kuching, one that everyone called *Warong Muhibah*. (*Warong* is a Malay word for a shack where someone sells food and drinks, and *Muhibah* means living amicably.) I was sitting at a table with a bus conductor, Ah Fon, who still lives in Tapah, and her friend, Toni, an Iban bus conductor from a longhouse close to the township of Simanggang. At some point during our conversation, Toni told me that she had to drive all the way to *Da Fu cun* on her motorbike to pick up Ah Fon to watch a movie at a cinema in Kuching. Toni complained, "That's more than forty miles round trip just to watch a movie," to which Ah Fon responded, "I can easily take the bus to Tapah." The difference is right there: *Da Fu cun* and Tapah. Others who were at the *warong* asked if I was aware that Ah Fon came from the *Thei Chui cuns* (Hammer Villages), or more accurately, one of the *Thei Chui cuns*, a place-name that indexes the operation that forcibly relocated 8,000 Hakkas into the *new villages*.

Naturally I began to ask who came up with the umbrella place-name *Thei Chui cuns*, but my investigation proved to be inconclusive, largely because the residents at these *new villages* were not as enthusiastic as I was about determining its genealogy. A few residents at Beratok and Tapah told me rather nonchalantly that *Thei Chui cuns* was just the name others would sometimes use to invoke the bluntness of the name of the operation that relocated them, and would mention it with a slight smile on their faces. Similarly, a former communist leader told me that his relatives at Beratok did not take offence when others used the Hakka place-name of their village or the umbrella place-name. The joke, he said, was not on the residents but rather on the emptiness of these names, not to mention the absurdity of the names of the rest of the relocation operations.[32] Having said that, it remained true that most of these residents chose not to talk about Operation Hammer, for it has reached, to use a phrase from Michael Taussig (1992), the status of a public secret; something known, but unspoken and unacknowledged.

Once, on the bus, I asked a Hakka bus conductor if she had ever heard of *Thei Chui cuns*. Instead of offering a straight response, she turned to one of her passengers and mimicked my question, "Have you heard of *Thei Chui cuns*?" before proceeding to "hammer" the passenger with her fists. She never did answer my question, at least not directly, and both of them were laughing. Their *performances* signified not only the absurdity of my enquiry but also the violent genealogy that inscribed their sensibilities. I had encounters with other residents that invoked the same ironic gesture, hammering each other with their fists. In many ways, their cynical performances were tragic reminders of the very operation that had literally hammered away their earlier livelihoods.

From these episodes, it is clear that the names of the *new villages* (whether they are in Malay or Hakka) and that of the umbrella place-name are proper names in a rather strong sense, specifying referent properties rather definitively and explicitly. They refer to some "willful act" (Carroll 1981) – the inscription of a certain landscape and its sacrificial victims. However, even if we were to acknowledge that the baptismal event – the operation and the name of the *new villages* into which they were forcibly relocated – involved a "willful act," it remains indeterminate if indeed the baptism was successful. Temporally speaking, there is always a tension between history and *ahistory*, between the non-historical, detemporalized perpetuation of a moment and the historical changes that surround these place-names, between the name as marking a perduring event or reality and the event as marking a particular moment – the moment of utterance. It is this tension that seems to be so salient here.

This tension recalls Searle's (1958) position on the need to focus on the necessary conditions and the immediate speech context in order to account for the meanings of proper names. Sometimes called the "use theory," it emphasizes that the essence of names resides in their intrinsic vagueness;　not only might different individuals understand the meaning of a proper name differently – a position taken up by Frege (1960) – but even the same individuals in different speech contexts might intend to use or understand the same proper name differently. To put it another way, proper names "function not as descriptions, but as pegs on which to hang descriptions" (Searle 1958, 172). However, proper names are not just labels or pegs on which to hang descriptions. They are also active, and context-creating as well as context-reflecting. They have a strong indexical function. What is at issue here is that the adoption and creation of different place-names was deeply embedded, if not invested, in a political and spatial-territorial context that changed over time (Lefebvre 1991; Arrighi 1995; Agnew 2005). The baptismal event which occurred with the construction of the three *new villages* and their place-names was governed by intention, here reflecting the ideology of the nation state – democracy versus communism – and all the mystifications that accompany such an inscription. Thereafter, every use of the place-name not only reflected present circumstances but also, to varying degrees, the original baptismal event. That is to say, the event left a trace. The creation of an umbrella-name by non-state agents can be read not only as a mockery of the state impressions on the national landscape over time but also as residues of the original baptismal event scattered among the present circumstances.

A subject's adoption or refusal to articulate certain place-names in a specific language can also be seen as an action to help alleviate the insult and injury of their past and current situations and, at the same time, to remind themselves of their biographically specific history (Agha 2005). Following Benjamin's (1999) concept of a critical historiography, "their biographically specific history" refers to what the past meant to them at the moment of utterance, "in the time when they are produced, the time which recognizes them – that is, our time" (464). What is happening here is a contestation over the different place-names, over the specific state-inscribed territory (and thus the language, Malay versus Hakka) that my subjects chose to adopt, and, in essence, over its meanings (Sinn) and its power. Indeed, their utterances can be seen as social dramas that are "embedded in and constitutive of political action" (Duranti 1994). In both large and small ways, their social utterances are speech acts that express their own sense of places – and also, inextricably, their own understandings of who they are.

Chapter Three

The Sri Aman Treaty

Today many countries in the world are still faced with a similar internal armed struggle of one sort or another. Some have inherited the problem from past regimes, others have only themselves to blame for causing the problem. The Sarawak Coalition Government has thus become the first government in the world to successfully deal with a well-established communist armed struggle by means of a *political strategy – a humanitarian approach* based on the simple human virtues of understanding of our fellow beings, their weaknesses and emotions, their strengths and rationales. In other words *a political solution to a political problem.*

Sri Aman: Peace Restored in Sarawak, 1974
(March 6, 1974, 3, emphasis added)

According to the "official" Malaysian history of communism in Sarawak, even though the Clandestine Communist Organizations (CCOs) waged guerilla warfare against the state for twenty-seven years (from 1963 to 1990), the beginning of the end of communism in Sarawak is said to have occurred in 1974 when close to 500 guerillas from the North Kalimantan People's Army (NKPA), one of the communist guerilla groups that operated between Sarawak and West Kalimantan, laid down their arms and rejoined society under the Sri Aman Treaty (Asli 1993; Mahmud 1993; Pusat Arakib Negara 1994). Following the "aestheticizing impulse" of the nation state, the state *broadcasted* that it was the concerted, benevolent effort of the Alliance Government in awakening and educating the public of the communist threats within Sarawak that ultimately led to the movement's disintegration.[1] Although I am in no position to challenge the validity of such assertions, it is significant to note that more than a hundred of those who "came out" (in Hakka, *choo-loi*; a euphemism for surrendering) under the Sri Aman Treaty retreated to the jungles in less than a year and, together with guerillas from other organizations, continued their struggles until a truce was signed in 1990 (Porrit 2004).

But as far as Malaysian authorities are concerned, communism is considered a past phenomenon, an anomaly in the script of nation-building. Much of its censored history is treated as archival material, doubly silent.[2] In fact, communism is now considered so benign that the Malaysian government recently restored several underground tunnels and caves at the Malaysia–Thailand border as a museum project for tourist consumption. Or perhaps this was a way to remind its populations of the bleak living conditions of former communists who have since "returned to normal lives." Seen in this manner, communism in Malaysia is portrayed as an aberration in the writing of the history of nation statehood, one of its struggles towards an "assured" specified nationhood.

It is this assuredness that provided the framework for my interruption. Focusing on the official claims of the history of communism in Sarawak, and, conversely, on what it silenced and aestheticized, I seek to interrupt the naturalness of Malaysia's claim to Sarawak and about the procedures of nationhood, history, and particular forms of sociality. If the history of communism is treated as an aberration in order to deny its eventfulness, have the events that transpired during the 1960s and 1970s been forgotten, erased from the consciousness of those who were affected by them? However, if the events are still in the consciousness of a section of the population, how can we write the dimension of disdain and its messiness back into the fore of history – in short, how can we restore their eventfulness back into history?

However, it would be one thing to say that this book is about the stories told by a certain population who were displaced as a consequence of a series of legal ordinances and operations carried out by the state government during the 1960s and 1970s. The problem goes deeper. In my discussion of the twin problems of silence and forgetting, this book also deals with the problem of stories that cannot be told by the victims whose lives were immersed in communist revolts and government repression. Besides touching on the struggles of a community to cope, to survive, and to build anew – in essence, "a history of contending politics and contending subject positions" (Pandey 2005, 18) – I am also seeking to understand their evasions and refusals to articulate and engage with their recent past. Some of the questions I asked were: How were families dislocated and divided and how did they cope with the trauma? Indeed, how did they rebuild their lives and what resources, both physical and mental, did they draw upon? And how did the experience of dislocation and trauma shape their lives and the *new villages* and towns they settled in? All of these are essential to our knowledge of the Cold War in Sarawak.

In this respect, my approach is like many approaches that stress historical forces and cultural discourses when speaking of the shaping of self and personhood of a specific community of individuals. In this respect, I am influenced by scholarship that stresses the importance of everyday life and livelihood, and the specificity of space and time in the shaping of the self.[3] To be sure, it is my focus on the quotidian that allowed me to emphasize the dilemmas I experienced in talking to my subjects about their histories.

I also want to make two general observations. First, the prevailing ideology of the progress of democracy against the evil of communism (to be sure, it was also about two competing economic methods of extraction and exploitation) needs to be re-examined. Such a dichotomous view of democracy and communism not only risks exaggerating the coherence of state objectives and their implementations, but also falling prey to the illusion of a unified "state" opposing a united communist movement with a singular rationality and purpose, which brings me to my second observation. Even though several communist organizations operated in Sarawak, they were conveniently labelled by the state under an umbrella name: the Clandestine Communist Organizations (Hardy 1963).[4] Consequently, there is an active silencing in the literature whereby the relations, or the lack thereof, between what assembled and divided the communist organizations in Sarawak are left out of history. Elsewhere I have written about the messy and competitive nature of the communist movements in Sarawak by using my interactions with two groups of former guerillas from the North Kalimantan People's Army (NKPA) and the Sarawak People's Guerrilla Force (SPGF), who had a history that was anything but amicable.[5] Here I want to turn my concern to the effects of systematic violence orchestrated against alleged communists and communist sympathizers.

To import the language of the Sri Aman Treaty from the epigraph of this chapter, I want to delegitimize its moral high ground. The hypocritical phrases *"humanitarian approach"* and *"a political solution to a political problem"* amount to nothing more than empty quotes. The enactment and re-enactment of various bills and ordinances, the launching of relocation operations and the corresponding construction of *new villages*, the imprisonment of communist cadres or communist suspects, the mobilizing of its whole military might with weapons far more modern than those of the communists,[6] and the harassment of farmers and cultivators were hardly humane, nor were they part of the dialogue of political process. Moreover, there has been a silence from "official historians" and within the popular discourse on the systematic and random raids of the sacrificial victims in the *new villages* and other so-called communist-influenced areas.

Commemorative Rituals

Maurice Halbwachs ([1950] 1980) was one of the pioneers who argued that the way we remember our history is determined by the circumstances and conditions of our remembering. Halbwachs was also one of the first to emphasize how treaties and commemorative rituals shaped narrative memory.[7] But there were issues that remained unexplored by Halbwachs: issues of divergent or contradictory memories in any memory community, and the question of who among the community has the power to do the remembering and to what ends (Cole 2001). Moreover, it is important to note that even though treaties and commemorative rituals might shape memories, memories are not determined by them (see, for example, Connerton 1989; Ho Tai 2001; Jing 1996).

I will follow the arguments made by these studies to analyse the degree to which the Sri Aman Treaty – a treaty that supposedly marks the beginning of the end of communism in Sarawak – determined people's memory. The Sri Aman Treaty, signed at Simanggang on March 6, 1974, had all the commemorative rituals. The Governor of Sarawak, his entourage of high-ranking officials, and several representatives of the North Kalimantan People's Army (NKPA) attended the event. Under the treaty, the leader of NKPA, Bong Kee Cheok, and 482 comrades "laid down their arms and rejoined society" (Sri Aman: Peace Restored in Sarawak, 1974, 2). The event was broadcasted as a victory for *democracy* and an accompanying official document, *Sri Aman: Peace Restored in Sarawak* (1974) was published and widely distributed. To further commemorate the significance of the treaty, the name of the township of Simanggang was changed to Sri Aman – *Aman* being the Malay word for peace, safe, or calm. Since then, Simanggang has no longer existed in the grammar of state language – on road signs and maps, in newspaper reporting, on buses, and so on.

However, even with all these *legalized* state *performances* and the paraphernalia that went along with it, there has never been any consideration on the part of the Alliance government as to how the local communities might feel about the change of their town's name. Were they supposed to acquiesce? Indeed, I was struck not only by how uninterested people were in talking about the treaty, but also how their selective memories of the event illuminate much of their political commentaries on the treaty. In trying to understand the apparent erasure of a certain past among people whose life must have been affected by the treaty, I am not suggesting that their memory of the treaty had been repressed, in Freudian terms, by some internal psychodynamic processes. Nor am I suggesting that there was a social injunction that forbade them to talk about it. But there seems to be a prevailing ethos, a tacit indifference towards the topic. When they chose to talk about the treaty, I was also struck by how frequently the theme of complicity, if not duplicity, cropped up in their narratives, forming the subtext to political jokes and cynical reflections on the treaty.

For example, a few bus drivers and conductors at Simanggang often joked about the alleged connection between the rank of a communist and the *gifts* one received upon "coming out." They would offer such clichéd, if not indexical, comments: "The higher you were, the more you will be rewarded," or, "If you want to be a communist, you must aim to be the captain." It was widely rumoured that Bong Kee Cheok, the leader of the NPKA, and his brothers received a substantial amount of land and cash from signing the treaty. It was also rumoured that they coerced their comrades into "coming out." Some even went so far as to suggest that one of Bong's brothers collaborated with the Special Branch in torturing their own comrades at the police station in Simanggang.[8] These comments were not isolated sentiments.

At the Sri Aman bus station, a middle-aged Hakka woman and a younger man assured me, sarcastically, that I would not miss Bong's house since it was the biggest one in Simanggang. Without my asking, the woman went on to say that she had not seen Bong's white Pajero that morning (a Mitsubishi SUV). I sensed she was hinting to me that Bong spent a lot of his time in his white SUV. She then proceeded to talk with the others in Iban and they started to laugh.[9] A younger Hakka woman echoed the same sarcastic remark about Bong: "He is now a big *towkay*" (rich businessman), which the middle-aged women interrupted by saying: "He is a very busy man ... many businesses." On another occasion, an Iban driver raised his voice at his Malay coworker, saying, "This is an Iban area and it hasn't changed." He then looked at me and said, "And this Bong. He is nobody." He seemed annoyed but I wasn't sure why he shouted at his colleague when it was I who was asking about Bong. But what his outburst did point out was that indexically, not only was Sri Aman a loaded place-name, but adopting it would signify a conscious acceptance of the enforced reality of the treaty and agreement to the adoption of a Malay place-name for an Iban township – in essence, acquiescing to one of the modern state projects designed to shape and reshape territorial spaces into nationalized racial entities.[10]

What is striking about these commentaries is the degree to which Bong's complicity with the State was mentioned – commentaries that bear the imprint of local discursive formations and practices that are stretched intersubjectively across actors of different ethnicities and the socio-political environment they inhabit. Their negativity towards Bong can also be read as a kind of moral policing that questioned the "appropriateness" of the latter's good fortune.[11] When I asked the bus personnel and a few passengers at the station office in Sri Aman why they continued to use the name Simanggang, a few of them seemed both scandalized and nonplussed by my question. Others claimed it was out of habit but I suspect there were other reasons; after all, the name change took place twenty-five years ago. Even if there was a se-mantic and linguistic shift that signified the alleged end of communist movements in Sarawak, the process by which Simanggang became Sri Aman was not discussed – at least not openly – by these residents.

I got a similar reaction from the passengers at the Kuching bus station. Whenever I was there – and when I was not on the bus talking with bus conductors or drivers, or having lunch or coffee with them at the coffee shops or at *Warong Muhibah* – I would frequent the ticket windows and chat with the station personnel. Late one afternoon, after the bus to Sri Aman had just left the station, I asked Geok Bee, a ticketing clerk, how the passengers inquired about the Sri Aman buses. She looked con-fused about my query and her initial reaction, in Mandarin, was, *"Wau pu tar ching choo"* (I am not sure what your question is). I repeated it, but this time I was more specific: "Do the passengers ask for Sri Aman or Simanggang when they buy their tickets?" Her response this time was, *"Ni wir se-mor yau che-tau?"* (Why do you want to know?), before adding, "They usually ask for the Simanggang bus." She then looked around the office and, much to my surprise, whispered the following sentence: "I understand you have been asking about Bong." She was clearly alluding to a certain link or complicity between Bong and the township of Sri Aman (Simanggang), or more precisely, the Sri Aman Treaty. I remained silent, hoping she would elaborate. She did not. Realizing that she was not going to divulge anything more, I asked if she could tell me something about Bong. Immediately, her facial expression changed as she realized that she had crossed the invisible line she had drawn since the first day we met. She had never allowed herself to indulge in topics even remotely tied to communism in all our previous conversations. Quite predictably, she gave me the trademark response, *"Pu chee tao"* (I don't know), before walking away.

The semantics and context of a name may play a role in the indexical drama, and they may mask what is really happening. Hence, the political uses of place-names like Sri Aman (peace) always need to be deconstructed, for, in the episodes I have presented, they mask a range of indexical political plays. Of course, masking can be done intentionally, as in private innuendo or clandestine communications that occur in non-clandestine situations. But there was a masking that seemed to take place when Geok Bee suddenly understood what I was driving at, not referentially but indexically, and it prompted her to note that I had been asking about Bong.

Geok Bee's colleague, a bus driver that everybody called "Tall" Tan, was more responsive. More than once he confided in me about Bong and his brother's complicities in the Sri Aman Treaty as a public secret. Tan reasoned that Ibans, Chinese, and Malays living in Simanggang and its vicinities retained the place-name Simanggang because it is an Iban area. He even managed to conjure up a statistical figure, saying, "Ninety per cent of the time, *they* (the passengers) ask for Simanggang, even the Malays." I made an effort to observe this myself by standing next to the ticket counter. Even though the signs on the buses and the tickets indicated the name of the township Sri Aman, the majority of the passengers would utter Simanggang when they wanted to buy bus tickets to Sri Aman.

Inasmuch as the so-called democracy versus communism ideology was reflected in the process of naming places in Sarawak throughout this period, in the few episodes cited, my subjects' indifference or reluctance to adopt the official place-name (Sri Aman) can be interpreted as a vehicle of personal (or group) criticism of state discourse. There were layers of contestation here: the renaming of an Iban township with a

Malay place-name, the questioning of the treaty commemorating the end of communism in Sarawak, and how my subjects felt about Bong and his brother. All of these did not sit well with the community at Simanggang, be they former communists, communist sympathizers, or just plain Simanggang residents. In many ways, their refusal to adopt the official place-name, Sri Aman, can be seen as part of their effort to delegitimize the institutional and social conditions that *legitimized* the name change.

The Hawker Centre

In 1975, a year after the Sri Aman Treaty was signed, another group of guerillas from the Sarawak People's Guerilla Force (SPGF) "came out." But unlike what was said about Bong and his comrades, the leader of SPGF, Chao Kui Ho, his wife, and about a hundred comrades were never given any land or cash for "coming out." Instead, the *gifts* they received were vendor licences to operate at a Hawker Centre by the SOC Kuching bus station.[12] Built in the mid-1970s, this single-storey Hawker Centre accommodates sixty retail lots in a space about three-quarters of the size of a basketball court. Though it used to be a relatively busy shopping spot in the past, in part due to its location next to the bus station, by the 1990s it had declined into a sordid recess as the number of modern department stores in Kuching continued to grow.

The first thing I noticed about the centre was that it was dimly lit and overcrowded – every inch of space was used to its maximum, as each vendor displayed his or her merchandise onto a third of the passageway. Aside from two food stalls and a tailor shop operated by Malay vendors, the rest of the lots were taken up by Chinese clothing vendors, the majority of whom were former guerillas.[13] The Hawker Centre has come to be considered old and dilapidated, catering mostly to rural residents looking for cheaper clothing and window-shopping to pass time while waiting for the buses. Quite ironically, it also appeared to me that these former comrades were competing with each other as they all seemed to be carrying pretty much the same merchandise – the same shirts, pants, and T-shirts. Often I would find them chatting among themselves or reading the Chinese dailies and it was not uncommon to find some of them dozing off in the afternoon breeze coming from the river. This lack of business did serve as a convenient pretext for me to spend many afternoons there, but I was concerned about them. Most of them were in their early sixties with no alternative incomes. Of the thirty-five vendors I met, only two owned their houses. The rest rented low-cost housing built by private Chinese developers on the outskirts of Kuching, and three of them could only afford to rent rooms.[14]

When I became aware that Chao Kui Ho, one of the former leaders of the Sarawak People's Guerilla Force (SPGF), was one of the vendors, I reasoned that I should get to know him –hoping to thereby gain acceptance from the rest of his former comrades. I began to see Chao on a regular basis. Even after twenty-five years, Chao's former comrades at the Hawker Centre still regarded him with respect and afforded him a certain distance. They would never stop by his lot when we were having a conversation. At his insistence, Chao and I often had coffee at the same table located right at the back of a particular coffee shop across from the Hawker Centre, and our conversations were always held in private, regardless of how sensitive or mundane the topics were. He once smiled but did not respond when I asked if the authorities are still watching him and his comrades at the Hawker Centre.

Chao liked to talk about the history of communism, beginning with the Paris Commune, the Bolshevik Revolution, and the Chinese Revolution. He was most interested in topics of universal conflicts and concerns, but always fell short of offering any prophetic call for social action. When we talked about Malaysia, especially the NEP and how it affected the standards of the universities, the civil service, government loans, businesses opportunities, poor public medical facilities, and so on, he would ask for my opinion. He once spoke softly, with a degree of resignation: "Put it this way, we lost to *Di guo zhu-yi* [imperialism]. Look at us. Seven days a week we are open for business even though there are hardly any customers. What future do we have?" Indeed, the arenas of their "battlefields" had shifted from the jungles to the dilapidated Hawker Centre. It would seem, far from the appearance assumed by the logic of exchange, the *gifts* they had received for "coming out" had always been – to once again invoke Deleuze and Guattari ([1972] 1983) – an inscription, and one made in the economy of debts over their marked bodies.

Once, forcing a smile, Chao offered a rather evasive, if not poetic, response that served as a paradigmatic model and interpretive device for giving meaning to his past and for acting upon the socio-political present: "Every *hao zi* [good mouse] has a home but not all of them leave their home at the same time. Some in fact never do." There is something philosophical and euphemistic about this. By identifying himself and his comrades as *hao zi*, meaning good mice, he was rejecting the pejorative term *swa ngiau chee* (jungle rat) that was commonly used by the general Chinese communities in Sarawak for communist guerillas in the area. There was also an admission on his part that, after being forced to go underground, they had come to accept the jungle as their *home*, and when they had to leave their *home*, they would refer to the act as *chor lai* (Mandarin for "coming out") instead of *toar ysiang* (surrendering). Besides, it was true that not all of them "came out." Some never did. Or perhaps he was referring to himself – given that, even though he "came out," he still retained a socialist outlook and used a class-based perspective for talking about the welfare of Sarawak and beyond. It is also interesting to note that Chao was profoundly indifferent when it came to discussing Bong or the Sri Aman Treaty. I am not suggesting that he was uninterested, but indifference provided a tactical shelter of a certain kind for him so that he would not have to openly expose his true feelings towards Bong – something that will become clear in the following pages.

Over time, my friendship with Chao promoted envy and, to a degree, discomfort among his former comrades and others by the bus station. Some of them even avoided having any association with me, while a few food vendors across from the Hawker Centre started calling me Mr. *Swa ngiau chee* (Mr. Jungle Rat). It was their way of teasing this nosy ethnographer who was asking a lot of questions about communism. Some of the clothing vendors would respond with a polite smile and say that they had forgotten about the past, or would give this characteristic response: "What is there to tell?" Perhaps they felt that it was no longer worth the trouble of remembering when the issues they fought for were dead, or because what they thought they were fighting for turned out to be something quite different, a disparaging theme throughout my fieldwork.[15] For the moment, it may help to think, as Thongchai (2002) suggests, about the complexity among former guerillas towards their past activism – ranging from pride to suffering, sacrifices, disillusionment, even shame – when the past has become a spectre of moral ambivalence that makes it so difficult not only to evaluate but also to find an expression of their remembering/silences, especially when their trauma has not been publicly acknowledged.

It took more than a month, which I spent hanging out at the Hawker Centre and talking about casual topics, before some of them felt comfortable divulging a little of their past. Perhaps they reasoned that Chao had already told me of their past. When some of these vendors talked about their lives in the jungle, their narratives were mostly within the realm of the pragmatic, even to the extent that they represented their experiences as being routine within the extraordinary state of siege that so many of them had lived in the jungles of Borneo. Their recollections hinged on the notion of *accommodation* as opposed to that of heroism and consisted mainly of fear and avoidance of confrontation, as captured by statements such as: "We saw *them* [the Allied forces] all the time, sometimes daily, but nothing happened. We would ignore each other. Nobody wanted to die." In fact, the following statement would suggest that fear and avoidance existed among the Malaysian, Indonesian, and the British soldiers as well: "Sure, *they* were just as scared ... Being a soldier is like taking up a job, earning a living." I mention this because fear and avoidance in these contexts are usually obscured behind the veil of machismo depicted in the majority of war movies or books.

This would seem to be in contrast to a highly publicized movie, *Leftenan Adnan*, that came out while I was doing my fieldwork. Set in Malaya during the Japanese Occupation, the film was yet another engine to broadcast the heroism of the Malay armed forces against Imperial Japan. Obviously there was no mention of the Malayan People's Anti-Japanese Army (MPAJA), the military arm of the Communist Party of Malaya (CPM) who fought alongside the British forces against the Japanese in the Malayan jungle. Indeed, time is not an empty passage and official history is not without its ironies, as it is produced and always sustained by silencing. In a matter of less than a few years, images of the bravery of the MPAJA were erased from Malaysia's master narrative about its memorable pasts.

When I was describing the movie *Leftenan Adnan* to a few vendors one afternoon, explaining how the protagonist Adnan and his *compadres* defended their station against the Japanese soldiers that heavily outnumbered them, one of them interrupted my detailing by stating the obvious: "It's a government movie, isn't it?" The rest of the vendors laughed but they also seemed to be in deep thought. Like *lieux de memoire*, my description of the movie triggered one of these vendors to recall an earlier episode:

> Once we were at Gunung [Mount] Gading.[16] We were convinced the British special unit was aware of our whereabouts. Their camp was stationed less than a kilometre from us, further up on the slopes. Their helicopters were flying over us but they left us alone.

He went on to say that it would have been suicidal to attack such a special unit, which was heavily armed with heavy machine guns and helicopters. Realizing that they now seemed moved to discuss their past, I asked if there was much fighting in the jungle, which prompted them to laugh. Another vendor commented,

> The truth is that there was a lot of sitting around. We made our daily patrol just like the soldiers did theirs. The whole idea was to get by each day without being killed. You need to understand what it was like in the jungle. After a while the only thing that occupied your mind was to get out alive. We knew it was only a matter of time before we had to leave the jungle.

Being caught up in my seduction by the chronology of historical events, and in an attempt to invoke their feelings, I asked, "So you were aware of the Sri Aman treaty?" I was hoping he might reveal his feelings towards Bong. He winked and spoke with an evasive obscurity:

> We heard rumours but nobody was sure. There were plenty of stories, mostly *rojak* [a Malay term for "mixed up"]. You need to understand … Communication with other cells was infrequent and it was mainly through our cell leaders or those higher up. You must know about the nature of our operation from *him* [he nodded towards the direction of Chao's lot].

There was a twitch on his face as he threw a glance at the others, perhaps feeling sorry for acting so overtly. Clearing his throat, he continued, "We knew the odds were against us. We were under-armed and outnumbered. And don't forget about the wild animals, snakes, crocodiles, and insects. *They* [the soldiers] were facing them as well." This provoked the rest of the vendors to laugh and another vendor interrupted, "They needed to stay alive to get paid." As a way to get back at the soldiers, these vendors often referred to them as mercenaries. More than once they would ask, "Do you really think the Gurkhas were loyal British subjects?"[17] This reminds me of Amitav Ghosh's (2001) description of soldiers all throughout the British Empire: "In this sense all soldiers, in all modern armies, were mercenaries. Soldiering was a job, a profession, a career. Every soldier was paid and there was none who was not a mercenary" (301).

Very Green about a Lot of Things

Most of these clothing vendors were in their mid-teens during the 1960s. When asked why one became a communist, this particular statement seems to reflect many of their responses: "I was very young ... very green about a lot of things." One of my interlocutors told me that his cousin introduced him to some communist books when he was only ten years old. He said that most of the former communists he knew only had a superficial understanding of communism. Indeed, there were many circumstances in which these teens became involved in or seduced by activities that could be interpreted as communism. Perhaps its ideology of equality became attractive to them after they were forced to live in the squalid conditions of the *new villages*.[18] In some cases, one became a communist because one was labelled as such by the government, and was detained and forced to sign on the dotted line. Other times, one was associated with a certain organization that was labelled as communist by the government. This happened to teachers and students at local Chung Hwa Chinese schools and members of the Overseas Chinese Swimming Club. In other cases, it was because one's siblings, father, or relatives were communists. Indeed, notions of camaraderie as well as adversity materialized out of each individual's respective complicity with communism, which I believe was a direct consequence of the economics and politics of the Cold War and the pre-existing *bangsa* politics in Malaysia – the policies and practices of sacrificing a certain rural population in Sarawak as communists, communist sympathizers, or socialist inclined.

To be sure, the people I worked with were not pawns in the plans of distant powers. There were local stakes involved in communism – they had hopes of getting back their land (or gardens), of getting rid of the state government that made them became part of Malaysia, and continuing the struggle for equality, but it was no coincidence that "bread-and-butter" issues – cries of "food" and "land" – so often lay at the core of their struggles.[19] Of course, the parameters of their struggles were set, in part, by the institutions of repression. As such, the roots of being communist might lie less in an individual's mind than in racially, geopolitically, economically, and historically systemic ways of meaning and knowing.

In any of the circumstances, once an individual was labelled as a communist, it produced a certain lasting identity – or, if I may, a certitude of identities – both by the parties who were doing the labelling as well as by the subjects who were labelled. To borrow from Roland Barthes ([1957] 1972), the essence of being a "communist," "communist sympathizer," or "subversive" was the direct result or casualty of the "disease of thinking in essences" (75). But for those who were labelled as communists, the subject positions and subjectivities have never been fixed. They can be positive or negative, or in-between, ambivalent, contradictory, and in constant flux depending on the circumstances and contexts. It is my hope that this will become obvious as I attempt to write about the lives and livelihoods of these individuals.

However, those who did the labelling often ignored this heterogeneity of thinking and feelings. When used, the noun "communist" is all-encompassing but nevertheless remains in the singular. Government officials, pro-government journalists, and others often speak of a "communist" with the same certitude that they identify someone as a "doctor," a "lawyer," and so on. But in this case, labelling someone as a communist reifies a particular identity, that of being subversive, rather than acknowledging that he/she has multiple identities such as a father/mother, brother/sister, son/daughter, teacher, students, and so on, and not just communist. This is ironic especially when one considers the inherent problems of defining what communism or what a communist was/is in any context. The way that this identity was singularized raises questions not so much about what communism was or who the communists in Sarawak were, but about power and representation.

People's Court

Even though I was getting closer to Chao and some of his comrades, there were times when I felt that I was building up a rapport with some vendors and that they were beginning to tell me fragments of their pasts, only to find them resuming their silent stance upon our next encounter. Even with Chao, though we had established a relationship, it did not mean that we were always at ease with each other. There was one incident that brought this home. One afternoon a middle-aged woman was screaming at Chao in front of his lot. As I walked over to figure out what was happening, there was only one vendor trying to calm her down while the rest remained quiet at a distance, seemingly at a loss as to what they should do. Apparently the woman was accusing Chao for her son's death. I found myself confronting something I had read about in the archives – the "people's court." These were trials that usually took place at rural basketball courts for communists accused of being government informers where the penalty was death if the "defendant" was found guilty. My level of comfort and closeness with Chao was momentarily shattered that afternoon.

For almost a week I couldn't bring myself to visit Chao, as I was afraid to confront him with the woman's accusation. It was only after I received snippets of the overall story that I began to catch a glimpse of the complexity of the situation. Chao might have given consent to the sentencing in order to set an example to those alleged to be betraying the movement. But still, why did it take the woman so many years to finally gather enough courage to approach Chao and vent her anger in public? In describing the violence suffered in Japan and China in the twentieth century, Kurt Radtke (1999) points out that, "Having gone through traumatic events, societies need to 'go on living' ... 'forgetting' is one way to achieve this" (19). It would seem to me that this woman did not just "forget" about the "execution"; she had been painfully silent about it until that afternoon. Could it be that the circumstances that led to the death of her son became too much for her to engage any longer with "active forgetting," and that her confrontation with Chao was her way of confronting the spectrality of a certain past that had been haunting her into remaining silent? To invoke Derrida (1994), perhaps it was her way of taking cognizance of the production of these silences in order make this oppressed past come alive, a reckoning of its repression in the present in order to say, "I would like to learn to live finally" (xvii).

When I brought up the incident two weeks later with Chao's former comrades at the Hawker Centre, I was told to let it rest. I was perhaps touching on a public secret. A month later, bus driver "Tall" Tan urged me to grasp the complexity of the situation before attempting to comprehend the stories I had been told. He warned me not to believe all the stories I had heard, something that Chao himself had also cautioned me on several occasions. In referring to the woman's son, Tan historicized the complexity of the situation:

> Many communists were betrayed, arrested, or killed. Some of them were not even communists. But guess who determined their fate? *Choo kuo* [traitors], of course! They handed out names to the Special Branch ... But it's not that straightforward either. Many of them did not have any choice. They had sons and daughters, brothers and sisters, and fathers in prison. They were forced to tell, to lie ... make up names.

Tan's two older brothers were killed during the late 1960s – when they were eighteen and twenty years old. He believed that they were betrayed but he did not have the proof, or perhaps he did not want to reveal it to me for his own reasons. He explained to me that because of his brothers' deaths he had never thought of joining any communist organizations. He went silent. After a very long pause, he continued, "Many times *they* approached me [long pause] … but after seeing what happened to my brothers I knew there was no hope. They were fighting a losing battle." I left him that evening thinking about his brothers and the many more people who had lost their lives at such an early age. I was also thinking about anthropology's theoretical silence when it comes to the meaning of the long pauses we often encounter in the course of our engagement with our subjects.

The Canals Are Gone

A few months later, during one of his days off, "Tall" Tan took me to the house where he grew up at *Hai Wai,* in one of the coastal areas. His relatives now occupied the house. As soon as we got there, he led me to the spots where his brothers were shot, less than 100 yards from the house. The day I was bidding him farewell at the bus station, he took me aside to reiterate a point: "Make sure you put down on your notes: I was never a *swa ngiau chee.*" My conversations with Tan helped me to catch a glimpse of the area residents' past. From that point on, I would always remind myself that I was not *there* and did not *experience* what had transpired during that period. I realize that there are certain things we cannot ask or that are best left within the realm of silence. Issues of my interlocutors' own complicity in the general scheme of things are an example of this. In the case of collaborating or selling out, or if an interlocutor did in fact sentence his/her comrades to death, how does the ethnographer even begin to have the stomach to ask about it?

Besides Tan's family, I met other Hakkas at *Hai Wai.* As in other *communist-influenced* areas, most of them sent their children to urban centres during the 1960s and 1970s in order to avoid unnecessary problems with the military personnel and, I should add, with the communists as well. Because of these "forced" migrations, *Hai Wai* is now a Malay area as evidenced by the proliferation of Malay *kampungs* (villages) like Atapak, Nonok, Jemukan, Simunjan, Sebujau, and so on. I once went to *Hai Wai* with a bus conductor, Mrs. Wong, to visit her brother, whom I shall call Mr. Tan. Once we got to her brother's house, the first thing Mrs. Wong said to me was how self-sufficient they had been back then, that they used to have plenty of pineapples, jambu (water apple), starfruit, papaya, banana, and a variety of chilies and vegetables, and their main cash crop, copra. To elaborate on his sister's nostalgia, Mr. Tan pointed towards some small drains, saying, "See that over there. They used to be part of a canal system, wide enough to transport our copra to the ferry. Now they have turned into tiny drains, pretty much dried up." He laughed before continuing, "The whole area has changed after *they* [the local government] filled up the land. The canals are gone."[20] His laughter, to be sure, was producing a memory landscape, and it did so by expanding nostalgic memory that was flowing through the fruits, vegetables, and past canals, making it subtle, even three-dimensional.

By the same logic, their imaginative remembrance is a discursive subordination of time to the immediacy of space or, rather, a fusion of the chronotope of time and space (Clark and Holquist 1984; Fabian 1983). It is through the evocation of the daily use of the canals that their narrative develops a description of social life and economic conditions at *Hai Wai*. As Bahloul (1996) puts it, "Remembered objects and places are made historiographers, sociologists of the past" (129). Both siblings' comparisons of the past and present are attempts to revive a past universe but, inadvertently, their comparisons resonate with the ways in which memories can be burdensome, for they testify to the gap that separates images of the past with abundance from the present experience of loss. What were once the waterways are elevated to iconic and mnemonic status as if they were the web and filiations of memory, evoking social worlds of the past. We spent an hour walking around the vicinity and our conversation was relaxed and lighthearted – that is, until I asked them what was it like during the 1960s and 1970s. Both siblings looked at each other but remained silent. I have heard of rumours about mass graves at *Hai Wai* but, like I said, they were rumours.[21] Later, during lunch, under an air of hesitation, Mr. Tan spoke rather softly (and this was within the confines of his own home), "Sure, the soldiers were nasty, but they were from where you came from. They were Malay soldiers from West Malaysia. They were not like the local Malays." That was not the only time I have heard Sarawakians express contempt for the presence of Malay military personnel from West Malaysia.

I believe Mr. Tan emphasized the difference between the Malays from West Malaysia and the local Malays because he wanted to talk about his relations with the latter. Some of his fishing partners were Malays from Atapak. He also hired them periodically whenever he needed some extra help with picking coconut or pineapples, or with loading copra onto the truck now that the drains had all dried up. On the whole, he assured me, everyone got along – all except for a few Malay ethnic brokers who would go around mobilizing fellow Malays to build themselves a constituency come election time.

From my visits to *Hai Wai*, even though I would consider the interethnic relationships between the Hakkas and the Malays to be amicable, I noticed there was a very peculiar pattern in how these Hakkas would make reference to the Malay *kampungs* – as markers of stateracial spatiality that materialized out of Cold War politics and economy, and only on very specific occasions – when instructing the Malay minivan drivers where they needed to get off. They did so speaking in the Malay language – statements like "I am getting off just before Nonok," or "Just after Atapak, by the bridge." Initially I thought this had to do with the ethnicity of the drivers. But I have had numerous conversations with these Malay drivers in Hakka and Mandarin. I also recall a time when Mrs. Wong was chatting away with the driver in Hakka about the welfare of his family but when it came to communicating where they were getting off, she switched to the Malay language: "*Kami turun dekat jambatan, selepas Atapak*" (We are getting off near the bridge, after Atapak). Regardless of the communicative goals of the speaker – to ask the driver to stop at such and such a place – the question I ask is this: how does he, the Malay minivan driver, understand this particular usage? Is it just a reference to a multi-named place in a polyglot world, or does it indexically mark a particular identity of the speaker – and therefore that of the driver? And is the driver cued into the privacy of the speech act? What is important here is that the directions do not rest with the language themselves but have a private value for Mrs. Wong and the Malay driver. Let me explain.

The Hakka families I met at *Hai Wai* were aware that the permits to operate minivans in the area were out of their reach. They were given to the Malays, or more accurately, to Malays with the proper connections. I should also mention that these minivans are a source of convenience more to the Malays than non-Malays. Only the roads connecting the Malay *kampungs* were asphalt-finished; the minivans are essentially a Malay inter-*kampung* transportation system. Mrs. Pang, another Hakka bus conductor I met in Kuching, had this to say when we visited her sister-in-law's house, located next to an asphalt-finished road: "We don't have to worry since their house is close to the road. We can stay until six, perhaps five-thirty, before catching the last minivan to the ferry. From there we can take the bus to Kuching."

The other Hakka families I met at *Hai Wai* were not so fortunate. To get to their houses, I had to walk for an hour or more on uneven, stone-covered, dusty roads after getting off the minivan, and all that in stifling heat. They seemed resigned when I asked when the dusty roads might be asphalt-finished. This remark from a fifteen-year-old Hakka girl summed up their feelings: "This is how things are around here. Only the Malay *kampungs* have proper roads. *They* [referring to the governing elites] do not need our votes." In other words, unlike the Malays or most of the indigenous communities in Sarawak, the state has no need to invoke the rhetoric of development (something most Sarawakians would call "election time instant noodles gifts") to the Hakkas at *Hai Wai* to get re-elected. Due to the conscription of *Hai Wai* as a communist-inflicted area and the consequent forced migration of most Hakkas from the area to urban areas, *Hai Wai* is now a Malay area and the votes of the remaining Chinese are insignificant. In the social and political context, her statement indicated that the welfare of the Hakkas at *Hai Wai* was not only contingent upon a racialized division of space but articulated by the exclusionary power of political elites to exclude those affiliated with a certain "problematic" past – of being communist inclined. These Hakkas are the infinite others who see without being seen. Consequently, their interest fell beyond the pale of concern and, as such, beyond the hope of acquiring some measure of what they sought.

Considering the memories of their past – the experience (real or imagined) of constant curfews and military surveillance – and the circumstances of their contemporary landscape in which all facets of their lives continue to be affected by NEP and its *bangsa* political economy, I suggest that it was at the particular moment when they were travelling in the minivans along an asphalt-finished road that the coefficient of the severity of state power was at its greatest, and where the demands of the state-inscribed territory were most oppressive as to weigh on their consciousness and thus give rise to their acknowledgement of the Malay *kampungs* as points of state spatial references at *Hai Wai*. However, I must stress that this habit is limited to the instances I have described and is in no way necessarily total or static. It is what defines the singular relation of these Hakkas to the order of conscripted reality.

Their speech or language is the product of an interaction between language and the situated materiality of circumstances. It was at those particular conjunctures where they were forced to acknowledge their circumscribed positions – but, at the same time, those moments enlivened a sense of their mockery towards the power that stemmed from that discourse. To be sure, the geography of *Hai Wai* is full of gaps and contradictions, official and unofficial markers into which these marginalized Hakkas have been able to inscribe for themselves new mappings and sites. I have come across makeshift Chinese signposts marking the directions to this or that Chinese household. If anything else, this illustrates the impossible totalization of official discourse as seen in its unintended production of politically and conceptually ungoverned effects.

What seems important in the cases at *Hai Wai* is that the directions do not rest within the language of directions themselves, but have a private value for the speaker. When Mrs. Wong used the Malay language to tell the driver where to let her off, it was certainly language, but it was no longer just language in the sense of giving directions. After all, she could just as easily instruct the minivan driver in Hakka or Mandarin. There was something else at work. If to speak is to transmit a message intended for a receiver, then Mrs. Wong's request to disembark at a village using Malay names can be read as facilitating a relationship, if not affecting a social hierarchy within the existing political, economic, state-inscribed landscape at *Hai Wai*.[22] Through her conformity in using these Malay village names, and her requests in the Malay language, both Mrs. Wong and the driver were evoking the political events and demographic transformations that have reshaped the landscape where they lived. Her request was not only intended to exchange a message but also to confer a relationship to the Other. The language had a private value for both Mrs. Wong and the driver. As Tzvetan Todorov (1984) notes, "[c]oncretely, one always addresses someone, and that someone does not assume a purely passive role ... the interlocutor participates in the formation of the meaning of the utterance, just as the other elements – similarly social – of the context of uttering do" (30). Like Bakhtin's notion of the dialogic, the understanding of Mrs. Wong's utterance as one with a certain value draws out the driver's obligation to respond; to cue him to his position with the social, if not racial, hierarchy at *Hai Wai* and by extension, that of Sarawak and Malaysia.[23]

In acknowledging the very existence of a Malay *kampung* and in giving the instruction in Malay, Mrs. Wong was expressing both the knowledge of her lot as a marginalized subject and, at the same time, her protest against that designation. Mrs. Wong's social utterances can be read as "unpalatable words" that challenge celebratory or comforting accounts of history, self, and nation. As unfortunate as it may be, the Malay minivan driver was conveniently used as a token symbol of state ideology, a symbol on which Mrs. Wong vented and overcame her displeasure. But as a Malay, and having the proper connection to obtain the minivan's operator permit, it is fair to assume that the driver was aware of his privileges and connections, and that he was entirely cued in to the privacy of the speech act in that moment.

Chapter Four

Any Other Day at the Bus Station

From the very beginning of my fieldwork, I was curious as to why so many rural Hakkas who had been forcibly relocated into *new villages* ended up working at the Sarawak Omnibus Company (SOC). Of the close to 800 total employees that had been working there since the 1960s, the overwhelming majority of them were rural Hakkas from the *new villages*. Was it because the company and the rural Hakkas shared a certain synthesis between the socialist agenda of the SOC and the political motivations of these Hakkas? Most likely there was a bit of both. A few drivers confided in me that it was their way to get involved with a company that, by way of its connection with the SUPP, opposed the government that had inscribed them and their families into the *new villages*. I should mention that the majority of the SOC employees would stress that their employment at the SOC had inevitably led to them being labelled as socialists, if not communists. There were also instances when some of them would hint to me that they were involved in *activities* that could be construed as socialist, but would later deny this. For instance, a female Hakka bus conductor once told me that she had been sent by her cell leader to pick up some Marxist literature at a jetty near the bus station, and she left it at that as she rushed off to her bus, which was leaving the station. But when I approached her the next day, she refused to talk with me, and she proceeded to avoid me for the rest of my fieldwork. She was even angry with me on several occasions. After a while I reacted by avoiding her altogether.

Very early during my fieldwork I ran into two Hakka bus drivers at the SOC canteen. This was immediately after I saw their former general manager, Hong Hee Siaw. I had the feeling that they must have known that I had just seen Hong, because as soon as I walked into the canteen the two of them asked me to sit with them, putting their arms over my shoulders and ordering coffee for me. They started asking where I came from and how long I planned to stay in Kuching. Before I could talk about my research, they told me that there were many communists in Sarawak, that they saw them at the outskirts of Serian as they travelled on their daily route from Kuching to Serian. I recall how excited I was, thinking that I would be getting a lot of juicy material from these two. Unfortunately, since I had already made an appointment to see someone else at the bus station, I had to leave, but not before assuring the two drivers that we would meet again soon.

As it turned out, such accommodating responses about communism in Sarawak were extremely rare throughout my fieldwork. When I approached the same drivers two weeks later at the same canteen, I was rudely awakened by how unresponsive and indifferent they had become. Their uncomfortable smiles made them appear a little apprehensive about my presence. This time around they told me they knew nothing about communism in Sarawak. You can imagine how dejected I felt, that it couldn't be true. I noticed a slight twitching on one of their faces when he replied, "We were joking with you then. We heard about your project … something about communism." His colleague started to laugh before adding, "We just thought it was funny. No, we have nothing to tell you. We have never *walked that path*," speaking flatly without any attempt to explain or elaborate further. "Walked that path" is a euphemism for belonging to a certain organization or adhering to a certain ideology.

I tried to assure them that any information they were willing to provide would be kept in utmost secrecy. I even showed them my "Human Subject Interview Consent" forms as well as the letters I had obtained from their former general manager, Hong, which authorized me to interview SOC employees. They read the letters with enthusiasm but reiterated that they could not assist me since they had never "walked that path." I realized there was nothing I could do at that moment and hoped that things would change on another occasion. It took me another two weeks to realize that the drivers' change of attitude had to do with the directives coming from their current management (something I will elaborate on in the following pages). From then on, it became incredibly difficult to get any of SOC's employees to talk about anything, let alone about things concerning communism.

The sudden change of reception I experienced illustrates the dynamics that transpired and inevitably affected the level of interaction between my subjects and myself. Still, there were many other factors that affected my relationship with them – factors that were more nuanced or hidden from me, things that were more difficult to uncover, let alone analyse. But through such a retelling and refutation of it, even in their unwillingness to recall it, we see a possible glimpse into what was experienced by my subjects (and the anthropologist). This is what Austin (1962) means when he insists that we need to analyse speech acts with reference to the context of the interlocution, to the concrete and conventional discursive situation in which speech acquires value above and beyond its meaning (noted by Felman 1983). In a sense, I am not only concerned with the total speech act through which a speaker actualizes his/her vocabulary in a certain language and in a particular situation of exchange, but also in situating the very act of enunciations within the network of social practices: the speakers' past and current situations at SOC; the place where the conversations took place (at the canteen, on the bus, at the coffee shops, in their home, at the bus station office, etc.); who was present at the time (not forgetting the anthropologist); whether any significant or insignificant event had happened prior to or was happening during the encounters; snippets of the different, if not conflicting, accounts from different interlocutors that allowed me to comprehend certain stories, and so on.

The History of the SOC

Among the old timers of the SOC, the most accommodating were Poh Shui Kim and Lee Shee Kang, two retired managers.[1] I first met them at Poh's house in late November 1999. His house is located some ten miles along the Kuching-Serian Road, one of the many places that was considered "communist-influenced" back in the 1960s and 1970s. Poh was waiting on the front porch of a rather simple wooden house when I got off the bus with Lee. Poh immediately led us to the living room and instructed me to take a seat across the table from him while Lee sat further away from the table. There were other household members in the house – his wife and grandchildren – but they stayed away from the living room. Poh was in his mid-seventies and had just retired a few months before we met. Lee, the former assistant general manager at SOC, was in his early eighties and had retired several years earlier. But both of them remained active shareholders and little of what went on in the company was beyond their knowledge.

There I was, sitting in the living room with these old timers, all the while thinking, "What if the materials I have read in the archives were inadequate preparation for having a proper conversation with two experts on the history of communism in Sarawak?"[2] Sure enough, I started on the wrong foot by asking if they could tell me about SOC's past relations with issues or activities that might be interpreted as socialism or communism. This made them rather uncomfortable, judging by the way they looked at each other. Poh responded by stating that they were not familiar with such things. Lee was silent and continued to look at Poh.

Our conversations were punctuated with intermittent silences and all the while I was aware that Poh's family members were within hearing distance. I realized I was at a loss as to what I should be asking. There was no flow, no continuity in our conversation. I would start by asking a historical question about the year in which the SOC was formed, only to juxtapose it with a more contemporary one about whether the SOC was going to automate its fleet of buses, thereby retrenching some of its employees. Less than twenty minutes into our conversation both of them began to talk to each other instead of responding to my questions. That happened after they requested I turn off my tape recorder.[3]

By now Poh and Lee had begun to reminisce about the early days of the SOC. Perhaps it was their way to get me to settle down as well as to suggest that I might want to pay more attention to listening to their stories instead of presuming I needed to direct our conversation. In a sense, instead of being an interlocutor to the dialogue, they wanted me to be an interauditor, privileging the discourse of listening over that of talking.[4] Since this meeting took place at an early stage of my fieldwork, most of the issues about which they were talking were new to me and I found myself desperately trying to keep up my note-taking, scribbling as fast as possible for fear that I might miss out on important details.

I should point out that when they were talking with each other they conversed in Hopo, a different Hakka dialect from the Taipu I am familiar with.[5] But when they conversed with me, we mostly spoke in Mandarin and Hokkien, interspersed sporadically with Hopo Khek. There I was, listening to their dialogue in an unfamiliar dialect and jotting it down in English, a daunting task by itself.[6] Moreover, since my initial meeting with Poh and Lee took place during the early phase of my fieldwork, not only had I not had enough time to reacquaint myself with Taipu, the same was true for all the other languages I needed – Hokkien, Teochiu, Mandarin, Cantonese, Malay, and a little bit of

Selako.[7] In fact, the Malay language in Sarawak even sounded differ-ent from the West Malaysian version. It also took about the same time for me to reacquaint myself with multilingual conversational habits to which most Sarawakians (and Malaysians) are accustomed. I do recall how awkward it was during the first month of my fieldwork when my interlocutors sensed that I was struggling to find the proper words, not only in terms of dialect but also idiomatic expressions.

As I listened to Lee and Poh, I realized that all they had been talking about was the origin of the SOC and its business-related matters. There was almost no discussion on, to paraphrase Lee's expression, *pu-see sen-zhi see-ching* (in Mandarin: "non-business-related matters").[8] Perhaps it was a tactical move on their part: by avoiding non-business-related matters, they had hoped to divert from talking about sensitive topics that, once invoked, they might have to confront. But as it turned out, discussion of business-related matters and Cold War issues were not easily separable. This will become evident in the following pages.

As they reminisced about the SOC's past, it almost seemed as if they were competing over their preferred versions of events that had transpired. For example, they would go into minute details such as the number or types of buses, kind of taxes, the start-up capital, number of partners, and the few financial crises the company went through – all without any sense of chronology. They were also quite reluctant to talk about the current situation of the company, especially the new manage-ment or the subject of unionization. Each time I tried to get them to talk about the current situation at the SOC they would switch to other top-ics. For instance, when asked about the current management, in partic-ular the new general manager and the recent partnership with Sarawak Multipurpose Holdings (SMH), a *bumiputra* company, Lee and Poh pro-ceeded to tell me about Stephen Yong (the former SUPP chairman) or Lee Kuan Yew (the former prime minister of Singapore) who, as it so happened, were Taipu. I couldn't help but smile when they commented that the Taipu were generally very talented and possessed exceptional *"liu"* (talent) among the Chinese communities in Southeast Asia. Time and time again, they would refer to Stephen Yong and Lee Kuan Yew to substantiate their claim.

In any case, here is the story of the SOC that I have put together in a somewhat chronological order. Prior to 1951, there were no bus com-panies in Sarawak. All that existed were individual operators – about 156 of them within the Kuching area – and the vehicles they operated, which were not what one would normally think of as buses. These were vans with a capacity of five to seven passengers. Poh laughed when he said, "And they had no tops on them. When it rained, the driver had to rush out the canvas from underneath his seat and the passengers had to help ... they were soaked before the covers were up." Lee was laughing as well, interjecting impatiently, "You should have seen those vehicles," before adding, "It's a shame none of them survived. Otherwise we could restore them for the museum ... They were antiques." Poh nodded in agreement, sighing, "It's a pity. They were what we started out with. They were our history."

There were also no regulations on bus routes or the bus fares each operator could charge. As a consequence, quarrels and fights were frequent among the operators. In an effort to regulate and control these operators, the colonial office issued a directive in 1951 ordering all the operators to form a bus association, to which Lee quickly asserted, while smirking at Poh, that there was another motive behind the directive. It was Poh's turn to jump in, saying, "This was what happened. After the bus association was formed, several individuals consolidated their vehicles to form different bus companies. That was how SOC started. The main directive of forming a bus association was to restore some order ... but my colleague here is right." Poh turned and looked at Lee before continuing,

> It was for tax purposes ... Before that it was impossible for the government [the colonial office] to collect taxes. There were no records. How can you know who were the operators? ... When it comes to having proper records, you tip your hat to them. They cannot live without proper records, proper bookkeeping.

There was a slight sneakiness in his smile when he uttered his last remark about the British colonial regime's ways of doing things.[9]

His remarks reminded me of a discussion on modernity: that the practices and interactions learnt during the colonial encounters gave birth to modernity in Europe (Mitchell 2000).[10] Of course, this is not to suggest that modernity came from the colonies, but without them; without the sites that offered numerous sites for practising and sharpening administrative skills, bookkeeping, transportation of raw materials and labourers (slaves and coolies), and so on, modernity would never have materialized the way it did. What better place could there be for the colonial powers to sharpen their skills but in their colonial laboratories?

Besides the SOC, another group of operators formed the Kuching Transport Company (KTC) a year later. Soon after that, a third company called Hap Tong Fatt Bus Company was formed. But all three companies were losing money during their first two years of operation as they were heavily burdened by the taxation system. Between 1951 and 1952 they were taxed not according to a percentage of revenues earned but on the number of vehicles owned. They all had to pay a certain amount of taxes regardless of the revenues generated, and the SOC owned about eighty vehicles that they had to pay tax on; they would not get rid of extra vehicles for fear they might be bought by individual operators or the other two bus companies, resulting in unwanted competition. Also, there were some colonial officers who were demanding more than the official rate per bus – as many as three to four dollars per vehicle over the official rate of fifteen dollars per vehicle to be paid every six months. Lee reminded me that these were English Straits dollars and not Malaysian ringgits. He added, "That was not easy on cash flow." In order to stay solvent, the SOC had to borrow from its partners as well as from outsiders to pay the taxes. Consequently, some of these "outsiders" became SOC partners.

Business began to pick up in 1953 after the colonial office realized that it had to change its policies if the bus companies were to remain solvent. Bus routes were determined and awarded to respective companies and the system of taxation was changed to one based on percentage of revenue instead of the number of vehicles owned. Poh was quick to assure me that the colonial office was once again looking after its own interests when he asked, rather disingenuously, "Who do you think benefited the most from the changes?" before adding, "The colonial office needed us to remain in business. We were their source of revenue." The SOC was awarded quite a substantial number of bus routes, in particular the highly profitable Kuching to Serian and Kuching to Bau routes. The other main competitor, KTC, was given most of Kuching's domestic routes, but Hap Tong Fatt Bus Company was only allocated some rural bus routes.

It was then that a few SOC partners thought they should expand the company's operation by acquiring more buses to cater to the lucrative routes they were awarded. Its former general manager, Hong Hee Siaw, invested another 40,000 Straits dollars of his own money. Both Poh and Lee made sure that I understood that that was a lot of money at that time.[11] To further emphasize their point, they told me that Hong had to sell most of his property, even his wife's jewellery, to come up with that kind of cash. But that made Hong the general manager. The SOC not only acquired more buses but bigger ones from Singapore that had the capacity for twenty-five seated passengers. Poh reiterated, "The new tax system was better for us and the English. For every six cents [of revenue the SOC made], the colonial office took one cent as taxes. On top of that, they also made sure that there were no more private operators that dared to cut into our business. The colonial officers personally undertook the task of ..." Here, Lee interrupted impatiently before Poh could finish his sentence, reminiscing,

> Those were the good old days. The colonial officers did their best to deter individual operators from picking up our passengers. Some did but they were heavily fined when they were caught. Some even had their vehicles confiscated and that really scared them off. Mind you, most of them did not own their vehicles ... Most of these operators eventually ended up joining the SOC or the other companies.

"How did they end up joining the SOC? As employees?" I asked.

"No, more like partners. The SOC took in their vehicles as part of our operation. That made them partners. Remember, the tax system was no longer based on the number of vehicles owned. They would continue driving their vehicles, but now as part of the company," both of them explained. Poh turned around and looked at his son, who had just walked into the room, before commenting rather proudly, "I don't care what you have to say about the English ... they were good for business. Things were much better. So many things were better then. Take education for one." His son remained silent.

Lee agreed with his colleague, nodding, "Everything they study nowadays is in Malay." He looked at Poh's son before continuing, "Besides, the current tax system is quite stiff when compared to how it was under the British. And bus companies are again facing all sorts of competition. I am not talking about other bus companies but minivans, tour buses, and taxis, even school buses. The worst are the minivans. Do you know who gets these minivan licences?"[12] He looked at Poh, as his old friend had not been to Kuching since his retirement, before adding, "You should take a look at the bus station. Sometimes even our buses cannot get in. The minivans are everywhere. Who do you think are driving these minivans? Look at their 'road taxes.' Most of them have Malay names, a few *la chi* [indigenes]. If you see Chinese, they are mainly employees."

It was Poh's turn to respond: "They were there before I retired. Some of them are actually owned by Chinese, but their licences were issued

to Malays – the usual *Ali Baba*." He turned around to his son who nodded his head in agreement. "The Malays get the licences but the Chinese own and operate the businesses," said Poh's son as he smiled at
me before introducing himself. But Lee intervened to note that there
was a slight difference here, saying,

> Most of them are not your typical *Ali Baba* business. They are not even
> supposed to operate beyond their village areas.[13] Their licences were only
> for the *kampungs*, taking passengers from one village to the next or to the
> nearest bazaar. But they now pick up passengers wherever they fancy
> them ... operating on routes that are in direct competition with bus com-
> panies. Isn't that against the law?

Immediately Poh and his son interjected, laughing somewhat, "Law?
What law? Whose law? Laws are for us but when it comes to their
own ... [referring to the Malays]." I laughed along with them, and Lee
laughed as well when he realized he was asking a rhetorical question.
When I asked them whether it was by design that the majority of the
SOC's employees in the past happened to be rural Hakkas who fled
from the *new villages*, both Poh and Lee said that much of the hiring was
due to a matter of timing. They did not offer any political reason behind
these recruitments.

The Human Dimension of History

I met up with Lee and Poh again a week later. This time I informed
both of them, as I had with most of my subjects, that my research
was not about the leaders in their communities but about them –
bus drivers, bus conductors, and other ordinary people – whose histories should be given the "human dimension" that is missing from
official history. Somehow this would usually make them slightly uneasy when they thought of themselves as agents of history. It would
also make them less willing to talk about their past. In fact, they
would always give credibility to those "higher up" as the purveyors of
knowledge, as if material well-being corresponded with knowledge
and truth.

But I was glad that Lee and Poh acted differently. They felt a little
more comfortable this time around on some of the sensitive issues from
the Cold War period. Once again, Lee would reminisce, "The 1950s
were good for us. Everybody was happy. The company, the staff, even

the colonial officers [laughing] ... Then things changed." I waited for him to continue but both Lee and Poh remained silent, perhaps still somewhat reluctant to dig up the past. I let the silence linger as I had the feeling they had suddenly realized that they were faced with the decision of whether or not to tell me something they had been avoiding. As I mentioned earlier, it was not easy to separate business from non-business-related issues in the case of the SOC's history. Although it was by definition a business entity, it had a certain political anchor to it (even if it was not that of communism) as it navigated through the stormy passage during the 1960s and 1970s. After a long silence, they told me that the changes had nothing to do with taxation or competition, but with something else. But before they resumed, they begged me not to write it down. As they put it, "treat this like a friendly conversation between friends. There is no need to write down everything." Adding some humour to it, Poh joked, "Don't be like the English. Not everything needs to be recorded."

According to Poh and Lee, things quickly turned for the worse in the 1960s. This was when the SOC's operations were thoroughly affected by the various anti-communist campaigns. For one, they were getting summonses for all sorts of offences – ranging from broken tail lights, or dimmed lights, or not enough air pressure in the tires, to faulty brakes or speeding – that caused the company a lot of headaches, not to mention the expenses incurred engaging lawyers to deal with those summons. Incidentally, Stephen Yong, the outspoken secretary general of the SUPP, was also the SOC's lawyer.

Poh and Lee assured me that ordinarily the police would have overlooked such minor offences. As Poh puts it, "None of that happened in the 1950s. Even today, you might get one or two summonses for broken tail lights and what not, but these are what we call Chinese New Year summonses ... These are our yearly gifts to *them*." Besides summonses, Lee asked if I had ever been subjected to curfews. Curfews were not only common during the 1960s and the first half of the 1970s but were usually enforced without any prior warning, thereby creating chaos for the public transportation companies. Since SOC had the outstation routes, it had to service all the towns and rural areas within the so-called communist-influenced areas regardless of the inconveniences and the risks involved. As Lee put it, "What choice did we have? Regardless of whether we ran our buses or not, we still had taxes to pay, salaries, all sorts of expenses. Do you think our creditors would extend our debts if we did not pay them on time?"

Furthermore, Poh added, "Quite often our buses were stopped and told to turn back. Sometimes the soldiers would harass our drivers and conductors. Some were slapped." He began to laugh and turned towards Lee to see if this was funny. Lee did not laugh. When asked why their buses were at the curfew zones, Poh raised his voice:

> Why? How could we know if this or that area was off limits on any given day? Let me tell you … we were at a loss as to which routes we could operate on any given day. Nobody had any idea. Isn't that right? [Again, he looked at Lee.] Not only was it inconveniencing those of us in charge of operations, but what about our bus conductors and drivers? They were the ones who were screamed at and sometimes slapped before they were told to turn around and head home. And where do you think they headed first when told to turn back? Our depot at the fifth mile, and I was always the first one they came to see.

As chief mechanic, Poh was in charge of the depot. I sensed a tone of pride in his voice when he commented, "But you know what? There was not even a single resignation. Sure, everyone was angry, but we stood firm. Many could have resigned and worked elsewhere or joined the KTC, but no, everyone stood firm." Both of them said – and I heard this from other old timers as well – that the company was like one big family with very resilient individuals who stuck together during this chaotic period.

After this, it was time for Lee to leave, and I took a ride with him on the SOC bus back to Kuching. He made sure I paid my fare.

Warong Muhibah

Whenever I was at the SOC bus station, I always made a point to hang out at *Warong Muhibah*. It was there that I could always find some bus conductors and drivers to talk to. If not, there were other regulars. Compared to the other coffee shops at the bus station, this *warong* had a lively and friendly vibe. It was located next to the river and one could always feel the afternoon breeze, a way to escape from the black exhaust of the aging SOC buses, if that was even possible. Quite often I would sit there observing the interactions between the Chinese, Malay, and Dayak bus conductors and drivers as they chatted about their workdays, teasing each other, complaining about the company, making jokes about the government, or just about anything.

I often found myself engaging in more than one conversation at *Warong Muhibah*. For instance, I might be talking with an Iban bus conductor, Tonlin, about her longhouse, while Zuariah, her Javanese colleague, was asking what I was doing at SOC head office. Pak Buang, the half-Malay, half-Chinese *sampan*-man who had just arrived to exchange some coins with the *warong* owner, interrupted to find out when I planned to visit his *kampung* across the river or his brother's house at one of the *new villages*. Ah Fon, a Hakka bus conductor, might interrupt our conversation by talking to Tonlin, and others might be teasing each other about different things. On top of this, these conversations were happening in different languages – Hokkien, Malay, Hakka (Hopo, Hwee Lan, and Taipu dialects), Bidayuh, Mandarin, and Iban. These conversations continued simultaneously, with each of them trying to be "with" me or to be "with" another individual, and me and others trying to engage with all of them, if that was even possible.

As I have mentioned earlier, in the beginning it was difficult for me to follow what was going on in all these concurrent conversations as I tried to acquaint myself with their strands of space, time, and meaning, not to mention their different personalities, mannerisms, speech patterns, and so on. In sociolinguistic terms, I was grappling with the disparate subjectivities of my interlocutors as they talked about a number of diverse issues and concerns that were still foreign to me. One might even say that there were too many disparate subjectivities and not enough intersubjectivity. It took me about two months before I could honestly say that I was able to follow the dialogues closely, and before I was able to engage with just about anyone that showed up at the *warong* – bus conductors, drivers, the store owners, their regular customers, even bus and *sampan* passengers who were passing by. Underneath these concurrent dialogues there were often some forms of collaborative discussion pertaining to the pressing concerns of their most immediate environment – their workplaces and their livelihoods. Obviously certain topics would also capture their attention, for instance, the first Anwar Ibrahim sodomy trial, the "Armed Heist" in West Malaysia,[14] or the number of headless victims showing up in Sarawak that many locals believed belonged to illegal Indonesian immigrants. Through what I took to be our mutual enjoyment in talking with one another, not to mention my paying for drinks and food from time to time, I was learning about their lives and livelihoods while they raised their concerns and frustrations about their company, the State, and other issues.

Most, if not all, of the different cliques congregating at *Warong Muhibah* and the other coffee shops transcended the usual race, class, and gender concerns. Malays, Javanese, Hakkas, Hokkiens, Chao Anns, Teochius, Bidayuh, and Ibans, all men and women of different age groups, would mingle at any available table – teasing each other, chatting, sharing food, paying for each other's beverages, and so on. Their sociability was also spatial in form in that most of their chatting took place in these spaces, which I would describe as being "anti-company" spaces where the levels of surveillance and restriction were markedly reduced. To be sure, the gatherings of different cliques in these anti-company spaces, even if they did not have any real sense of political and social resistance, was generating some discomfort for the management, as I could tell by the occasional glances by the station managers, or even by the security officer, as they walked past. Usually at these moments the employees would lower their voices, but they would burst out laughing as soon as the air was clear of any eavesdropping. They knew better than to raise their concerns and frustrations. Sometimes I would sit there with some of them without talking, observing the coming and going of buses and their passengers, or simply gazing at the *sampans* as they arrived and departed at the jetty about twenty feet from the *warong*. It was as if we were all searching for quietude amidst all the noises and the pollution at the bus station.

One afternoon, after I had been frequenting *Warong Muhibah* for almost a month, a rather reserved Hakka bus conductor who had the reputation of being unapproachable quietly confided in me that the SOC buses had in the past distributed anti-government materials as they travelled through the rural areas – in particular, landscapes that were inscribed by the state as *communist-influenced* areas. But before he could elaborate, some of his colleagues arrived and sat at the table next to ours. Even as he tried to speak softly, his colleagues stopped chatting and began to listen, making him uncomfortable. But they encouraged him, saying, "*Jangan takut-lah! Kami biasa cerita itu.*" (In Malay: Don't be afraid! We are familiar with those stories.) He proceeded to tell me that he was aware that certain former colleagues of his (underscoring that "they are no longer working at the SOC") had distributed *fan chin-fu* (in Hakka: anti-government) and *kong chang tong* (in Hakka: communist) literature back in the mid-1960s to early 1970s.

That was the first time anyone had ever mentioned anything that would directly link the SOC or its employees with anti-state or pro-socialist activities. I asked him what the pamphlets looked like. "They looked like any other one-page leaflet with Chinese characters written on it. Just like that red piece of leaflet on the lamppost over there," he said, pointing towards a one-page advertisement on the lamppost outside the *warong*, before continuing, "Usually in red paper with black inked Chinese characters. They were pamphlets calling for an end to *Di Guo Zhu-yi* [imperialism] and for Sarawak self-rule, that sort of thing." "They were distributed on the buses?" I asked. "No, not on the bus. They were dropped off at rural bus stations, or sometimes scattered alongside the road ... usually at entrances or pathways leading to rural villages, much like what you see during a funeral procession – papers thrown from the bus windows, scattered along the road. Sometimes they were handed out to passengers, but seldom," he responded without looking at his colleagues.

At that moment another bus driver, Keong Wen, who had just walked in and sat down next to me, interjected rather sarcastically, "Spies, oh, that's something else. The SOC is full of them. You have to watch your back." Then he started to laugh. I was annoyed with him not only for interrupting an important story, but also for bringing up the topic of spies at that particular juncture. Others that were present reacted by daring him to blare it out in front of the station office, to which Keong Wen proudly responded, "Me? I am not scared of them." Although his colleagues were a little put off by his remarks, I suspected they shared his opinions. They were unhappy with the company, especially when the issue of getting their bonuses was still uncertain. In any case, because of Keong Wen's abrupt, if not abrasive, interruption, the others started to disperse, including the rather reserved Hakka bus conductor. I thought of following him, but I realized he would not be talking about those pamphlets on the bus. I ended up alone with Keong Wen but he could not tell me much about the pamphlets since he had not joined the SOC until the late 1970s. He did, however, mention that he had heard of them.

The next day I tried to ask the group of individuals who had left after Keong Wen's interruption if they could fill me in on what they knew about the pamphlets. But like in so many other encounters, in a way that had become the routine reply to my queries, they denied my request by claiming ignorance. This time, one of them commented, "Oh! We knew nothing of it. We were just playing along to get him excited. We wanted to hear the stories as well." I should mention that even though those pamphlets were written in Chinese characters, it did not mean that they were targeted at rural Chinese residents. Many indigenous people in Sarawak do read Chinese. In fact, the trend had been growing, especially after the implementation of the national school system in the 1970s following the policies of the NEP.[15] Since then, a significant population of indigenous and Malay parents had been sending their children to Chinese Chung Hwa schools in Sarawak.

When I asked old timer Lee if it was true that SOC buses were once used to distribute socialist literature, he said, after some hesitation, that he was not aware of it. What was puzzling is that he did not ask whom I had obtained my information from, even after I specifically told him that I had heard it from a bus driver.[16] Another thing worth mentioning is Poh and Lee's timing in bringing up a question when I met up with them on another occasion. They asked if I was aware that Hong had been arrested and imprisoned in Kuala Lumpur in 1969. Were they implying that Hong had some affiliation with some communist organizations or was their response purely coincidental? Throughout my fieldwork I was never told that Hong was a communist. As in the case of the overwhelming majority of the arrests during the Cold War in Sarawak, Hong was never officially charged for his arrest and, subsequently, was never given a trial. He was released in less than two years, a sentence that was considered to be relatively light considering that many others I met were detained for much longer.

Poh said that Hong's arrest was the lowest point in the history of the SOC. Everyone was worried that more arrests would follow. Lee became the acting general manager then, but he was quick to point out that he had mainly been in charge of business issues, things pertaining to the operation of the company. It was interesting to observe him being so careful about things that had happened a long time before. When Hong was eventually released in 1971, he was not allowed to travel anywhere, not even to any of the company offices outside of Kuching. Lee complained, "He couldn't visit our office in Simanggang. That was absolutely unnecessary and unreasonable. Do you know anything about red identification cards? He was issued one after his release. With all these restrictions it was difficult for him to perform his job as the GM." The issuing of identity cards, a colonial invention, was the technology of biopower by which the authority could govern the movement of people, especially so-called dissidents, across the national landscape.[17]

"Why Simanggang?" I asked Lee, somehow feeling that there must have been a reason, or several reasons, as to why he had made reference to this particular township. I was preoccupied with Simanggang at that time of my fieldwork. Both Lee and Poh responded that Hong was forbidden to travel outside of the Kuching area. This included Simanggang and the other townships. However, I was not willing to let this slip by without further elaboration. I continued with my question, this time asking Poh why he did not mention Bau, Semantan, Serian, or any other townships, but instead spoke of Simanggang. Both of them appeared a little uncomfortable but fortunately, once again, Poh's son bailed me out when he interjected by repeating my question, almost disingenuously: "Was there something about Simanggang?" He was grinning and nodded to me that I might have touched upon something worthwhile.

I was glad that the two old timers took it well and Lee even teased Poh's son that he should be on his way to work. Eventually Poh tried to answer my question, though indirectly. He said that it was true some SOC employees were revolutionaries, but at the same time he was quick to point out that not all of them, using the familiar phrase, "walked that path." He reiterated that the bottom line was that the SOC was a business entity. Both of them wanted me to understand that because of its connection with SUPP the company was inevitably affected by the policies of the government of the day. As Poh put it, "The SOC had a unique relation to SUPP and SUPP was an opposition party back then. What more can I say?"

Besides this, from what I have gathered from other employees, things were not so black and white concerning activities that might be construed as either communist or business related. It was certainly true that when the SOC was set up in 1951 its primary motive was to make profit. But among the original partners that formed the company, some were definitely socialist inclined. And during the 1960s, especially when government policies were determined primarily by the Cold War geopolitics, economic issues became more and more entangled with political complexities. Otherwise how could one understand the constant issuing of summonses and the harassment of SOC bus conductors and drivers inside the curfew zones? In the face of the constant harassment, wouldn't the management and employees have reacted with disgust, if not hatred?

I believe part of my initial problem in determining if the company (or part of it) was communist lay with my tendency to adopt a prior understanding of what constituted communism and then to use that understanding to determine if my interlocutors fitted into that paradigm. My inquiry about communism or the history of communism in Sarawak, whether consciously or otherwise, lay in my preoccupation with debates or critiques of capitalism, democracy, and communism that were always clouded by notions of equality, progress, and civil liberties. Perhaps it comes as no surprise that these notions lay at the root of most of our investigations on topics such as egalitarianism, exploitation, genocide, unionism, labour issues, migration, immigration, and so on. Having said this, shouldn't equalities, progress, and civil liberties (to mention just three) be considered concepts that arise out of specific contexts instead of being treated as givens, unchanging and ontologically unchanging prior to the situations in which they arise? This question or tendency, however, is not easily answered or avoided. One is constantly reminded how prior understandings affect our consciousness by witnessing just how resilient they can be when adopted into our investigations. Nietzsche, for one, was never tired of telling us that consciousness is notoriously error prone.

"What about the fact that the SOC was predominantly a Chinese company in the past? Do you think that might have determined the government's attitude towards it?" I asked Poh and Lee. Lee responded by noting that this was probably true, but quickly retracted it when Poh reminded him that their competitor, KTC, was also a Chinese company and had not been harassed like the SOC. At this point Poh even confided that there were communist elements within the KTC, but with a qualitative, if not ironic, difference. I detected a sense of pride when he said, "Unlike the SOC ... how can I put it ... they did not have the kind of connection we had with SUPP. Most if not all of our employees were SUPP members."

Whether these individuals ended up as communists or not remained a fuzzy question. Most individuals would not openly admit to it but there were certainly indications, either coming from the way they talked or addressed certain issues, or from third parties confiding in me about their past identities, that they were influenced by socialist ideas of equality and a way out of their positions. Moreover, there were different roles and responsibilities for communists in Sarawak during the Cold War. Some went into the jungle to wage guerilla warfare against the Allied forces. Many remained in *society*, where they were responsible for disseminating communist literature to the general public (mostly in the rural areas) and for providing information, food, and any other assistance they could muster for their comrades in the jungle. The SOC's involvement, I believe, if there was any, was mainly with the latter. However, I was not able to determine what proportion of its employees was involved and in what capacity.

I should also mention that whenever I approached the bus conductors and drivers who I had been told had distributed anti-government pamphlets in the past, and whenever I asked if they could tell me anything about the content of the pamphlets, time and time again they would repeat that they hadn't the slightest idea since, as they put it, "*Ngai mo hang ke tiu loo*" (in Hakka: "I don't walk that path"). However, as I reviewed my field notes, I realized that not once did any of them refute the assertion that the distribution of socialist literature by SOC employees took place. I was also surprised that none of them were upset with my persistency, but would typically respond with a smiling refusal. In fact, some of them tried to convince me that those who liked to brag about things had misled me. They were not the only ones who stated the last point.

One afternoon as I was having coffee across from the station office, two Hakka old timers advised me to be cautious about what I heard. Choosing his words rather carefully, one of them said,

> Mr. Yong [all of my interlocutors would call me Kee], there are some folks who think there is something heroic about being a communist. The way they would talk about the communists, as if they were heroes. A few hundred fighting thousands of soldiers, fighting *Di Guo Zhu-yi* [imperialism], you know ... that big word. Not to mention they [the communists] were under-armed ... People like to make things up. You need to be careful when you hear these sorts of stories. You are new to Sarawak and people are aware of that. It is not easy for you to double-check their stories. You should be aware of that instead of wasting your time.

I told them that I had received similar advice from others and for that reason alone, I wanted to seek their proper advice and guidance. I continued, "After all, both of you have worked for the company for over forty years and as drivers operating on the Kuching-Serian road, you could tell me about your experiences." But all they did was smile and reiterate the same response others had before them – that they did not *walk that path*. I smiled back and paused before I was overtaken by the temptation to find out more about Bong Chee Cheok, a name I was then preoccupied with. I asked if they could tell me something, anything, about Bong and the Sri Aman Treaty. It turned out to be a mistake, if not an opportunity for them to terminate our conversation. They gave me a typical response: "Who hasn't heard of Bong? Everybody in Sarawak knows Bong but that's all we can tell you since we don't know him personally. If you are so interested you should interview him at Si-manggang. Sometimes he is in Kuching. Or you can contact his brother here in Kuching." After saying that, they got up to excuse themselves, saying, "We have to make the next run to Serian." I asked if I could go along but they smiled and walked away. I walked across the street to *Warong Muhibah*, just like any other late afternoon when I was at the bus station.

This Thing about Indonesia

Social scientists are not alone in being attracted to a comparative view of things.[18] Most of my subjects shared the same habit. The theme of comparing Sarawak with West Kalimantan (Indonesia) was constant throughout my fieldwork, especially when my subjects dealt with their dispositions. It was common to hear them talking about the high level of unemployment in Indonesia, riots, corruption among the government officials at all levels, the illegal Indonesians in Sarawak and their willingness to work for very low wages, and so on. It was as if by making referential claims to the bleak situation in Indonesia, especially about the situation of the Chinese there in the mid-1960s[19] or in 1998,[20] to name only two sets of dates, they were creating excuses to tactically resolve their own powerlessness – a sort of mental shield that helped them to live sanely in an unjust situation. I should state that the comparison with Indonesia is often part of Malaysian state rhetoric to tell its population that they are better off than those violent perpetrators in Indonesia. Therefore, to hear my subjects making this comparison is not just a reflection of their specific dispositions but also a use of official rhetoric. In other words, their narratives reflect part of the state narratives.

One of the reasons these bus drivers and conductors would not want to dig up the past was the relatively peaceful situation in Sarawak. They emphasized that Sarawak was relatively calm nowadays when compared to other parts of Southeast Asia, especially Indonesia, and that it was inappropriate to dig up stories of the past. Strangely enough, their reluctance to talk about the past only heightened my conviction that there is a connection between this reluctance to talk and the awareness of their current positions. The bitter fate they experienced during the Cold War was not the end of the story. Those who joined the SOC because it offered them a venue to express their dissatisfaction against the government now found themselves facing a management that bore no resemblance to the one they once were loyal to, a topic I will address in chapter 7. But first, let me recount their ambiguity – if not indifference – to the SUPP.

Many of the SOC employees I spoke to not only said that SUPP had gone "soft" since joining the Alliance government in 1971, but even went as far as suggesting that it was a Faustian pact. Past battles against imperialism, against colonialism, and so on, now seemed like an illusion. It is no wonder that some of them even joked sarcastically about those battles – for instance, about a few hundred communists fighting thousands of soldiers who were far better equipped. I have the feeling that quite a lot of them felt jilted, betrayed by SUPP, and now by the changes at SOC, especially with its recent *Ali Baba* Malay partnership. This latest move had, for many of the bus conductors and drivers, severed all links with their past struggles and aspirations. I am convinced that my queries must have been painful for some of them, since they reacted so defensively and often dispensed so much effort to convince me that I had been misled.

Were These Communists?

Reading my field notes, I regret how irrational I was in some of my interactions with these interlocutors. I recall when Lee once told me rather flatly that I was asking about something that was no longer relevant to their lives. He even got a little poetic, saying,

> A lot went on in the past. It's like the water flowing under the bridge, a lot has swept by. Sure, the government used to accuse us of being infiltrated by communist elements. It was the same rhetoric they used against SUPP. You told me earlier you have read some literature from the SUPP library. Well? Don't you see the similarities? As we have been telling you all the while, the company has always been a business entity and like any business entity, we operated in the hope of making a profit.

That was that. He had said what he wanted to reveal. I realized that in many ways both of them had given me as much information as I needed about how the SOC was construed by the government as pro-socialist. In short, to understand the situation, one has to decode the hidden message behind the narratives, to situate them within the politics and economies of the Cold War and the *bangsa* relations that existed in Sarawak. By treating Lee and Poh's analogy between SUPP and SOC as a performative utterance, I understood that they were producing at one and the same time a meaning effect, or effects, that there were communist elements within the SOC and that both of them might have been treated as communists during the 1960s and 1970s.

Borrowing Austin's (1962) theory of illocution, I might state that, paradoxically, Lee, Poh, and my other interlocutors were attempting to offer the heterogeneous images of what was considered to be communist or communism during the Cold War. They were trying to emphasize that there were many more referents as to what one might call communist or communism and a lot of it had to do with certain links, a certain history. In the case of Lee's indirect response (as it was with most, if not all of my interlocutors' responses), his language was already imbued with all sorts of referents to that chaotic era. The referents, being communist in this case, were no longer simply a pre-existing substance, but an act of being communist. Lee's performed utterances of drawing an analogy between the SUPP and SOC was an action that exceeded a simple response to a query, but it nevertheless left traces on the real or intended query, that is, "Was he a communist?" By being indirect or using an analogy, Lee's responses or performed narratives can be seen as analogous to the speech act of practising discreetness or of being refractory in that they contain within them the possibility of different interpretations or miscues, thereby allowing him, the interlocutor, to deny or refract any direct reference to the real or intended query – in other words, "by committing speech acts [Lee] literally escapes the hold of truth" (Felman 1983, 31). Identity, in this case, becomes a site of contestation.

Unlike the constative discourse of language, the performative does not refer to a perfect symmetry between statement and enunciation. On the contrary, it is from asymmetry that Austin's thought proceeds, from the excess of utterance with respect to statement. In fact, one would argue that analysis using the performative discourse of language is the only way to read into Lee's (and Poh's) knowledge of what transpired in the past. More importantly, the performative has the property of subverting the alternative, the opposition between referentiality and self-referentiality. In a sense, there was a kind of intelligence in Lee's narratives that was so submerged in the logic of tactical practices that it can only be communicated or decoded within the contexts of the Cold War in Sarawak. To paraphrase de Certeau (1984 79), narrative does have content, but that content is also part of the art of "scoring": it makes a detour through the past ("in former times"), or by the way of a quotation (a "saying," or a proverb, or an analogy), in order to seize an occasion and make an unexpected modification in the precarious balance of things. These kinds of practices play on time; they wait for the right moment, which comes at the moment of interlocution between different interlocutors.

The reluctance of revealing one's past identities – in this case, of being a communist – was in no way unique to Lee or Poh. To be sure, my interlocutors' reluctance to directly answer my queries would suggest a few levels of possible interpretations. They were (still) uncomfortable with the researcher at that juncture; they were no longer proud of their past; it was still too risky to reveal their previous identities; they did not find it empowering to talk about their past when their current positions were just as bleak; or in fact they had already revealed their past to me, but in a disguised fashion. It seems to me that there was a correlation here between their lack of attribution towards memory (here I am treating memory as an act, as the process of reminiscing or recollection) and their reluctance to be politically engaged, especially if one were to take their current dispositions into consideration. One might even call it the abeyance of agency seen from the context of indifference or even resignation towards life rewards or aspirations. Most, if not all, of the bus conductors and drivers at the SOC (as well as at the KTC) had not attended any of the SUPP meetings for more than fifteen years. They were neither interested in the opposition parties, nor did they believe the opposition could challenge the fully oiled election machinery of the ruling regime.

Chapter Five

What's There to Tell?

As they became evil, they talked about fraternity and humanitarianism and came to understand those concepts; as they became criminal, they invented justice and drew up voluminous codes of laws to enforce their justice ... and built a guillotine to enforce their laws.

Fyodor Dostoyevsky ([1834] 1980, 221)

"What's there to tell? One might go to prison for it," was how Huah Li, a bus conductor from the KTC, responded to my queries about the *new villages*. Even though there is no law in Malaysia that forbids people from talking about communism or the history of communism in Malaysia, my observation with former guerrillas and other subjects affected by the War on Communism in Sarawak would indicate that they were still haunted by it, so much so that they would rather not talk about it. Moreover, there was always the fear of being watched by the Special Branch.[1] Huah Li was one of them. Her father and brother were killed in one of these *new villages*. This chapter deals with the experiences of those who were forcibly displaced and relocated into the *new villages*. In this regard, I am dealing with aspects of how dislocation and trauma shaped these people – how families were divided and how they coped with that dislocation and trauma. I am also concerned with how they rebuilt their lives, what resources – both physical and mental – they drew upon, and how that shaped the *new villages* and towns they settled in.

Narratives of random as well as systematic violence experienced by these subjects, their family members and friends will weave in and out of the texts, much like the asymmetrical warp and weft of an Iban *ikat*

(a traditional Iban weaving). The manifestations of certain vocabularies in the lives of these subjects, their refraction from the wielders of
power, so to speak, in dealing with the social realities both during the
Cold War as well as in the historical present is the underlying theme of
this chapter.

In his essay "Ideologies in Social History," Georges Duby ([1974]
1985) notes that quite often "non-verbal documents are likely to provide even more information, since ideology sometimes finds more direct and richer expression through visual signs" (157). Even though
Duby refers to signs like emblems, costumes, festivals, monuments,
art and so on, when he talks about non-verbal documents, the concept
can be applied to things that are less glamorous (if not just opposite of
glamorous) in excavating the meaning of a particular discourse or ideology. I am referring to the state-inscribed spatiality and architecture of
the *new villages*, including the arrangement of social space within them,
which stand as *lieux de mémoire* through which memories of a certain
past are perpetuated.

During one of my visits to Siburan, a few teenagers, much to the displeasure of their elders, showed me a few blocks of cement with metal
stems at various spots that were supposed to be remnants of the watch-
towers. They also led me to where the perimeter of the fences were once
located. Other detritus from the past included a few fading trespassing signposts that had clear indications of the territory, both forbidding
outsiders from entering the village without proper authorization and
confining residents within the fences. Beneath the bold letters on the
sign that reads No Trespassing is a caricature of a man being fired upon
as he tried to escape. These are memories. To pick up from Pierre Nora
(1996) again, these were the traces left behind by actions that materialized from the Cold War, as if aging into modernity through the passing
of violent time. It was not difficult to visualize what life must have been
like as the residents were allowed to "suffer peacefully," living under
constant curfews, restrictions and harassments, the occasional firing of
shots followed by anxious silence, wailing, and funerals.[2]

Similar to the *new villages* studied by Judith Strauch (1981) in West
Malaysia, these controlled settlements in Sarawak persisted as viable
social units long after the fences were taken down. Obviously there had
been changes. There were now new families who had moved in, families
that were related in some way to the original residents through kinship.
There were also a few Ibans and Bidayuhs who moved in through inter-
marriages with the Hakkas. But overall, the three *new villages* remained
as Hakka villages. Just as in any community, there was a barbershop,

several grocery stores, a meat market, a couple of fish stalls, and a few Taoist temples. But the liveliest places in Siburan were the few coffee shops that lay adjacent to the Kuching-Serian Road. This was similar to Tapah and Beratok. I often hung out at these coffee shops, usually on Sundays when some of the villagers and a few pepper farmers from the surrounding area would congregate to play mah-jong. Most of these pepper farmers were former residents who had since moved back to their land after the "restrictions" were lifted. They would now sell their peppers to the grocery shops at these *new villages* but, if they had a good season, they much preferred to sell them to the merchants at the Main Bazaar in Kuching for higher prices.

To most of the residents of these villages, the pepper farmers were considered the fortunate ones who managed to renegotiate their leases with the indigenous landowners after the fences at the *new villages* came down.[3] Others who were not so lucky ended up working at the various shops in these *new villages*, and quite a few were unemployed, picking up odd jobs here and there during the fruit tree season, or working for these pepper farmers if they needed an extra hand or two. I was told that some of the younger men travelled as far as the interior north-east of Sarawak to work at the various hydroelectric dams or at some logging sites. Many would also often travel to urban centres for work. Some even had their children working at factories in West Malaysia, Singapore, Taiwan, and Japan.

Quite often I would detect elements of envy towards the pepper farmers in the tone of some local residents. The usual comments I got were *"Goyang kaki!"* (Shaking one's legs!), or *"Senang!"* (Easy!),[4] or "Pepper prices have been really good over the years." These would usually be followed with "You know, I used to have acres of land myself, more than ... [so and so]." One might even say that they have become jealous of their own past, that their envy of these pepper farmers was born out of the dislocation of that period and the subsequent forced abandonment of their vegetable gardens. In response, these pepper farmers would tell me that life was not as *senang* (easy) as one might think since there was a great deal of work and risk involved in cultivating peppers. It is true that pepper plants are extremely prone to all sorts of diseases and that prices do fluctuate rapidly, which are beyond the control of these farmers.

Another possible reason they were so envious of the pepper farmers might have to do with the sense of spatial compression at the *new villages*. In terms of the spatial arrangement, each family was allocated less than an eighth of an acre of land on which to build their house. On top of that they were told to cultivate vegetables and fruits. From the comments I got, once the house was up, there was hardly any land left and the most one could do was rear a few chickens. That was a sharp departure from their pre-relocation notion of space when most of these residents had *access* to Native Customary Rights land that they informally leased from indigenous landowners.[5] After years of transforming tracts of primary forest into vegetable gardens, they were taken away from them. They now lived more on the memories of these gardens than from the gardens themselves.

The residents at the *new villages* not only complained about the size of their houses but also the size of their bathrooms.[6] All of the households I visited had layers of thick cardboard and posters, which had been accumulated over the years, covering the wooden plank walls that separated one household from the next. A grandmother told me they helped insulate the noises between households, as well as the visibility from the spaces in between each plank. Still, she complained to me she had not been getting much sleep lately because her neighbours had a new baby. She whispered, pointing towards the wall on her left, "They have many children. Very noisy! It makes my heart restless … baby cries day and night." It was true. As soon as the grandmother mentioned this, the baby started to cry. I could also hear occasional chatting from the houses next door, or sounds from the chopping block or when someone was taking a shower.[7] One could hear everything through these walls. Could that explain the level and frequency of whispering among these people? This was an observation I had working with these displaced subjects.

All throughout my conversations with these residents, I was struck again and again that they much preferred to talk about the jobs that were (un)available at the villages, the part of southern China their parents or grandparents came from, their children's educational details, and so on. Each time I enquired about the 1960s and 1970s, their standard response was that they have forgotten about that period, or that it was pointless. Or they would say, "Come on … Why talk about those unpleasant things?" Some of them even stated that they were not familiar with the background information I had gathered. Over time I came to suspect that unfamiliarity was deliberately used to obscure their cooperation, facilitating forgetfulness as public practice.

As it turned out, it was from a group of bus conductors and drivers at SOC and KTC that I first learned about the violence at the *new villages*. Unlike the residents of the *new villages*, they were more willing to talk about their villages' violent past because they no longer lived there, and they were no longer inscribed by its social architecture and its names. Obviously, we were more familiar with one another as I had spent most of my fieldwork at the bus stations, in their anti-company spaces, and on *their* buses. According to the drivers and conductors, there was strict monitoring of movement within and beyond the fences. To venture beyond the village gate, one needed a pass and a soldier escort. And during the dusk-to-dawn curfew (from 7:00 p.m. to 6:00 a.m.), nobody was allowed to leave one's house, not even to go to the bathroom that lay beyond the back door. Sometimes the curfew went on for days, if not weeks, to the point that it became the very fibre of their existence. But, in retelling the past, I noticed there was a certain detachment in the way they talked about the conditions of the *new villages.* There was this lack of emotion in the way they talked about them. Interestingly, they too could not remember when all the restrictions were finally lifted, or when the fences came down.

After I told some of the residents what I had learned from the drivers and conductors, some of the men began to divulge a little information, but not the elderly and middle-aged women. They remained steadfast in not wanting to disclose anything to me. Paradoxically, their refusal to speak is the loudest silence in my effort to catch a glimpse of this past. But I had to respect their decisions. I would enquire about the welfare of their children – some of them working in Singapore, Taiwan, or Japan – and refrained from touching anything remotely connected to the past, especially after I realized that I had touched on a sensitive topic that was best left unsaid. This happened one afternoon as I was getting my hair cut in Tapah. I had been to this barbershop a dozen times, chatting with the barber and others who were there. One of the main topics on everyone's mind was the upcoming election in Taiwan. This was true with the rest of my Chinese subjects in Kuching.

Somehow, that afternoon, without my asking, the barber told me how worried and disconcerted both he and his parents were when they were first relocated. He said he could still remember vividly the morning they were woken up by a banging on the front door and were given four hours to pack. He recalled how confused he was and the frightening feeling he experienced of being *taken* from their home. He was fourteen years old. Forcing a smile, he said that since all of *them* were "cooped up like chickens," it did not take long to be acquainted with strangers. Plus, they were mostly Hakkas. So language was not the problem. However, this did not mean they trusted each other since rumours were spreading quickly that someone within his *new village* might be a communist, or that certain characters were government or communist spies.

Like many others who were willing to divulge a little about the past, the barber said his father would not let go of the idea of getting back their garden years after they were forced to abandon it. Forcing a smile, the barber said that was why he was probably fated to be a barber. He then proceeded to talk about the soldiers, that they would confiscate any household materials they deemed suspicious, objects like bamboo sticks, axes, and even alarm clocks because the soldiers claimed they could be used to detonate bombs.[8] And then the barber said something he should not have. As soon as he said that the soldiers were *daring* (in Hakka, *tai tum*), he tensed up, hoping that the three elderly men at his shop would say something. They too appeared ill at ease and remained stoically silent. One of them was quite talkative a few days earlier, giving his analysis of the upcoming election in Taiwan and telling everyone at the shop he was being given first-hand information about the election from his son who worked there, his son who was getting married to a Taiwanese woman. This time around he was silent. I too refrained from asking and remained silent. After a brief period, perhaps to indicate to the barber that he had spoken about a public secret, the man with his son in Taiwan asked the barber if he was referring to "the evening hours." I could sense that it was his way of hinting to the barber how close he was to evoking a path towards something that had reached the status of not just public secret, but sanctioned denial.[9] The barber acquiesced by saying that it was best to leave those unpleasant incidents behind. At this point, one of the men left the shop, making me feel slightly guilty that perhaps I was the source of his departure.

It should be clear from the above that much of what the barber and the rest of the village residents could tell me, or what they chose to recount, is entangled by what is not available immediately as a story. For the most part, their retelling was a reminder of their *peaceful suffering* that remained the very texture of the hidden but active contemporaneity of their lives, a contemporaneity that did not provide an imagination with which they could reach forward. It should not be forgotten that they were forcibly dislocated and forced to pledge allegiance to a country not of their choice. Metaphorically, they were sacrificed in return for the military Cold War economic exchange that benefited the elites within the Alliance Government in their continued effort to plunder this Land of the Hornbill.

Paradoxically, the residents' silences and uneasiness in talking about the past attest to the fact that what appears to be forgotten is nonetheless powerfully alive. Violence exists in the past, silences in the present. Their remembrances, however reluctant, are encapsulated into the material and physical structures of the *new villages*. Here and elsewhere in this reconstructive enterprise lies the evidential paradox: I was subjected to the same dynamic of silence, but this is a case where I, as an anthropologist, had the task to, in John Berger's (1972) formulation, "conjure up the appearance of something that [had been silent or] absent" (10), to confront the events in the villagers' pasts that loiters in the present. The purpose here is to give recognition not only to the silences, but also to what silences represent.

To grasp the significance of the terms *daring* and the phrase *the evening hours*, I once again relied on the bus drivers and conductors. Whispering rather softly within the confines of their kitchen one evening, two conductors confided to me that *the evening hours* were the dusk-to-dawn curfews when no one was allowed to leave his/her house, not even to use the bathroom that lay beyond the back door. And it was during these hours that the soldiers would conduct their random household searches. It was also during these haunting moments that they were most *daring*. The two conductors and some of their colleagues confided to me that they knew (or heard) of incidents whereby husbands or fathers were forced to watch while their wives or daughters were being molested. And those who retaliated were beaten. Some families tried to conceal the shame by remaining silent, but the porous walls between each household made it impossible to keep a secret, even with thick layers of cardboard and posters that covered them.

Similarly, a pepper farmer living close to Tapah had this to say: "You would only be giving them excuses if you retaliated." His wife, somewhat smiling, perhaps feeling embarrassed, recalled an incident at Siburan, in which a group of women were ordered to strip. She would later make it a point to tell me that the incident she was referring to happened at a village along the coastal area, and not in Siburan. Suffice it to say that no reports of police or military personnel brutality on Chinese residents in any of the controlled areas were ever published by the media, although numerous complaints were lodged with the Sarawak United People's Party (Porrit 2004). It was not until 1998 when Stephen Yong – the former secretary general of SUPP – placed on record in his autobiography, in carefully crafted words, what he called "the misbehavior of some military personnel ... [who] were in the habit of slapping the villagers and molesting young women. [That they] forced some Chinese women to strip naked" (Yong 1998, 207). To this day, this is the only "official" record of these *daring* incidents by the military personnel at the *new villages* and other so-called communist-infested areas in Sarawak during the 1960s and 1970s.

Besides issues of overcrowding, lack of adequate water supplies, the policing of movements within these controlled settlements, and curfews, it was not practical for residents to attend to their gardens, which lay outside of the village fences. They said that not only would they try not to inconvenience themselves if by chance they were confronted by the communists at their gardens, but that they were also afraid of the soldiers who, they said, "would come up with all sorts of wild accusations" – providing rice or strategic information to the communists were two of the most common. As far as they were concerned, they wanted minimal contact with these soldiers, and some of them wanted to avoid the communists as well. But that was not easy, considering that these controlled settlements were essentially, to repeat the SUPP representatives' remark, "concentration camps." Soldiers were constantly patrolling within the fences and making random checks or raids on individual households, especially during *the evening hours*. I have also heard similar remarks from the few Hakka families living at *Hai Wai*, the coastal villages. Those who ventured out of their house in the evening hours or during curfew hours did so at the risk of getting shot at.

Communist-Infested Areas

Besides those who came from the *new villages*, many young Hakkas from other "communist-influenced areas" also ended up working as bus drivers and conductors in Kuching. I met Soo Li Yi on a very hot and humid afternoon by the SOC bus station. He was from Betong. Soo was dozing off under the warm tin-roofed passenger seating area, as anybody would have under the circumstances. He had become a "spare driver," that is, he only worked when needed by the company. In his case, it had to do with the kidney complication he had developed two years before and since then his health had deteriorated rapidly. But he still showed up at the bus station, thinking that by showing up the supervisors might contemplate asking him to drive. It hadn't happened for a while.

For income, Soo was receiving 300 ringgits per month (around $90 Canadian) from the SOC, inadequate to put food on the table for his wife and son. His wife could not look for work since she had to take care of him, and his twenty-year-old son had just started apprenticing at a mechanic's shop. Fortunately, Soo was getting some assistance from the State Social Welfare Department to pay for the renal dialysis treatment as well as 265 ringgits (around $80 Canadian) per month for living expenses. It had taken Soo a great deal of effort and time to secure this assistance, spending months obtaining letters from different community leaders in support of his application to the agency. However, even with this money, all he could afford was to rent a room for the three of them, costing him 82 ringgits a month ($25 Canadian).

I was feeling uncomfortable when Soo went on to tell me about his contempt for some of his colleagues. He believed that some of them and the company wished him dead. He says, "If I die, they can each donate a few ringgits towards my funeral expenses and be done with me. I know they think of me as a burden." Not knowing how to respond, I asked him to have coffee with me across the street. I noticed he was limping badly, and he appeared weaker than I thought he was. He attributed his weakness to the kidney treatment he was having three times a week, something that had also greatly diminished his appetite. Citing his loss of appetite, he kindly declined my offer to buy him lunch. But after my insistence he finally agreed to have his lunch packed so that he could eat it when he was hungry, or at least his wife or his son could have it.

While we were sipping our coffee he confessed to me he had been observing me after he heard that I had been asking a lot of questions about communism. He was curious as to why I was interested in communism in Sarawak and, for that matter, why I was not approaching people like Bong Chee Cheok or other leaders of the various communist organizations. In fact, it was through Soo that I learned about the former communists at the Hawker Center. I was thrilled with this discovery, but at the same time, felt somewhat disappointed that others whom I had interacted with at the bus station had not mentioned this at all. Like his colleagues, Soo was quick to assert that he had never been a communist. He did go on to say that given the complexity of the situation during the "chaotic period" (in Mandarin: *how ruan te see chien*), it was extremely difficult to tell who was a communist and who wasn't. Speaking softly and rather seriously, he offered a rather elaborate remark that captured the opaqueness of the period:

> It was not that simple. Everybody was caught up in the whole mess. The government thinks you are a communist and the communists expect you

to help them with food and information just because you happened to be Chinese. Quite frankly, most of us were simply bystanders, mostly scared. But after you were constantly harassed, sometimes slapped and kicked by the soldiers, you tend to hate the government as well as the *swa ngiau chee*. We were trapped, you know. A lot of us young people left our village because of that. We were fed up. Why do you think many of us refuse to talk about it?

Soo's remarks reminded me of what James Scott (1985) once said – in any war, hostilities are conducted over a shifting terrain where there are many neutrals and reluctant combatants. Soo *escaped* to Kuching while still in his teens. As with many rural Hakkas, his family used to "own" plots of vegetable gardens close to the township of Betong before circumstances forced them to give it up. Like most rural Chinese, the land they "owned" was land *leased* from the indigenous landowners, in the form of verbal agreements. Because of that, there were plenty of ways they could lose their leases, as for example, when the indigenous owners or their relatives decided to cultivate the gardens themselves, especially after they were abandoned, a precarious position that was so aptly described by Soo:

> Things were really fuzzy then, and even today when it comes to land issues. I am not even sure if my dad had a lease. Perhaps he made an agreement with some *la kia* [Hokkien for indigenes] to work on his land in return for some cash. You know, if there is one thing *la kia* have in Sarawak, it is land. Some of them have as much as an entire mountain. The only thing Chinese are not allowed to own in Sarawak is land.

He was generalizing of course, but it is true in the legal sense when one talks about designated Native Customary Rights land. Obviously, there are other channels of obtaining land for farming. Marrying an indigenous woman is a common practice. Soo told me that none of his siblings had the urge to go back to Betong after moving to Kuching more than thirty years ago and he was not even sure if his parents' house is still there or if they are still entitled to live on it. I had heard similar stories.

After seeing Soo for more than a week, he told me about a personal experience that took place back in 1968. This was an encounter he had with a Malay commanding officer when he was eleven. He made it a point of mentioning that this Malay officer was from West Malaysia, as a way to compare the West Malaysian Malays with the Sarawak Malays, which

I had often been reminded of throughout my fieldwork. The incident took place when he was a student at a primary Chung Hwa Chinese school at the 32nd Mile on the Kuching-Serian Road. This was in the Serian district. He was interrogated and detained in the lock-up (a cell) for more than three days because he had absent-mindedly forgotten to carry his "Transfer Identification Card," a document authorizing him to be in the district of Serian (since he was from Betong). For three days his family members were not informed of his whereabouts. While he was being held, he was slapped several times for reasons that were beyond his comprehension, saying, "They slapped me for no reason. I was thrown into this lock-up with the others. There must have been twenty of us. We were treated like dogs. I also heard screaming and crying in the other cells. I believe they were the *swa ngiau chee* [jungle rats]. Sometimes I would see soldiers carrying slabs of ice. You know what they were for." I nodded.[10] On the fourth day, Soo was removed from the lock-up only to be tied to a tree. He recalled, "I am not sure why they tied me to a tree, but I was there for an entire afternoon." Luckily for him, a local army officer from Betong recognized him and spoke with the Malay commanding officer from West Malaysia. Still, that wasn't enough to get him released immediately. In fact, Soo recalled how irritated the commanding officer was that a local officer would dare to interfere with his authority. Soo was eventually untied and released that evening. Since then, he never forgot to carry his "Transfer ID" again.

The routine checking of identity papers or "Transfer ID" was one of the technologies of biopolitics by which the police and soldiers governed the movement of people within Sarawak, in particular within the so-called communist-influenced areas. The restriction on travelling between districts was not the only hindrance for many rural Chinese during the chaotic periods. As in the *new villages*, curfews were another source of danger. The curfews not only gave the government a means of "controlling" the movement of its rural populations, but also gave the soldiers a means to abuse their power. Being trapped, many of these rural Hakkas would pray that the soldiers would not raid their houses, because it was during these haunting evening curfew hours that they were most *daring*.

Violence Out There

Similar to Gyanendra Pandey's (1999) convincing elucidation of the violence during the Partition between India and Pakistan, narrations of the ill fortune that befell others are dictated by a discourse of "violence out there." For instance, in referring to accounts of those who were sexually assaulted in the *new villages*, such stories were told to me not by members of the victims' families but always by an "outsider." Thus the narratives went something like this: "There were these brutal incidents that happened to this or that family where ..." or "My neighbour's daughter/wife was ..." In all of these accounts, only the men speak.[11]

But unlike the Partition when violence occurred at the boundaries of communities, the violence that occurred within the *new villages* in Sarawak was described as occurring at the boundaries of other households or other controlled villages. Most, if not all, of the accounts of atrocities were almost always told to me not by the immediate family members or relatives of the "victims," but by others. It was always this or that family, their neighbours, or someone from the adjacent village who suffered from the violence. Could it be that violence always lies beyond the boundary of each household so as to constitute and reconstitute "us" and "them" within the sacrificed communities; to constitute "us" who did not experience sexual humiliation, torture or death, and "them" who unfortunately did? In a sense, everyone appears in the position of "sacrificial victim," but there is a differential degree of being sacrificed. Somehow violence and household appear to constitute each other.

For instance, several bus conductors and drivers told me what happened to Huah Li's father and her brother, something I mentioned at the beginning of this chapter. When I tried to gather more information about the nature of her father's and brother's deaths, my queries became the conversational gambit at the KTC bus station. This is what I gathered. Huah Li's father was shot and killed when he had to visit the bathroom during the curfew hours. What was so tragic was the way he was killed: he was drunk one evening and was shot when he absent-mindedly stepped beyond his backdoor to visit the bathroom. Their collective stories were unanimous as to how he was killed.

However, there were conflicting stories about her brother's death. Some said he had suffered the same fate as his father. Others said he was killed while fleeing the village. Still others said he died in a cross-fire between the soldiers and the communists. Some said he was a communist. Another version said that he was killed when caught in his garden trying to pass information or food to the communists. I must emphasize that many of the stories I collected have differing, even contradictory, details coming from different individuals. Sometimes the story was told differently even by the same individual at a different time, and it could get extremely fuzzy, if not outright inaccurate.

To illustrate, here is another example. During my fieldwork I often accompanied bus conductors and drivers to their villages or long-houses, or just about anywhere during his/her day off. I even had a conversation with a bus conductor at a hair salon while she was having her hair permed. One time I went with four female bus conductors – a Hokkien, a Hakka, a Bidayuh, and an Iban – to a Chinese temple located at *Hai Wai* (the coastal area). As we were waiting for more than an hour for the bus to take us back to Kuching, the bus conductors, almost out of nowhere, began to talk about one of their colleagues, a C61 (a Mrs. Pang).[12] They said that they felt remorse for C61 because her husband had recently passed away and he was only in his early fifties. On top of that, her youngest son was a *si lepak*, one who stayed at home and woke up late. All of a sudden, perhaps because we were then at *Hai Wa*i, a former State-inscribed territory alleged to be "communist infested," they started to tell me about C61's father. It turned out that the story they told me was simply untrue.

According to them, C61's father was tortured and killed because he refused to surrender a pipe gun to the soldiers. The Hakka conductor mentioned that many of her families back in the day had pipe guns hidden in their houses just in case they had to use them in one of those *daring* evening hours. Still, with a touch of ingenuity, the Iban conductor interjected: "No! Sharpened bamboo sticks or a pot of boiling water were better. You can always say they are for cooking purposes." Somehow none of her Chinese colleagues were laughing. At that point, Mrs. Yeo, a retired Hokkien bus conductor quipped, "Who would not retaliate if they intend to rape your wife or daughter? Pipe guns, bamboo sticks, boiling water, anything."

I have often asked myself, and you can take this as a measure of my naïveté: What have these rural Hakkas in Sarawak got to do with the ideological battle of the Cold War, an ideological confrontation that originated in the Western and Northern Hemisphere that affected their fates, thousands of miles from the epicentres of the Cold War capitals? What of the other lives in the other counterinsurgency sites where the Cold War was fought, sites that were anything but cold? I am more convinced, after reading Bataille (1991), that the Cold War was a war for profit, the battle between two models of economic extractions. When asked if anyone in the *new villages* had ever reported these brutalities, Mrs. Yeo cried out:

> What would the point be? Do you think those soldiers would be so brutal
> if they were afraid of being caught? Those curfews gave them the perfect

atmosphere to do those things. It's the same during the Japanese Occupation. The Malay government (*Malai chen fu*) has always hated us. They think all Chinese are bloodsuckers, that we are robbing their land. At one minute the government thinks we were Kuomintang, the next ... we were communist.

The discussion became even more illuminating and insightful with this remark from Mrs. Wong, usually a very quiet person, "It is funny that they think poor people can be pro-Kuomintang. How can poor people afford to buy those titles from the Koumintang? Only the rich *towkay* can afford them." Many scholars have touched upon the tapping into the resources of the various Chinese communities living outside of China by successive Chinese governments. The Manchu government gave out titles and rich overseas Chinese reciprocated with interest. The revolution of 1911 was partly financed by the overseas Chinese communities (Yen 1976). In fact, remittances and investment by overseas communities were a major preoccupation of the Kuomintang and the Chinese Communist Party (Williams 1960). One of the main functions behind the establishment of Kuomintang consulate offices throughout Southeast Asia was to woo Chinese contributions and investments. In return, rich Chinese merchants were awarded with titles from the Kuomintang regime (Yen 1970; Toer 1996). It was all about gifts and counter-gifts. If anything else, Chinese education was always used as a pretext for their involvement in the affairs of the overseas Chinese communities, but underlying this was primarily a financial motive – with every new pronouncement on education, there was always a call to increase the flow of money to China (Yen 1970).

Concerning C61's (Mrs. Pang's) father, I knew I needed to get the story from her but I was not sure under what circumstances it would be appropriate. Luck was with me. Within two weeks, Mrs. Pang agreed to see me on her day off. When I arrived at her house at two o'clock in the afternoon, her youngest son appeared from his bedroom, apparently just waking up. Feeling rather embarrassed, Mrs. Pang shook her head: "He's out late every night." As we chatted, I took the liberty to browse through a photo album that was lying on the table next to me. Inside there were some old family photos, judging by how yellow they were. When I showed them to Mrs. Pang, she told me the man in the middle was her father. It was the opportunity I had been waiting for and I told her the story I had heard. She looked puzzled, but was not angry. She assured me that her colleagues must have been referring to someone else. I told her I had double checked with them the employee ID numbers of the person they were talking about. In this case, it was C61, which belonged to Mrs. Pang.

Mrs. Pang told me her father was a river peddler, selling pots and pans and other merchandise to the indigenes from whom he would also buy jungle goods. On one of those trips, her father was attacked and beheaded by certain Ibans for reasons that remained unclear. There were many incidents of Chinese river peddlers or *singkheh*, as they were called back then, who were beheaded when they took the risk of peddling deep into indigenous territories. Local historian Daniel Chew (1990) refers to these river peddlers as the "unsuccessful" Chinese pioneers who never got written up in the usual "triumphalist" history of the overseas Chinese.

A few weeks later, as I was having coffee with Mrs. Pang, she told me it was imperative that I double check my sources as well as the stories I had collected. She cautioned me, as did a few others I have mentioned, saying:

> Many people like to spread rumours or exaggerate their stories because these stories do not affect them directly. It is difficult for the living members of the victims to tell them. Tell me, what do you know about the *swa ngiau chee*? Let me assure you ... the real *swa ngiau chee* are usually very discrete about their identity. Those who boast about it are often fakes. [As if not satisfied with what she said, she added after a short pause] You need to understand. There was and is something heroic about being a *swa ngiau chee* ... even today. It still has that stature of a fighter, this allure (*yóuhuò*), something brave about it.

Chao Kui Ho, the former leader of the Sarawak People's Guerilla Force, offered a few reasons as to why people liked to exaggerate or boast about being communists. First, it had to do with the perceived idea of having the courage to stand up against capitalist imperialism, this "never-give-up mentality."[13] Second, he felt that, and this was rather ironic, it had to do with the current economic and political stature of a few former *swa ngiau chee*. Chao would not directly refer to Bong Chee Cheok. Chao also thought that there were a lot of people who would either lie or hint that they were once a *swa ngiau chee*, or that their father or brother had once been a communist because they were probably covering up their own guilt, if not their lack of courage, to stand up and fight imperialism and capitalism. He also felt that it had to do with me being an outsider – I would not have the same familiarity or channels of network to confirm or refute their claims.

But to my mind even if some stories I collected were exaggerated or outright lies, they were not produced in a vacuum. The Cold War in Sarawak is handed down to us through memories (usually impure and mediated), individual and collective, through the divisions it has unleashed and through the histories it has produced. Allow me to reiterate, Bakhtin would say that the past is continually confused, rehearsed, and performed (Clark and Holquist 1984); it is often selectively both used and abused (Lowenthal 1996). Tambiah (1996) has noted in his studies of riots in India, Pakistan, and Sri Lanka that rumours – specifically, exaggeration and fabrication of events and stories – always exist and operate in any period of violence. In a dialectical sense, there is, on the one hand, the government-controlled mass media and, on the other hand, the role of rumour. Both are responsible in transmitting information and misinformation during any period of crisis and violence, albeit in an asymmetrical sense.

I submit that a lot of these contradictions or different versions of the same story I have collected pertaining to the experience of dislocation and brutalities within these controlled settlements have to do with the rural Hakka population's sense of dispossession and, by extension, the resulting level of exaggeration that produced all sorts of gossip and rumours. In the aftermath, those who heard of them either directly or indirectly continually reproduced rumoured stories. However, this collection of memories – individual and collective, familiar and historical – is what makes up the memories of the Cold War in Sarawak, even if they are shifting, changing, ambivalent, or even unreliable.

Uneasy Encounter

It is not you who will speak; let the disaster speak in you, even if it be by your forgetfulness and silence.

Maurice Blanchot ([1980] 1995, 4)

After I heard about *what* happened to Huah Li's father and brother, I tried to approach her, but each time the encounter turned out to be quite awkward. I recalled the first time when I walked up to her while she was having her quick lunch between bus runs.[14] She snapped at me, saying, "You must be crazy. Why are you listening to rumours?"

She stood up and left in a hurry, making me feel sorry for interrupting her lunch. After that incident, each time she saw me, she would either avoid any eye contact or would hurry off in some other direction, as if carrying a banner that said Leave Me Alone.

During the early part of my fieldwork, I made the mistake of enquiring about marital status. I learned very quickly that such line of inquiry could be quite embarrassing for unmarried women as they were one of the favourite "backstage" topics of conversation among their married colleagues. This was frequently reflected by such remarks as "*lau-chei-poh*" (old female spinster) or, in a rather condescending fashion, "Oh, you know! So-and-so has a good life since she has only one mouth to feed. And besides that, she is such a *kedicut*, a *kiam siap*" (*kedicut* in Malay: a stingy person; similarly *kiam siap* in Hokkien means the same thing). I bring this up to note that these bus conductors and drivers were preoccupied with many other quotidian things instead of dwelling on sensitive or painful events that transpired during the Cold War. In a sense, the individuals I worked with resemble what Walter Benjamin was talking about in his idea of the ordinariness of the everyday collective, a collective "in which the joins, the disagreements, are allowed to show" (Buse et al. 2005, 39).

Huah Li was a target of their gossip. I often heard remarks of how "tomboyish" or hot-tempered she was. She was tough; the way she walked; always fast paced, even to the point of running. For her part, she told me that she was not concerned with what others said about her. I do not recall ever seeing Huah Li having her coffee break with her colleagues. When I asked her colleagues if they had seen Huah Li, their usual response was "*Pu-chee-tao*" (in Mandarin: Don't know), or more forthcoming from a Bidayuh colleague, "*Dia tak campur*" (in Malay: She doesn't mix). Others would say that Huah Li had never wanted to talk with her colleagues for as long as they could remember. I wondered how she managed to play this solitary game for so long, for more than thirty years on the job.[15]

It was more than a month since that first awkward encounter that Huah Li finally spoke to me. Well sort of, since she only said two sentences before hurrying off: "Be careful. You might get blacklisted by the Special Branch." I have often thought about what she said, about being blacklisted by the government. After all I was often reminded that I was this nosy researcher that was asking all sorts of questions about communism in Sarawak. I would have to wait for a few more weeks before Huah Li finally agreed to meet. We met for lunch at a hawker's stall located at one of the free trade zones – one of those apparently homogenized modern State abstract spaces that Lefebvre alluded to – whereby the State could procure its source of cheap labourers for Japanese and American factories as part of its obligation to reciprocate with interest the aid it has been receiving since the days of the Cold War. Huah Li suggested we eat there because the food was cheaper, catering predominantly to factory workers. My lunch with Huah Li was especially late that day considering she usually ate around 11 o'clock in the morning to compensate for not having breakfast. But this proved to be more conducive for talking since the place was empty. Huah Li made a similar comment to what she had said when I first met her on the bus that morning a few months before, "What is there to tell?" The she added, "The soldiers shot my father. He got drunk and was careless. They didn't care if you needed to visit the bathroom or not."

"Just like that?" I asked, unsure if I should show some sympathy or not. She was silent. After a brief moment, in between bites of food, she continued, "There were others who died the same way. Our neighbour across from us! People got shot when they tried to run away." "Why were they running away? I asked. "Oh ... I'm not sure. They thought the soldiers were coming. There was so much confusion. People were worried. Everybody was extremely cautious ... easily panicked. You didn't trust your neighbours. No one knew who might be selling you out. No one knew who the soldiers would harass the next evening."

"What do you mean 'selling you out'?" I asked. "Do you mean somebody informed the army that so-and-so was a *swa ngiau chee* or they were assisting the *swa ngiau chee*?"

"Well," she paused for a brief moment before providing a somewhat elaborate response:

> You really didn't know who was a communist. Say you were working at the garden and a few of *them* suddenly appeared ... and asked for rice or something to eat. Sometimes they asked for information. What could we do? ... They had guns, too. [Without looking at me, she continued] Eventually we had to abandon the gardens ... If you sneaked out to the garden someone might say you helped *them* ... If these stories ended up with the soldiers, or you thought they did, you panicked ... A lot of shooting started that way, when people panicked and ran.

"What about informers?" I asked. Again there was a long pause, but this time I thought her response was not only sympathetic to those

accused of being an informer, but also denoted the chaotic atmosphere
at the *new villages*:

> Sure, there were plenty of them. Sometimes they had no choice but
> to talk, making up stories … Say the soldiers found something at your
> house … an axe, bamboo sticks, anything … they would say these were
> weapons. That would get you into a lot of trouble. They then make you an
> offer in return for information. A lot of that sort of thing happened … You
> just don't know how things can be cooked up, stories made up. Eventually
> everybody kept things to themselves, within each household.

"Does that explain why a lot of you are always whispering?" I asked.
"Whispering?" she sounded puzzled. "Yes, whispering. I have noticed
that habit with you, most of you, including, you know, some former *swa
ngiau chee*. Every time I asked about certain events during the *Len Zhang*
(Cold War) … you know, suddenly most of you whisper. Are you not
aware of it?" She forced a smile before offering her famous response,
"*Pu-chee-tao!*" (Don't know!).

Not knowing if that was the right time, feeling rather uncomfortable,
I asked, "Can you tell me what happened to your brother?" She did
not answer my question, but directed my attention to the bus driver
who had been waiting for her to start their next bus run. I took the ride
back to the bus station. I was the only passenger since the factory workers were not finishing anytime soon. I was hoping that Huah Li might
want to tell me about her brother but she stood silently, holding on to
the metal railings next to the bus driver while I remained seated a few
rows back. We did not talk along the way and immediately upon reach-
ing the bus station she jumped off the bus before it came to a full stop,
as she did every time her bus reached the station. She rushed to the
office to have her bus-run sheet and tickets checked and signed by the
stationmaster and, before I realized it, she was out of sight. I waited for
her at the bus, meanwhile chatting with a Bidayuh driver. About five
minutes later, Huah Li showed up, but just as she had done in the past,
she avoided having any eye contact with me, in a way telling me not to
pursue my query about her brother.

Back at the station, I asked Mrs. Pang (C61) why they had the habit of
whispering. Like Huah Li, she looked puzzled as well before replying,
"Is it whispering or do we speak softly? Perhaps we are being polite. At
least we are not shouting when we speak." Of course she was teasing
me as most of the bus drivers and conductors tended to speak rather
loudly, considering the level of noise on the bus and at the bus station.

Later on, Mrs. Pang suggested that the habit might have come from living at under a controlled space. She added, "It was not polite to let your neighbours hear everything in your house. The walls were pretty thin," she smiled. "I know," I replied, "I have seen them." "Did you visit any pepper gardens when you were *there*?" she asked before adding, "Before we were relocated, one had to walk quite a distance before you got to the next house. Our houses were quite big, lots of rooms." She smiled before adding, "I think you might be right. We probably got the habit of whispering from living at the *new village*."

I recalled the many visits I made to *Jemukan*, one of the coastal villages that were once zoned as "communist-infested areas." Like those at the *new villages*, the Hakka families at *Jemukan* also had the habit of whispering each time they touched on issues deemed sensitive. But within these whispering tones, there was some inventiveness about it. Somehow as the conversation got more interesting I could almost see the glow in their eyes. Let me remind the readers that these conversations took place within the confines of their living room and there were no longer any soldiers roaming in their village. However, the degree of surveillance and control had penetrated so deeply into every form of social network such that it continued to influence these individuals. They were still acting and living in accord with it.

It was towards the end of my fieldwork that Huah Li decided to talk about her brother's death. I have reason to believe that she took pity on me because I had wanted to hear her version, and she knew I was leaving in a matter of days. As it turned out, some soldiers shot her brother at the family's vegetable garden. That might explain why she did not look at me when she spoke about attending to their garden. There was a conscious avoidance of distasteful facts that induces active silencing and forgetting. However, Huah Li could not remember the exact year her brother was killed, but thought it was around the same year as her father's death. "They were months apart," she said. "That I can never forget. I know I came to Kuching either in 1970 or 1971. I can ask my sisters when I see them at *Tapah*." Huah Li fled from Siburan by herself when she was sixteen, the same year her brother and father were killed. Her two sisters remained in Siburan, but they don't talk about their father and brother anymore. As she put it, "What is the point? When I visit them, we cook. I play with their children. Sometimes we play mah-jong." I had the feeling she did not like to be reminded of the past. The full story was not merely too complicated for a simple answer but, instead, introduced a painful memory. However, the past was hidden, but was not irrecoverable, and the combination of facts given at different times gives much more significant information than the bare facts themselves. It tells us why certain people were so unwilling to recall the past. It gives meaning to their silences.

The Atapak Resettlement Scheme

Most of my interlocutors also seemed to think that their stories had a "lesser," even invisible status as compared to grand events or the stories of the so-called leaders. As I have mentioned earlier, the usual responses I would get were: "Have you spoken to Stephen Yong" (the former secretary general of SUPP) or "I think you will be better off contacting this or that Y.B. After all, we are *tar-kong-chai* [in Hakka: wage labourers]. What do we know?" Y.B. is an acronym for the official title *Yang Amat Berhormat*, which means, "The Respected One."

I visited several VIPs for various reasons, one of which was to please these bus drivers and conductors. Interestingly, many of them would tell me, rather candidly, that they were aware of my visits to this or that VIP, sometimes within hours after my visits. On top of that, they never failed to comment that I looked rather "nice" with long pants and shirt as opposed to my usual shorts, T-shirt, and sandals. As it turned out, most of my visits were unproductive since the VIPs would profess that they were unfamiliar with what had transpired during the Cold War. If there was any discussion about the Cold War, their statements sounded exactly like any governmental reports: the operation and resettlement schemes were successful in protecting a certain section of the Chinese population from the communists.

But two of these VIPs brought to my attention a certain resettlement scheme that the Kuching Municipality had zoned sometime in 1998. They were for the resettlement of certain groups of Chinese squatters in Kuching. However, neither of the two VIPS would reveal who these squatters were or where they came from. As it turned out, these squatters were part of the massive depopulation phenomena from the "communist-infested areas," mostly from *Hai Wai* during the 1960s and 1970s, that have since been squatting along the Foo Chow and Chawan Roads in Kuching. When I revisited one of the VIPs he confided to me (on the condition that I would not reveal his identity) that some 50,000 Sarawak Chinese (20 per cent of the Chinese population or 6.5 per cent of the entire population) were resettled in one form or another by 1985, except the squatters along the Foo Chow and Chawan Roads. It was

only in 1998, after years of public outcry from residents in the area, that
the state government finally relocated these squatters on a piece of land
at Stampin, officially known as the Atapak Resettlement Scheme.

Even though the original plan of this housing scheme was designed
to solve the *problems* with these Chinese squatters, it turned out that
there were Malays and indigenes living under the scheme. On top of
that, the scheme was divided into different *bangsa* (racial) sectors: there
was a Malay sector, a Chinese sector, an indigenous sector, and a mixed
sector. Interestingly, the mixed sector applied only to the Chinese and
indigenes. An Iban bus conductor and her Chinese driver whose route
went through this resettlement scheme offered a factual, if not ironic,
comment as to why there were different *bangsa* sectors in the scheme.
They said it had to do with food taboos. The Malays found it offensive
if they had to smell their neighbours' food, especially if it was pork.

The few times I was at the scheme, I also noticed that the buses only
serviced the Malay sector. When asked, the bus driver responded,
somewhat puzzled by my naïveté: "Why? … It is convenient for *them*.
There is no bus stop here. They can have the bus stopped right up at
their doorsteps … almost like having your own car." On the other hand,
the non-Malay sectors were deprived of such luxury since the buses did
not even pass through them. For my benefit, the driver took a detour to
show me the non-Malay sectors. They were mostly located on swampy
land and, according to the bus conductor, the occupants had to spend
thousands of ringgits laying down truckloads of pebbles and sand to
strengthen the foundation of the houses they were allocated.

It is quite obvious, and ironic, that the Atapak Resettlement Scheme,
a project that materialized out of the outcries of Chinese squatters in
Kuching, continued to practise the *bangsa* division of space that fa-
voured the Malays over the non-Malays in terms of its zoning and
public transportation facility. After almost forty years of being part of
Malaysia, these squatters remained mired in a discriminatory limbo.
Local politicians remained aloof to their welfare unless an election was
near. As they put it in Sarawak, the visibility of politicians increased
as the elections drew closer and they just as quickly disappeared after
the event. Common remarks included "Days before any election, the
VIPs behave as if we were old friends, smiling, talking to us, shaking
our hands, handing out *Maggie Mee* projects,"[16] or "They would canvas
like door-to-door salesmen," or "They were nothing short of being in
the Chinese Opera" (*chor-tar-shee*). Saying that someone is performing
a *chor-tar-shee* refers to one acting as in a Chinese Opera or putting on

an act. Such refreshing candor serves to remind us that my subjects were well aware of the system they were conscripted by. Their predispositions and subjectivities were not based on the passive compliance of subordinate classes, ethnicities, language groups, and so on, but, rather, they were based on sanctions and coercion. In short, these were not subjects of ideological domination or the promulgation of false consciousness.[17]

Chapter Six

Virtuous Subjects

Even if ... protests may be sincere and often fruitful, it makes protesting too easy for itself ... The radicalism of these radicals would have more weight if it really penetrated the structure of reality, instead of issuing its decree from on high. How is everyday life to change, if even those whose vocation is to stir it up pay it no attention?

Siegfried Kracauer ([1929] 1998, 101)

Similar to other nation-states in the region, Malaysia has continued to cultivate ethnic differences as useful adjuncts of nationalism, in essence, muffling incipient class conflict (Ackerman and Lee 1988; Cushman and Wang 1988; Kua 2007). If anything else, the reification and performances of ethnic identities serves to bolster the overall power of the state and at the same time camouflage its fragile unity or unpopularity. This historical mix of bureaucratic ascription and social inscription along ethnic (and religious) realm has meant *freedom* and emotional well-being for some, while prescribing violent consequences for others. For instance, the regional economic and financial crisis in 1997 triggered waves of violence against various communities throughout Southeast Asia, most particularly in Indonesia where antagonistic nationalistic rhetoric once again scapegoated its Chinese communities as sojourners, undesirables, and disloyal Others (Chirot and Reid 1997; Purdey 2006). While this might not be the case for Malaysia, the ruling regime has often reminded its population of the indefinite detention power of the ISA, or the scare of another May 13 incident, proscribing any hope of political activities.

Many studies have argued that the cultural politics of the Chinese (and other non-Malay) communities in Malaysia must be understood by looking at the negative effects produced by so-called modernizing state projects, namely, since the NEP and its "geographies of state space" (Jomo 1986; Jesudason 1989; Osman-Rani 1990; Kua 2007).[1] For me, this is not enough. I propose that we also need to analyse the roles played by its Chinese (and other ethnic) politicians and/or "ethnic entrepreneurs" and their recruits.[2] In other words, an understanding of the extreme degree whereby ethnicity is being politicized and a critical analysis of the various collaborations – that is, explicating the degree of co-optations, competitions, alliances, and complicities between these "entrepreneurs" and the ruling regime – are not only vital but also necessary to understand how the majority of the country's populations remained inscribed by this so-called modernizing state project. Failing to do so, I believe, often results in some kind of dualism that either focuses on the centrality of the various disciplinary apparatus of the State or is couched within the notion of resistance, both of which have the tendency to obscure the multiple levels of agents' negotiation and creativity in everyday practices.

This is critical because if we have learned anything from the colonial encounter, it's that the discursive discourses of any colonial regime cannot be forced onto its subjects indefinitely without some kind of collaboration and/or cooperation from portions of the colonized Others. Some might want to call this "local hegemony" or "internal Orientalism."[3] Indeed, "local hegemony" often has an ethnic flavour in Southeast Asia and cultivating contrastive ethnic identity in Others is often the project of politicians and/or ethnic entrepreneurs who endeavour to mobilize their ethnic kind and thereby build themselves a constituency.

In this regard, anthropologists are no exceptions. In our well-intentioned effort to combat racist stereotyping, we are often moved to invoke essentialized tropes, often conflating description with interpretation. Perhaps this has to do with our age-old habit to categorize, to formulate taxonomies. Taking a cue from Kant,[4] this in fact illuminates the limits of theory when over the past three centuries what we have of different theories are "explanatory discourses that bring forth into light an inverted representation of its opaque sources" (de Certeau 1984, 72).[5] We are thus led to question the underside of such inquiries and to ask whether some of our observations, if not our theoretical urgency, does not in fact function as a collage – juxtaposing the "us" and "them," linking less and less effectively the theoretical ambitions of our pedagogy with the stubborn persistence of the opaque reality of the every day. This is rather unfortunate.

For more than half a million persons of Chinese descent living in Sarawak, the questions of how they identify themselves and what that means to them and to other Malaysians are important matters. What they have in common is not so much a language or a cultural inheritance but rather the "certitude of identification," both imposed by others as well as adopted by themselves as "Chinese." It is to this that I now turn. It might help to invoke Michel de Certeau (1984) when he insists: "We must first analyze its manipulation by users who are not its makers. Only then can we gauge the difference or similarity between the production of the image and the secondary production hidden in the process of its utilization" (xiii).

Very early on during my fieldwork, it occurred to me that most of my subjects – Chinese, Malays, Ibans, Bidayuh, Hakkas, and so on – were often too busy to deal with labels like ethnicity or identity. After all, that was the "job" of the State, as reflected in some of their usual responses: "Of course, we are Chinese. We are not Bumis, no land, no handouts. No *Amanah Saham Nasional* [a high yielding interest and dividend paying governmental bond that is specifically entitled only to Bumiputra], what we get is a big fat egg."[6] The materiality of identities seemed obvious and, in the case of the Sarawak Chinese, their casual remarks were tactical responses to the constant reminder of who they are and therefore existed outside of any governmental handouts. Paradoxically, they can also be seen as their stances to remain indifferent to rhetorical narratives on ethnicity.

Unfortunately, the anthropologist did not have such a luxury. I had to read, watch, and listen to these repetitive and rhetorical "speeches." I recall my earlier trips to some longhouses where village elders were often dozing off while government officials were delivering their speeches on *pembangunan* (development). Initially I thought it was the intense heat that created such a drowsy atmosphere or perhaps it was the monotony of the speeches. But then I realized it could not be the heat since these longhouse residents were used to it. Even though these officials were aware that their speeches during these pompous official functions were using recycled materials and that a huge segment of the population was not "buying into it," these speeches were continually being produced and performed on all levels of society – whether it was on the village, town, city, or the federal level, or even deep inside the rainforest.[7] As Philip Corrigan and Derek Sayer (1985) have perceptively noted, the production of discourse is an integral part of the state's exercise in legitimation, and as they put it, "the State never stops talking" (3).

But as storyteller, the anthropologist cannot afford to get bored for it is out of this formative experience that I am able to somehow jolt the emptiness of these repetitive speeches into meaning. The common theme underlying all these speeches was that the government was the unquestioned legitimate ruler of the nation and it was the sole guardian in terms of steering the populations towards a (read: politicized) just and moral society, towards progress and *development*. This is its *gift* to the nation. In the context of Malaysia, receiving the State's *gift*, obtaining a *just* and *moral* society, of achieving *pembangunan*, usually glossed as "development," meant voting for the ruling regime, *Barisan Nasional*. Furthermore, *Barisan* would regard its legitimacy not by revealing what was not working but by pointing towards any form of signifiers that suited its need. More reverential than anything else, patriotism or the popularity of the *Barisan* is usually marked by the outcome of elections and the inherent elements that determine the outcomes – limited and biased media coverage given to competing parties or candidates, the counting of votes, the jailing of opposition candidates just before the election, or how populations are coaxed into voting for certain individuals – are obviously left out of the equation. Given this fiction of legitimacy, the *Barisan* has the conviction that it is indeed succeeding very well in managing its affairs. After all, it only has to (re)count the citations of whatever phantom witnesses it can gather by surveys and statistics that are favourable to its goals, allowing the government to expand its authority, both material and moral, over the population (Hacking 1990).[8] Michel de Certeau (1984) has pointed out that such behaviour has as its corollary the conviction by State agents that although the public is more or less resistant, it is nevertheless moulded by the State. Moreover, the issue of legitimization or what may appear as moral truth was taken as a given and was not to be questioned. To question *Barisan Nasional* was unMalaysian, and the State has its draconian Internal Security Act and other *legal* ordinances to remind the population of the repercussion of resisting.

During my fieldwork, the prime minister of Malaysia, Dr. Mahathir Mohamed, would appear on the air at least once a week, reminding Malaysians of national unity, patriotism, and one of the nation's latest "common enemies," globalization. Unlike during the Cold War, the nation now had two common enemies – the evils of globalization, and the *Reformasi* movement. Ironically, this theme of two common enemies resurfaced only after the 1997 region-wide economic and financial fiasco, not before, and certainly not in the twenty-first century with the globalization of capital markets and trade, when every government in Southeast Asia began wooing foreign investment with as much zeal as they once condemned it (Reid 2010). However, the *Reformasi* movement remains UMNO's common enemy, especially when the *Barisan Nasional* regime lost its two-third majority in the 2008 general elections to *Pakatan Rakyat*.[9]

It was not surprising that my subjects had this nonchalant attitude about the surge of anti-globalization and anti-*Reformasi* paranoia. To them, the current "common enemies" had the same clothing "communism" used to wear. But I am not suggesting that they could live their lives unaffected by State discourse. Being displaced and outside of any governmental incentives, they had the tumultuous tasks of either having to obey laws whose authority they questioned or to remain indifferent to the authority of rules from which they could not escape. From this point of view, to acknowledge the authority of rules is exactly the opposite of obeying them (see de Certeau 1984). The point is that most of them had many other important agendas that were more urgent in their daily lives – they had to deal with responsibilities and the monotony at the work place, they had to negotiate with the new management (more on this in the next chapter), and they had their family and relatives to think of. On the whole, these employees realized the tactical role they needed to play in order to negotiate living in an unjust and "insane" world. Unfortunately, even as their tactics allowed them to buy time on one level, they also served to reinforce and legitimate their subordination on another level, since their use of tactics does "not manifest itself through its own products, but rather through its ways of using the products imposed by a dominant economic order" (de Certeau 1984, xii–xiii). And in the various *tactics* and *strategies* they deployed in their everyday practices, there was one common underlying component: they essentialized. Let me explain.

Zhong Yong

It is commonly perceived that there is a certain mythical synthesis (perhaps a chimera is a better description) concerning the level of understanding the Chinese have of Eastern philosophies. This is not entirely an Orientalism manufactured by so-called Westerners and inscribed on so-called Chinese bodies but exists even among most Chinese them-selves. Most Chinese assume they know about things "Eastern" – *Ying Yang, Chi-Qong, Feng-Hsui, Confucianism,* and so on. Or at least they pre-tend or allude to others that they do. Strategic essentialism, if you may. When my subjects spoke about Confucianism (or other Eastern phi-losophies), they implied, invoked, or alluded to having a certain under-standing of such philosophies. I am not concerned here with whether they were knowledgeable with such philosophies. Rather, my point is to explicate the meaning of this essentialism and my emphasis is on the "performance" of it, concentrating on the point of enunciation, privi-leging the act of speaking and how it effects an appropriation, or reap-propriation, of the self by the speaker. In other words, it is a tactic that promotes some kind of "knowledge" or "feelings" in the actor.

In an Austinian sense (Austin 1962), how do my subjects do things with words? Such elocutions, I would argue, at least psychologically, enable these Sarawak Chinese subjects to survive within the domi-nant economic order. I will use the concept of *Zhong Yong*, which was invoked by two Chinese subjects Hong and Pay, as an ethnographic canvas to elaborate my point. Hong and Pay were subjected to an es-sentialized notion of China and its philosophies, colonialism, Cold War geopolitics, *bangsa* political economy, and postcolonialism, yet they nevertheless managed to constitute themselves as subjects in their own right. Hong is the former general manager of SOC and a well-respected retired politician, and Pay was his employee, one of the many bus con-ductors who, among other things in their productive and well-rounded lives, have been alleged to be either former communists or communist sympathizers. But before that, here is a sample of how *Zhong Yong* is described:

> Being without inclination to either side is called *Chung;* admitting of no change is called *Yung.* By *Chung* is denoted the correct course to be pur-sued by all under heaven; by *Yung* is denoted the fixed principle regulating all under heaven ... The Book first speaks of one principle; it next spreads this out, and embraces all things; finally, it returns and gathers them all up under the one principle. Unroll it, and it fills the universe; roll it up, and it retires and lies hidden in mysteriousness ... When the skilful reader has explored it ... till he has apprehended it, he may carry it into practice all his life, and will find that it cannot be exhausted. (Legge 1971, 382–3)

From the above description, *Zhong Yong* denotes inexhaustible ele-ments, one of which is the "middle path." Moreover, the middle path

can denote "walking the middle-road," "balance," "avoiding the extreme," "avoiding attention," and so on. In fact, one could conjure up
new meanings of the concept as one goes along applying the term. In
essence, this reflects its usefulness, its pragmatism and its ambivalence.

Hong Hee Siaw was in his late sixties when I met him very early on
during my fieldwork. As I have mentioned before, he had just retired as
the general manager of the SOC and had been the former press secretary of the SUPP. This was an extraordinary person. There were articles
and government reports about him: that he was a people-oriented politician, frequenting correction centres, especially when there were hunger strikes, attending to victims of forced relocation, and that he could
pack an entire basketball court each time he gave a speech. Because of
his activities he was imprisoned right before the Sarawak state election
in 1969, thereby disqualifying him from running for office.[10]

During my first conversation with him at his office, I could not completely escape the historian's agenda by asking about "grand" subjects
like the Cold War, communism, the hunger strikes at correction centres, and *new villages*, or asking for his opinion of Malaysia, the British Administration, the United Nations, and, a touchy topic, asking for
the reason(s) his party – the SUPP – joined the Alliance Government. I
could tell he was uncomfortable with the last question, but I was hoping it might spur him on to tell me stories, events, and descriptions of
the atmosphere of the recent past. But he remained expressionless. I
waited for some signal, but there was none. I was faced with a practical
impossibility of speech. I tried to find excuses for his unresponsive-
ness: I heard that Hong had not been the same person after he was
released from prison, that he was no longer the explosive and captivating speaker he had been before. Others had told me he had not fully
recovered from a stroke.

Hong appeared to be gathering his thoughts before he said, "*Zhong
Yong*. It's the way to live one's life according to Confucius, our great
Shen-Shien [Great Benefactor]." I remember asking myself: What is
this middle path, of avoiding the extremes, of staying out of trouble,
even being a conformist? What had happened to his radicalism? Did
he think of *Zhong Yong* while in prison? It also occurred to me that by
invoking Confucius, "our" Great Benefactor, perhaps he was drawing
an analogy, inserting metaphors, and, precisely in that measure, they
become acceptable, taken as legitimate. But still. Was he trying to avoid
the issue of why his party joined the Alliance Government?

He seemed to realize I was mystified and decided to let the silence
linger. Taking his time, in what seemed like an eternity, he finally

commented: "We don't have to do the extremes to change things. Sometimes things change by themselves ... when and how much later, we don't know ... There are more ways to negotiate when one is in the middle. When there is *Zhong Yong*." He went on to tell me how he used to believe that changes could only be achieved through political process, in particular, through the SUPP's agenda of achieving self-rule so that Sarawakians could enjoy the fruits of their labour and the abundance of resources instead of being exploited by England. But he had come to realize that it was unrealistic to depend solely on politics for change as changes could also occur within the economic and the social. Moreover, he believed that economic and social activities were not as ideological as political activity, and they had longer lasting effects.

I was beginning to see his point, but I am not sure if one can in fact separate politics from the other dimensions of life. Besides, *Zhong Yong* is a political discourse, and Confucius was a political writer. Furthermore, considering the unfavourable situations SUPP was in, politics was *doing* economics in the 1960s. Recall Bataille's (1991) emphasis on the economic centrality of the Cold War and Schmitt's ([1932] 1966) reflections on economic imperialism. I went on to ask, "Doesn't *Zhong Yong* mean not causing any problems with the authorities even if you disagree wholeheartedly with them? Would that contradict what the SUPP set out to do, to fight for justice ... for independence ... to fight *Di guo zhu-yi* [imperialism] and policies orchestrated from abroad?" I took out my notebook and flipped to a certain page before adding, "I'm aware of the chilling reception Sarawakians gave to the United Nations' entourage in 1963. It's in the archives." He was quiet for a while before saying, "You do not understand what I meant by *Zhong Yong*. You are not seeing the bigger picture." Perhaps, and I was waiting for him to elaborate, but he did not. He mentioned to me that he had other engagements to attend to.

When I visited Hong the following week, I told him I was pleasantly surprised that he would grant me another interview. I confided to him that I had been thinking about *Zhong Yong* but failed to comprehend the concept in respect to his position, or rather, his former position vis-à-vis the federal and state Alliance Government or with the colonial administration. I asked if he could explain, but this time with concrete examples of how one's life could be deemed as being *Zhong Yong*. Hong smiled and asked if I was aware of the political development in West Malaysia – that the opposition *Parti Islam SeMalaysia* (PAS) had won the elections in two northern states – Kelantan and Terengganu. "With PAS," he said, "you don't have *Zhong Yong*. There is no middle path for the Chinese and Malays to work together. Sure, UMNO is an Islamic Party and Islam is the religion of Malaysia but they are not extremists like PAS." He continued, "If more states go to the PAS in future elections, Malaysia will no longer be *Zhong Yong* … We [Chinese] have to be careful. [Otherwise] *we* might have another *Woo Yeah See-san* [May 13th]." He asked if I was beginning to see the bigger picture, adding, "Think of the situation of the Chinese in Malaysia during the past thirty years. Also, compare that with the Chinese in Indonesia. Imagine what will happen if the PAS takes over. That will be like losing the *Zhong Yong* we have."

What Hong was alluding to was that there was moderation within the current coalition government but such moderate space would dissipate if the PAS was to win more elections in West Malaysia or in Sarawak. Not knowing what to say, I asked, "Weren't you and the SUPP opposing the formation of Malaysia in the early 1960s? That was not *Zhong Yong*, was it?" Again he smiled before responding:

> But things were different then. We thought we were fighting for what was best for Sarawakians. We wanted … independence. Things are different now. There have been a lot of changes and SUPP is working to achieve more developments for Sarawakians … bridges and roads … SUPP is no longer an opposition party but we helped achieve the same goals. Whatever political parties you are in, whatever your ideology, you still work for the same thing, progress. Otherwise you won't get re-elected. During the British Administration everything went to England. All our revenues! But now we have more infrastructures, a better standard of living. We have roads, bridges, electricity … even a university. We are peaceful, unlike Indonesia.[11]

He smiled after what seemed like a lengthy response.

At a few SUPP meetings I attended, I could not help noticing a somewhat similar language. The speakers would caution its members (mostly Chinese) to consider the adverse consequences in store for them should PAS become the government in Sarawak. All that SUPP had achieved for them and all that the Chinese had benefited from the coalition government would be lost. There were also references to sayings, idioms, and teachings from the sages of China at these events. Just like Hong, the way these speakers invoked *Zhong Yong* and how they appropriated it for their positioning had an ethical, aesthetic, and practical character to it. Coming from the sages of China, it strategically increased the saliency of its rhetoric, at least symbolically, both for the speakers as well as for their Chinese audiences. There is something quite interesting here. It seems to me that by invoking *Zhong Yong* and the sages of China, they were appropriating an avenue or a "knowledge" that in their opinion had a higher status or "civilization" than the dominant discourse they were subjected to. At these SUPP events, I could not help but feel the irony of having to hear members chanting their original party slogan, *"Sa'ati, Sa'ati, Sa'ati."* Before joining the Alliance Government in 1970, *Sa'ati* stood for the unity of all ethnic groups in Sarawak to fight for self-rule. Since joining the Alliance, its meaning had changed. Although *Sa'ati* was still the party slogan, it now denoted a moderate calling, "the voices of the people," in essence reflecting its acquiescence to the political, economic, and spatial reality of contemporary Malaysia.

A few weeks later I saw Hong at another SUPP event. When we had a moment of privacy I asked him if the federal government in Kuala Lumpur was not benefiting from the same position as that of England during the colonial era. After all, the chunk of the resources and revenues generated from Sarawak benefited Kuala Lumpur more than they did Sarawakians. Clearly, he must have agreed, but he chose instead to repeat what he had told me: "But we have made a lot of progress, whether for the Chinese or others. Things are in *Zhong Yong*. That is what I have been trying to tell you." What Hong was alluding to is that, given the minority status of the Chinese, to collaborate or to work out a middle ground within the heavily Malay-dominated government was the best alternative; the means to get the best out of what was available.

Following de Certeau (1984), it would seem to me that the ways Hong and the SUPP leaders invoked *Zhong Yong* were more strategic than tactical. According to de Certeau (1984), a strategy has the ability to "transform the uncertainties of history into readable spaces" (36). The type of knowledge derived from strategy is "one sustained and determined by the power to provide oneself with one's own place" (36). Strategy, therefore, belongs to an economy of the proper place and to those who are committed to the building, growth, and fortification of a "field."

The way Hong used *Zhong Yong* and the way he enunciated it alluded to the manoeuvring strategy that was available for "minorities" to use within the dominant structure, both for himself as a leader of a political party and for his economic and class interest. His appropriation of *Zhong Yong* was strategic since he had positions to secure and defend – his position in the SUPP, his ownership at the SOC, and even the very existence of the SUPP as a political party. One might even say they stood to have more negotiating power as part of the coalition government as opposed to being an opposition party, given that most of its leaders were also businessmen. To put it differently, it was their way of embracing political practicality and economic realism. They might still be "committed" to the oppressed, but they had switched the means of achieving it. Perhaps.

Furthermore, the way Hong and the leaders of the SUPP talked of the potential threats posed by the PAS had all the indicators of securing and protecting their own position and the existing status quo. Incidentally, contrasting the oppositional roles played by the leaders of the SUPP during the 1960s with their current favourable socio-economic and political positions attests to the overlap between communism and capitalism. Here is a case whereby the interrelatedness of their economic, class, and political orientation muddled the communist/capitalist dichotomy. One might even say that treating *Zhong Yong* as a principle of social life, Hong and the SUPP were politicizing the term, treating it like free-standing explanatory tools or like the terms "democracy" or "freedom." Seen in this light, Hong and the other SUPP leaders had made *Zhong Yong* something akin to their ethos, as opposed to using it for timely tactical ploys, as was the case for my other subjects who had no position to secure or defend.

In contrast, to the working poor Chinese population, their appropriations of *Zhong Yong* had less to do with securing or fortifying a position. They were local tactics as opposed to strategies. According to de Certeau (1984), a tactic bets on time instead of space, "a calculated action determined by the absence of a proper locus (37). For example, when I solicited information from the Chinese employees at the SOC about *Zhong Yong*, I would get anecdotal responses like, "sure, in that way we stay out of politics." Reading it against the leaders of the SUPP, staying out of politics could be read as being a non-conformist. It can also be read as adopting an indifferent attitude towards the government, of creating a mental space in order to protect themselves from the attacks of State discourse, or, as de Certeau (1997) suggests, as "shutting themselves off from [State's] injunctions" (ix). When I queried these working-class Chinese subjects further on *Zhong Yong*, they suggested that I see one of their colleagues, Pay Lai Eng, someone they considered to be a "scholar."[12]

Pay's wife was not happy to see me when I arrived at their house. She might have heard that I was this nosy ethnographer who had been asking a lot of questions about communism. Anxious to get things started, it should come as no surprise that the first question I asked concerned the chaotic past. Pay looked at his wife, somewhat nervously, before responding, "You are referring to the *Len Chang* (Cold War), a very hot and chaotic period." I smiled at the way he referenced the Cold War; that it was anything but cold. He became uncomfortable when I asked if he knew any communists and had this to say:

> It's not that simple to explain. [Long pause] Most of us were scared, confused ... trapped. [Again long pause] You have the soldiers and the *swa ngiau chee*. We had to be extremely cautious. Many [Chinese] schoolteachers and students were detained and some never made it back. They were exiled to China.

Again, he glanced over at his wife and suggested that we talk about something else. We spent the rest of the afternoon talking about the history of the SOC and his family background. The following week I asked Pay what he thought of the current situation in Sarawak. He looked at me in a rather nonplussed fashion, before responding, "What is there to say? You know how it is. Most businesses are in the hand of the Malays." But almost immediately he tried to state a case for the relatively peaceful situation in Sarawak compared to Indonesia in 1998, saying:

> Life is very difficult over *there* [in Indonesia] for the Chinese, even for most *Indons* [Indonesians]. The Chinese are living in very precarious situations. Those who can afford it have left. But for those who could not afford to leave ... or because they have to look after their house or their shops are living in constant fear. Their shops have burned down. You read about them in the [Chinese] newspapers. Burning tires thrown at Chinese shop houses, sometimes their wives and daughters were raped. Things are really bad.

Pay acknowledged that the intra-ethnic relationships amongst the Chinese in Sarawak had become businesslike. Chinese businessmen of different speech groups or even among the same speech group were competing against each other. He also pointed out that most Chinese today were uninterested in the political drama played out by the various parties, whether those of the *Barisan Nasional* or the opposition.

Commenting further on the political drama between the *Barisan* and *Reformasi,* Pay felt that the best thing for the Chinese community to do was to remain neutral, by remaining *Zhong Yong*.[13] I tried to reason with Pay (and with others) that the general attitude of being indifferent towards politics might send the wrong signal that the Chinese community as a whole was passive, divided, and unconcerned about their current situation. He smiled before offering a response: "Of course we are concerned but what can ordinary folks like us do? We used to be very active … getting involved in all sorts of communal activities. We attended political rallies, we thought about the future of Sarawak. Those sentiments are gone. Now we are just getting by. Of course we have to *be Zhong Yong* to get by."

Notice the idea of "getting by" – most of my subjects were "getting by with what they had" – and that kind of living necessitated conjuring up knowledge of local tactics in order to manoeuvre their way through the ruses of the dominant economic order. Looking at it from a different and yet related perspective, it was both creative and counterproductive. It is creative in that it could be viewed as providing the individual with the multifarious tactical positions for maximum manoeuvring but, by an ironic circularity, it was also promoting some sort of apolitical stances that could prove to be detrimental to the Chinese community as a whole. As I have implied on several occasions in the book, it was precisely because of the heavy politicization of *bangsa* that the majority of my subjects chose a route of indifference as their recourse. The way most of the lower-working-class Chinese population had been categorized and displaced in Sarawak and their cynicism towards the rhetorical discourse of the State (and this applies to the general public as well) contributed to a fortified separation between the general public and those in office – the VIPs and the VVIPs.[14]

I once told Pay (and others) that I was puzzled as to why the SUPP, including Hong, joined the coalition government when they were at the height of their popularity during the late 1960s. I was fully aware of the sensitivity since most of the old timers had an immense respect for Hong. Pay's wife, who was sitting across from us in the living room, interjected, "What do we know about such things? You should ask the politicians or the rich businessmen," before she went into the kitchen. Pay was slightly embarrassed before offering to elaborate:

Things were different then. They had to change with the times … They thought they had a chance to fight for self-rule … But being *Zhong Yong* was precisely that, to achieve the best overall positioning and the SUPP thought that fighting for self-rule was the best position for them at that time. [He then lowered his voice, this time almost whispering] What alternatives, what choice did Hong or the SUPP have? For that matter, even Ong Kee Hui and Stephen Yong had to bend.[15] Razak [the late deputy prime minister, Tun Abdul Razak] had a talk with them and before you know it, the SUPP became part of the government. It was like "take it or else ..." You need to understand ... many Chinese were arrested, including Hong. And there were no trials. Many confessed to anything they were asked to confess ... Many signed their names on the dotted lines.[16] Ice slabs were deployed. It was that bad. Are you aware of the series of hunger strikes?

Yes, I was aware of the hunger strikes. I read about them in the archives. "But ice slabs?" I asked. Again his wife overheard our conversation and spoke to her husband from a distance, this time raising her voice: "Old Pay, you better be quiet." She then walked out from the kitchen to bring me a glass of Milo (a local beverage). Fortunately she had to leave the house for errands in Kuching and the next bus was arriving in front of their house. As soon as she left, I asked Pay, very softly, "What ice slabs?" It occurred to me I was beginning to follow their habit of lowering our voices each time a sensitive topic was touched upon. Also in a whispering tone, Pay told me that during the course of interrogation detainees were often forced to embrace slabs of ice until they passed out. And if the interrogators were not satisfied with the confessions, more ice slab treatments would ensue. Most of these interrogations involved extracting the names and whereabouts of communists. This is a further irony, since the authorities were fully aware that each cell unit within the communist organizations was set up to prevent comrades from confessing too much information under interrogation. In fact, the structure of the various communist organizations and the notion of cell units were extensively written up in the government whitepaper *The Danger Within*. It would seem that the authorities were not interested in rounding up real communists but instead finding an excuse for detaining as many individuals as possible. It was about *inscribing* as many bodies as possible, to use a Deleuzian term, under the Cold War–based geography of fear.

Other forms of torture were also deployed. However, ice slabs usually did the job. A few of my subjects who went through the horrible experience confided to me (in whispering tones) that one's entire body would go numb after a while. The pain, they said, became internalized. After a few rounds of ice slabs, they said, one would sign anything, whether it were an admission to being a communist or revealing the names of fellow comrades, real or otherwise, leading to more arrests. Not forgetting that those who were detained did not have rights to a trial and could be detained indefinitely.

A plastic lighter repairman located near the SOC bus station had spent years being moved from one correction centre to the next on sus-picion of being a communist. He put it this way: "I was never charged, but they kept me for thirteen years. They never told me why I was be-ing detained all those years," forcing a bitter smile onto his face. They took away thirteen years of his life. His wife left him for another man while he was detained. Trying to justify why his wife had left him, he said, "It was quite common. Most women left their husbands to marry again. They needed support and we were not there for them. I would have done the same if I was her." I cannot comprehend how he must have felt all those years or even then as he sat there on the sidewalk repairing plastic lighters during the day and sleeping in a tiny little room at a cheap hotel next door at night. He had no family to go home to in the evening and always bought his lunch and dinner from food vendors. Somehow I had this uncomfortable feeling that there were many other sacrificial victims who went through the experience that this lighter man had experienced and who had also lost their wives and families.

Returning to the question of *Zhong Yong*, Pay repeated to me that Hong and the SUPP did not have any choice, saying:

> You either join them or you are out. That was the ultimatum. But that is precisely why *Zhong Yong* is useful. You take the middle path. You try to survive in light of the circumstances that are available. What is the point of fighting when you can't win? Obviously, it is better for them to be part of the Alliance than to be out of the political scene. Now tell me, what could they do for the people if they were declared an illegal party? Associations got deregistered, unions, even newspapers. And look at the *swa ngiau chee*. What did they accomplish? Most of them were starving in the jungle. In fact they had to depend on *us* [the rural Chinese population] to feed them, causing us many problems, even death.

It seemed to me that ambiguity as well as contradiction was inher-ently imbued in the manner with which both Hong and Pay spoke of, or invoked *Zhong Yong*. They invoked the concept without any reservation when it supplied them with an argument, a perception, or a weapon they could use in order to achieve an advantageous position at the moment of articulation. And in each incident they would conjure up the meanings of the concept. In many ways it is about pragmatism, as Pay summed it up:

> Being practical is *Zhong Yong*. You might have interesting ideas but if they don't work, you need to rethink. SUPP had to look at the bigger picture. They needed to be part of the government in order to serve the people. That's why I am still a SUPP member. What would you do if you were in the same position as Hong or the rest of *us* in Sarawak? It is also about flexibility. It is a form of living, a philosophy. *Ying and Yang* is similar to *Zhong Yong*. They are from the sages of China.

Like Hong, Pay was appropriating a genealogy or "knowledge" that in his opinion came from a "civilization" higher than the one he was being conscripted into. To bring back de Certeau (1984) once again, it was "an ethics of tenacity … the countless ways of refusing to accord the established order the status of a law, a meaning, or a fatality" (26). Besides, being *Zhong Yong* allowed for the possibility of having a high degree of manoeuvrability but within the constraint of "making-do-with-what-you-have." Its power lay in its capabilities to negotiate with the government but within the rules that were largely dictated by the latter, achieving a middle path in which the Chinese and the Malays (and other ethnic groups) could carve out a way of living without the open-armed conflict as they had experienced.

When I asked Pay why *Ying and Yang* was part of *Zhong Yong*, he asked if I was aware of the notorious *Ying Yang* split-voting trend among many Chinese in Sarawak, of how they tried to balance (or perceived they were balancing) their votes between the federal and state elections.[17] Here is how it was supposed to work. A bus conductor, Ms. Tan, once told me she voted for a *Barisan* candidate in the federal election. If the candidate won, she would make sure she voted for an opposition candidate in the state election. The idea of voting *Ying Yang*, according to Ms. Tan and others, was to balance things out by not casting both votes for the same candidate or party in the federal and state elections. That was their way of ensuring (or they believed they were ensuring) that they were not giving too much power to one candidate or one party. Thus the logic here, if there was any at all, was

more practical than ideological since most of my Chinese and indigenous subjects felt that there were no ideological differences between
the political parties in Malaysia. They also believed that all public officials had an immense tendency to be aloof once they were in office
(and hence the common anecdote: "You only see them right before the
elections"), especially when they felt that the voting population within
their constituents could not affect the election outcomes. It was with
this understanding that most of them believed the *Ying Yang* voting
technique could prevent a landslide victory, thereby sending the message to the public officials that they could at least be held accountable
for their actions once they were in office.

This voting technique, I would argue, is unfortunately only effective
when there are adequate opposition representations in the federal or
state governments, which was not the case in 2000. A different Mrs. Tan,
also a bus conductor, somewhat agreed with me, saying, "Running an
election campaign is very expensive. Besides, the oppositions do not
have the 'fully oiled election machinery' like the *Barisan*. But I voted
Ying Yang as well. You like to take some power away from *them* ... or at
least that is what we hope." She realized that was wishful thinking, and
quickly added, "Of course *Barisan* is too strong."

Obviously, there is a contradiction, if not illogical reasoning, but my
main concern here is on how she was appropriating *Ying Yang*. When
Mrs. Tan appropriated *Ying Yang*, she had a certain "intentional meaning," what speech-act theorists might call "illocution effects" (see Austin
1962) that made her utterances understood by her audience even if the
way she articulated the concepts, in this case, the voting techniques,
turned out to be quite illogical. My interpretation of her utterances,
that they were illogical, was a "perlocutionary effect" as far as my interaction with her was concerned. Her colleagues may have interpreted
the same utterances differently. This was possible because she was using the conventionality of certain interpretations, in this case *Zhong
Yong* and other Eastern concepts, that was partly defined by the norms
and social codes of these Chinese subjects and that were evoked in a
rather casual manner at a given time and place.[18] The *Ying Yang* voting technique was, in the opinion of some of my interlocutors, a small
measure of holding the *Barisan* more accountable. To be sure, such manoeuvring tactics could also be interpreted as partly psychological and
partly pragmatic. These tactical ploys survived on a daily basis as part
of the existing ruses within the dominant discourse, regardless of their
actual effectiveness.

Conscripts of Modernity[19]

Years ago, in a critical engagement with Eric Wolf's epigrammatic work *Europe and the People without History*, Talal Asad (1987) made the following vivid remark about history and change: "Historical conditions," he said, "change like landscapes created by a glacier – usually slowly, always contingently – on which old paths that followed old inequalities simply become irrelevant rather than being consciously rejected" (607). The geological metaphor is instructive for thinking about the transformations that constitute the making of the postcolonial subjects who find themselves as conscripts of that structure of power. For Asad (1987), therefore, if there is a story to be told about the choices people make in the course of acting historically, there remains nevertheless "the story of transformations ... [that] are not of people's choosing, but within which they must make their history" (607).

What Hong and Pay offer is a representation and mediated expression of that "story of transformations." They have a clear notion of themselves in proportion to the power they were conscripted by. They served as witnesses – with both a consciousness of the historical process and a conscientious intervention in that process – not only to the form of power that altered the rules of the games of sociospatial, political, economic, and cultural life of those opposing the Alliance Government but also the postcolonial power that reshaped and reorganized the conceptual and institutional conditions of possible action and understanding. In a sense, both men depended on the existence of a dominant chronological history to provide the necessary field to practise their local strategies and tactics – how the balance of forces was altered during the 1960s by the annexation of Sarawak into the Federated States of Malaysia in the context of the Cold War military gift economy and the *bangsa* political economy, and by the dominance of the *Barisan Nasional*, both of which affected their course of political practicalities.

Elements guiding Hong's and Pay's thoughts are not characteristic of so much contemporary social scientific discourse between local and global or resistance and power, but between responsible and irresponsible practice, right and wrong strategies or tactics. Hong and Pay viewed their situations and actions as products of "the times" and it was to an essentialized understanding of *Zhong Yong* (read: as their tropes) that they turned to for meaning and redress. The ways *Zhong Yong* was invoked and enunciated gave meanings to the various sets of practices and settings to which Hong, and, to a lesser degree, Pay justified the actions taken by the SUPP in joining the Alliance Government, regardless of how they were necessarily ambivalent, ambiguous, and tactical. In effect, whether it was Hong's (or the SUPP leaders) appropriation of *Zhong Yong* that had elements of both strategy and tactic, or those of Pay and others which was strictly tactical, such acts could not be described as mainly selfish or instrumental. They could be seen as manoeuvrings that were necessary in order to get by with what they had.

Unlike the State, Hong and Pay (and others) did not have the power to invent "facts" to support their own convictions, but they did have the flexibility of invoking *Zhong Yong* and other Eastern philosophies and concepts. They did not invent an idiosyncratic response to circumstance but rather deployed the means to address circumstance imaginatively. What they showed us was their practical wisdom in the articulation of the problems facing the displaced and marginalized. Their judgment was confirmed to the degree that their actions were acknowledged by others as fitting, and to the extent that it brought them a degree of equanimity and a consciousness of history and their place within it.

It is in this way that we can speak of them as virtuous subjects because they understood the practical and psychological role they needed to play in order to negotiate their lives in a discriminating world. This is not to suggest that there were no mixed emotions or that they did not harbour internal conflicts. But to argue that they were political, ambivalent, or indifferent does not preclude them as being moral and virtuous subjects. In Mauss's (1973) discussion on habitus, their actions were derived from a sense of cultivated sensibilities that had less to do with resistance than with the idea of living sanely in an "insane" world. Like most, if not all postcolonial regimes, the Malaysian government inherited its knowledge of government from the colonial regimes whereby "the very concept of right often stood revealed as a void … [whence] its one-sidedness … [Its] supreme right was simultaneously the supreme denial of right" (Mbembe 2001, 25). History taught these postcolonial subjects to view resistance as something unworthy of their time since they had been dislocated and continued to be subordinated by a government that politicized *bangsa* as a useful adjunct of nationalism, one of the main recurring forms of violence that constitute the cultural *imaginary* in Malaysia.

Chapter Seven

Sites of Impermanence

Since its formation and throughout the tumultuous years of the 1960s and 1970s, and up to the late 1990s, SOC was like a *family* to its employees. But by 1999, this was no longer true. Hong had just retired and the torch had been passed to his grandson, George. With it, things started to change with the management reorganization that instituted a sharp division between the management and the employees. This created not only an air of uncertainty and impermanence at the workplace, but also a feeling of betrayal and resentment towards the company, especially when it finally succumbed into the *bangsa* political economy of *doing business* in Malaysia. In 1999 SOC went into a business partnership with a *bumiputra* company, the Sarawak Multipurpose Holdings (SMH). SMH was not just any other *bumiputra* company, but one with ties to the chief minister of Sarawak. But it is worthwhile emphasizing here that it took nearly three decades for SOC, under a new management, to finally succumb to the *Ali Baba* business reality in Malaysia, one that started with the NEP in 1971.

And it was with this *Ali Baba* partnership that old timers Poh and Lee finally gave in one afternoon in late May 2000 to criticize SOC. Lee's justification for the *bumiputra* partnership sounded almost apologetic, saying SOC required a lot of capital to run its operation. Poh, who was usually the more expressive of the two, remained quiet and looked away in a somewhat disgusted fashion. When I asked if they were aware of SMH's connection with Sarawak's chief minister, they remained silent. I told them I was aware of how SOC's employees had volunteered in the past to help out the company with financial difficulties but their royalties had deteriorated, especially with the company holding back on bonuses for the past three years, something unprecedented in the company's history. I must have struck a sensitive chord because that was when both Lee and Poh decided to be frank with me. Speaking almost in unison, they mentioned "Sibu."

"Sibu?" I asked, pretending I had no idea what they were referring to. Sibu is the second biggest city in Sarawak. This time Poh started by saying: "We lost a lot of money in Sibu and it is still affecting us. You need to understand how unreasonable some of our suppliers are ... even long time suppliers. But everybody has been having cash flow problems since 1997 [referring to the region-wide financial crisis]. As a bus company, SOC needed to pay for spare parts and other expenses to stay in business." Lee interjected to remind me: "And we have more than 200 buses. That's a lot of spare parts we need to carry." I believed Poh was tired of beating around the bush when he finally said, this time addressing Lee, "We were stuck with a lot of buses from Sibu. We had to shut down that outfit and nobody wanted to buy our buses unless we sold them cheap. So you see! SMH was a way out." I noticed a slight hesitance in his voice pertaining to the last point, of finally succumbing to having a *bumi* partner.

"Why was Sibu a mess?" I asked, hoping they might add something. They did not. Again I asked, but this time in an insinuating tone, "So, how is the current management? How is George Hong, the current general manager of SOC?" I briefed them about what transpired during my meeting with George even though I was pretty sure they were aware of it, something I will touch on shortly. Many bus drivers and conductors, including those from KTC as well as those who worked or hung out at the bus stations, have hinted to me that the Sibu operation was George's pet project. A Chinese bus driver at the KTC once put it across rather sarcastically: "George took it upon himself to invest in Sibu. He decided on the scale [of operation], the number of buses, the workforce, and so on. He did it all by himself." There were many other more pejorative comments about George Hong. Some even said that George thought he had no need to consult any of the SOC managers because he had a business degree from the United States. In short, many of their descriptions would suggest that the Sibu operation was a total miscalculation by a novice who was too proud to take advantage of a pool of experienced staff with almost fifty years in the business.

Perhaps Lee and Poh talked to each other about George and the current management. I believe it was out of respect for their longtime colleague and former general manager, Hong, who is George's grandfather, that I did not hear them complaining, not even once, about

George or, for that matter, the current management. Very early on during my fieldwork, a SOC security officer interrupted and ended my conversation with a bus driver. This was less than a week after I had already obtained permission from Hong to "interview" his employees. From then on, I would carry the handwritten letters I had obtained from Hong in my backpack. There was a psychological reason I carried them – it was my acknowledgment that I had with me letters written by someone who had earned much respect from the SOC employees. In my opinion, the abrupt interruption by the security officer and the new directive preventing me from interviewing the SOC employees was an attempt to undermine not only Hong's authority, but also all the authority of the other old timers that had helped set up the company.

After learning that the directive came from the new general manager, George Hong, I knew I had to meet him if I wanted to continue working with SOC bus drivers and conductors. I had initially thought of consulting his grandfather to resolve the problem. But I was concerned that it might put Hong in an awkward position since the directives came from his grandson. I set up an appointment and saw George Hong at the head office. His office, like the other newly installed managers' offices, had one-way mirrors facing the general staff located in the middle of the floor. I was thinking of Foucault's (1977) panopticon. Although the office was not a prison or an asylum, or even a factory, it had this "all-seeing" structure that confined the staff in such a way that the managers could observe their actions inside their offices, an architectural arrangement of space conducive to creating a sense of exact legibility, leaving no zone of shade, so to speak, in which the office staff could hide. They were constantly visible and knowable, feeling the continuous power coming from those housed behind the one-way mirrors.

It was no coincidence that each time I was at the head office, I noticed how the general staff were glued to whatever tasks they were performing, such as auditing the bus schedules submitted by the supervisors of each bus station, tallying the ticket numbers and fares collected from individual bus conductors, and typing memos coming from the managers. They appeared so disciplined, so serious, and there were hardly any conversations between them. Their freedom of action had been taken away from them as a result of their visibility, their lack of *shades*. There was something else. There was no interaction between the office staff and the bus drivers or conductors who were there to hand in the daily schedules, behaving as if they were strangers to each other. I later found out from a cashier at the head office that the management discouraged interactions between the two categories of employees.[1] I once heard a manager asking a clerk if she needed more tasks to do when she was having a conversation with a bus conductor. Unlike the general employees at the head office, the bus conductors and drivers were not confined within this "all-seeing" structure. For them, there were zones of shade that were opaque enough to allow them to engage in some "outside" activities and even to "hide" their presence from management's gaze.

In my conversations with a few new managers at the head office, they often resorted to telling me about their effort to modernize by getting newer buses equipped with automated ticket dispensers (in essence, replacing the bus conductors), the plan to expand into other towns, or the ongoing renovations at the head office to accommodate new managers and additional directors from the SMH partnership. Not once did they talk about the welfare of their employees or about the plight of the old timers and their contributions and loyalty to the company. As a matter of fact, when I forced the issue on them, their response had been negative, if not outright demeaning. On several occasions, these managers spoke of the bus conductors and drivers as *kuo* (in Mandarin or Hakka: dog). In addition to being disrespectful, they were also distancing themselves from those they knew were their subordinates.

In reacting to the disrespect shown by the managers, many bus drivers and conductors would ignore their physical presence and directives. For instance, when asked if they were aware of the renovation at the head office or the appointment of new managers and directors, the common response I would get was *"kuan-tar"* (in Mandarin or Hakka: who cares), spoken without expression. This is rather strange if one thinks of it. Here you have a transport company whereby the new management is separated from one of the main components of the company, its bus drivers and conductors. This separation also explains why most of the bus drivers and conductors congregated at various coffee shops or at *Warong Muhibah* (the anti-company spaces) at any given workday as opposed to hanging out by the station office. There were also others who sought obscurity by remaining alone, trying to go unnoticed. These were some of the old timers who had worked at the SOC since its inception and by now seemed resigned to working the remaining days of their lives or quitting before that.

The "New Philosophy"

George Hong must have been in his mid to late-twenties when we met. We talked about general issues like the atmosphere of the bus industries in Sarawak and what my research was about. I did not bring up the abrupt interruption from the security officer during our conversation. Neither did I ask him about the Sarawak Multipurpose Holdings (SMH) partnership. In fact, he brought it up. According to George, SOC had accepted a partnership in September of 1999. Underscoring that SMH was a state subsidiary, he said: "This is a strategic move for *us*, to accept the modern reality of Malaysian governmentality." I was struck by the word "governmentality." Was he implying that with the political, economic, and spatial reality in Malaysia, it was best to have a *bumiputra* partnership not only to remain competitive, but also to stay ahead of the curve? That seemed to be the case in the following remarks: "Being in the public transportation industry, we have to be monopolistic and the way to do that is to have a *bumi* partnership. In fact we have been trying to get a *bumi* partnership since the early 1970s [since the NEP]. So, this partnership with SMH is perhaps the best deal we can ever hope for." He seemed to be smiling as he reflected upon what he had just said. I was still trying to swallow what I just heard, that SOC had "been trying to get a *bumi* partnership since the early 1970s." Surely, he must have some knowledge about the history of the SOC and the role his grandfather played in the company?

The partnership with SMH came with a new management and a new board of directors. Seven directors would be selected from SOC and three from SMH. George's father would be the executive director. His father and his uncle Hong Khai Seng, who was the mayor of Kuching South District, were also on the board. He then proceeded to tell me about the SOC's "new philosophy," saying, "The SOC is a company committed to growth and reinvestment. This is the philosophy of the present management." I felt this was rather disrespectful of him to say. It was as if he had forgotten that it was his grandfather who had founded the company and that there had been plenty of reinvestment since its inception. I was further bothered by his remark about the SOC's main competitor, the KTC.

"Unlike KTC," he said, "the SOC is committed to the long term." He smiled and leaned back in his chair, projecting a somewhat authoritative stance before continuing. "Every year-end if they make a profit, their directors split the profit instead of reinvesting it back into their operation. That is not the case for the present SOC. Reinvesting is one of our prime directives. We are modernizing our company." It got even better. "KTC is not like us. All their directors are old and when they pass away, the company will die with them." A rather harsh statement! Perhaps it is not superfluous to remind my readers about the Sibu fiasco.

As far as continuing my working relations with SOC's employees, George insisted that I make out a list of questions pertaining to my "interviews" and, in return, I would receive a letter of approval from the new board of directors. It took me more than a month before I finally received the letter. The letter contained a set of conditions, more like directives, that I had to follow if I were to interview SOC employees. One of the conditions insisted on the presence of management staff during my interviews and, on top of that, they had to be held within the SOC head office. I also had to arrange the time with the management a week prior to the interview and it had to be conducted during the employee's day off.

The last condition seemed particularly disturbing. If I could only interview an employee during his/her day off, did the managers even have jurisdiction over how their employees spent their leisure time? I did not, however, bring this up with George since it would not be wise to be confrontational. But I did try to explain to him that my research was not a survey and, as such, there were no predetermined questions. I had the feeling that he refused to understand the kind of research I was concerned with because he insisted that I follow those conditions, repeating each time that they had already been agreed upon by the new board of directors, of which he was one. In many ways it was the timing of the letter that made it harder for me to bear its content since it was only slightly more than a month earlier that I had received letters from his grandfather authorizing me to interview some station supervisors and managers. In a sense, the letter approved by the new board of directors undermined the authority of George's grandfather, one of the founders of SOC.

George was not at the office when I picked up the letter of approval from the new board of directors. As I was leaving, the office manager Chow Siaw Kwan escorted me out of the building. I had heard that this character was a *frog*, meaning he had switched alliances from being a union leader to an office manager. I was told to watch out for him. A Hakka bus driver informed me that Chow was a very capable union leader and that was the reason he was "brought over" by the management. As this was happening, I thought it was more than just coincidental that Chow escorted me out. Was he making sure that I did not wander into the canteen and start chatting with some bus drivers or bus conductors like I had done previously?

To resolve my problems with the conditions listed in the letter, I took the advice of some local scholars. They told me I should see a few VIPs, including Hong Khai Seng, George's uncle who was not only the mayor of Kuching South District but also one of SOC's directors. I did just that. I saw a few junior ministers and told them about my research before calling on the mayor. I was rather surprised that the mayor agreed to see me. I had the feeling the few VIPs I saw must have told him about my project since they belonged to the same political party, SUPP. After listening to my research plan, Khai Seng told me that using bus conductors and drivers to look into the social history of Sarawak was a unique and excellent idea. He was rather smooth, saying diplomatically: "Apparently there must have been some miscommunications. I am sure it can easily be sorted out. I will speak with George. Go ahead with your research." The meeting lasted less than fifteen minutes. After that I was never again interrupted or stopped by the security officer. However, since there was no official memo rescinding George's earlier directive, it continued to have negative effects on my working relations with some SOC employees. Many were not a hundred per cent sure if they should talk with me. Needless to say, others refused because they did not feel it worthwhile to talk about the past.

After my meeting with the mayor of Kuching South, I started seeing various station supervisors and managers whose names were on the letters written by Hong. Much to my chagrin, they were in favour of the changes at the SOC. Some even bragged about the company's generosity, as for instance, the size of its bonuses and housing loans. What they did not tell me was that the bonuses and the loan policy no longer existed. I mention this because it affected my trust towards them, and as I built up closer working relations with the bus conductors and drivers, it became obvious to the management whose side I was on. If there was one incident that made my position obvious to them, it happened when I was trying to assist a bus conductor who had been fired.

A Forty-Cent Bus Ticket

There had been various incidents in the past when bus drivers or bus conductors were fired when they were "caught" by ticket inspectors for failing to issue bus tickets, usually for only one ticket and for as little as a forty-cent ticket (less than fifteen cents Canadian).[2] One such incident happened early on during my fieldwork when George Hong fired a bus conductor, Kee Sey, for apparently failing to issue a forty-cent ticket. The incident took place during the rush hour when the bus was packed with students heading home from school. The day after Kee Sey was

fired a few bus conductors and drivers at the station office signalled me
to follow them to *Warong Muhibah*.

As I alluded to earlier, *Warong Muhibah* resemble Bakhtin's (1984)
description of the marketplace in Rabelais's time (1483–1553), a place
that has the reputation of shaping and inducing lively conversations
with the qualities of frankness, teases, curses, and laughter. Similarly,
I invoke Bakhtin's reading of Rabelais to make a contrast between the
spaces occupied by the drivers and conductors – the lively atmosphere
at *Warong Muhibah* and the other coffee shops – and the dry and rigid
atmosphere of the "official" spaces at the station office, the accounting department, and the head office. In the former spaces a different
sense of time and place was felt, one with a different ethos that not
only undermined and debunked the authority of the management, but
also offered a healthy antidote to the dullness and dryness of the language of the current management. It was in these spaces that I found
expressions of fearlessness in the drivers' and conductors' critiques
of the controls, the rigidity, and the disrespect shown by the current
management; where I witnessed their attitude of indifference towards
the management in their speech and gestures as they conversed among
themselves, with me, with the shop owners, and their fellow employees, or with other regular customers.

That afternoon, the *warong* was packed with the usual suspects. But
the lively atmosphere was replaced by the sombre mood over Kee Sey's
termination. Many of them were in disbelief, as if the whole thing was
not real. "George fired Kee Sey over a forty-cent ticket, just one ticket.
Just like that, thirty-odd years, without any compensation!" commented Lina and Tonlin. They were genuinely sad and angry since Kee
Sey's presence would be missed. He was like an elder brother. "It is
difficult to find such a nice and humble person. Perhaps that is why
the company always picked on him," said Zuariah, the Javanese bus
conductor. Ah Fon shared the same opinion, "That's true! Those heart-
less people! How could George do that?" I hardly knew Kee Sey but I
had noticed that he was usually very quiet when he sat among his colleagues, always smiling at them as they teased each other or cursed the
management, or the politicians.

"What about the union? Has he consulted Robert [the union head]?"
I asked, even though I was aware that it would be pointless. I wanted
to hear their responses. All of them looked at me and laughed. "What
Robert? Don't talk about that *binatang* [in Malay: animal]," Lina said
in a raised voice, laughing at my silly question. Zuariah added, also

laughing, "Robert is scared of the managers. He always disappears when there are problems." Again I asked, even though I could easily imagine the answer myself, "Then how did he end up as the union head?" Zuariah replied after a brief pause, waiting for others to fill in, "*Entah! Kami pun kurang faham*" (in Malay: Don't know! We are also unsure). Her response was interesting, for clearly they knew that the management had appointed Robert. By saying "We are also unsure," she left open the possibility of challenging this. After all, the union head was supposed to be elected by union members and not appointed by the management. For the rest of the afternoon, before most of them took off for their respective bus runs, they talked about Kee Sey's situation, wondering how he was going to take care of his wife and children. Kee Sey married late and his children were still at school.

Although issues of race, gender, marital status, and wealth played themselves out daily, and some of the bus conductors and drivers – including other regulars at this *warong* – could be blatantly racist and sexist at times, these were not the most important social categories being discussed. On an afternoon shortly before Kee Sey's firing, a regular customer that everyone called *Pak Gemuk* (in Malay: Mr. Fatso) had said, "At this *warong*, we like to joke and tease each other but there is no trouble here. That is why this place is called *Warong Muhibah*, you understand?" There were other more pervasive dramas or referents of differences that took place in which those identified as the regulars at this *warong* tended to orient themselves towards values derived largely from criticizing the present management of the SOC or that of the State. It was these values that I had often observed the collective *kami or kita* (in Malay: *kami* – we exclusive, and *kita* – we inclusive) using in their speech. For example, the collective *kami* (we) was used by Zuariah – *Kami pun kurang faham* (We are also unsure) – in response to my question as to how Robert became the union head. Similarly, whenever I asked someone about his/her relationship with the management, the most common response I would get was "*Kita tak campur*" or "*Kami tak campur*" (We don't mix), instead of "*Saya tak campur*" (I don't mix).

Besides the clique at *Warong Muhibah*, there were other smaller cliques at the various Chinese coffee shops located across from the station office. Each had its own regulars. Initially I thought there was an ethnic consideration behind each "anti-company" space. But that was not to be the case. For instance, Yong Pau Sau and a few Malay, Bidayuh, and Iban colleagues would hang out at a particular coffee shop in the middle of the block. Meanwhile, Yong's partner, Tonlin, an Iban bus

conductor, would frequent *Warong Muhibah*. There were a few old timers who would have their coffee at the shop furthest away from the station office. Obviously, the preference for which of these anti-company
spaces they hung out also had to do with the level of comfort they developed from years of familiarity with the owner or employees of each
shop, as well as each individual's preference for the quality of coffee or
food. Everyone, I was told, had his/her own favourite coffee and it was
common to hear them arguing over which *warong* had the best coffee
at the bus station, or for that matter, in Kuching. The same is true with
chicken rice, noodles, or just about any other Malaysian cuisines.

Like the Malay owner at *Warong Muhibah*, the Chinese owners of
these coffee shops were familiar with the history of the SOC. Most
of them had been around for as long as the bus company and quite
often they were quick to interrupt, interject, or add to the conversations
I was having with the bus drivers and conductors, especially about
the deteriorating working conditions at SOC. There was another
issue that occupied the community's consciousness at this bus station.
The entire area by the waterfront – the bus station, the wet market,
the Ban Hock Hawker Centre, and the hawker stalls next to the river –
would soon be redeveloped into a tourist centre with "modern" retail arcades. But nobody had any idea who the new tenants would be.
To once again invoke Lefebvre, this whole business of redevelopment
and relocation, this modern state mode of spatial production was
constantly on the minds of the bus conductors and drivers, including
those whose livelihood depended on the traffic of customers at this bus
station.[3]

In this regard, within the context of *bangsa* spatiality, there was an air
of uneasiness and impermanence. Just like the *new villages*, the redevelopment of the waterfront had its politics of inclusion and exclusion.
The Chinese hawkers and stall owners suspected that the new facilities
would be reserved for the *bumis*, if not the Malays, as reflected by such
comments as "Anytime the government developed a new facility, they
were always reserved for *their* own." Still, others, perhaps putting on an
air of optimism, welcomed the potential of catering to the supposedly
more lucrative tourist business. But if and when the redevelopment
happened, SOC would have to relocate its bus station to the outskirts of
Kuching, and with it there would be plenty of readjustment, not just in
terms of operations but also in terms of the lives of drivers and conductors as well as others whose livelihoods had centred around the current
bus station for as long as fifty years.[4]

That evening when the station was empty, I approached "Tall" Tan to talk about Kee Sey. There were two other bus drivers at the station office, but they remained silent, not wanting to offer any opinion about the episode. Tan said he wasn't clear on the matter but confided to me that the two station supervisors, old timers Mr. Fong and Ah Pin, were not consulted about the firing. Tan emphasized that that was a new development since Mr. Fong and Ah Pin had overseen the welfare of the bus drivers, bus conductors, and the ticketing personnel at this particular bus station for the past fifty years. With the new management, it would seem that they had been sidestepped, considered "old school." Indeed, I often saw Mr. Fong spend most of his time sitting idly at the station office, reading the Chinese afternoon papers, passing each day before he decided to call it quits.

With no reason whatsoever, I asked Tan if Robert, the union representative, had been notified. As I had expected, the two bus drivers burst out laughing. Tan commented, "Why even mention that *hantu* [in Malay: devil]?" Derogatory words like *hantu* (devil) or *binatang* (animal) were often used by most of my subjects to refer to traitors, brownnosers, the new station manager, the new management at the head office, or any politician. I could not help laughing myself as Robert had been called an animal and a devil within the same day. Ten minutes later, Tan dragged me to our chicken rice shop. While there, he decided to be frank, albeit with slight hesitation since Kee Sey was an old colleague. "What happened to Kee Sey is a horrible thing, but he does have a history. He was short by fifty cents on his daily collection [around fifteen cents Canadian] last year. The company forfeited his 1999 bonus for that." But as soon as Tan said that, he shook his head and laughed, saying, "But so what? What bonus? None of us have seen any bonus. Besides, there was nothing any of us, not even Mr. Fong, could do for Kee Sey." He was right. With the perilous status of their union and against a management that distanced their subordinates, Kee Sey's firing was a done deal. Another bus driver put it this way: "The management is not interested in our complaints. Our concerns are like pieces of rocks that sink to the bottom of the river."

The atmosphere at the station office was still gloomy two days after Kee Sey was fired. Both station supervisors, Ah Pin and Mr. Fong, looked away when I arrived. So did "Tall" Tan. Mei Mei, the other ticket collector, who was usually extremely agreeable and gregarious towards me, pretended not to see me. Geok Bee, who usually was the first to say hello, kept quiet. They clearly were not in the mood to deal with me that morning. Only the *Warong* regulars – Tonlin, Ah Fon, Zuariah, Lina, Fuad, and a few others – were talking quietly among themselves at one corner inside the station office, but they soon dispersed and headed to *Warong Muhibah*.

History as Promises

One of my fieldwork routines was to travel on the buses in order to work with these bus drivers and conductors. That was how I met Ms. Chin, as I was riding on *her* bus one afternoon. Ms. Chin started working as a bus conductor for SOC when she was fourteen and she had been working on the Kuching to Bau route, a route that travelled twenty-eight miles each way, for the past forty years. Every day, she started her workday by getting on *her* bus at six in the morning as it journeyed back and forth between Bau and Kuching, making five runs each day, an average of two hours each way. She normally got home at eight in the evening.

Ms. Chin smiled when she saw me sitting at the rear end of *her* bus. When it came to my turn to pay, she asked, "What are you doing here? I have no stories for you." I smiled and paid for my fare. By the time the bus was at the outskirts of Kuching, when most of the passengers had gotten on and paid their fares, she approached me and started to chat. Ms. Chin lived in Pasar Paku with her younger sister, one of those one-road bazaar towns located close to Bau. Like many Hakkas from Bau, her parents were farmers back in the 1960s before the Bidayuh owner took back the land in the early 1970s.

Ms. Chin was annoyed when I asked if she was a union member, saying, "Why talk about the union? All it does is collect money. I pay two ringgits every month [sixty cents Canadian] and on top of that there are always other dues ... like funeral monies. Funerals are expensive, even the simplest ones. Just last month ... I paid nine ringgits for three funerals. That's eleven ringgits if you add the two ringgits."[5] She was not the only person who complained about the costs of being a union member. However, the issue was not so much about the costs but its entrapment. These sentences from another Hakka bus driver, Yong Pau Sau, denoted such entrapment: "We have already been paying for so long. It would be giving up a lot if we stopped. Once you are out, you are no longer entitled to any funeral contributions should you or someone in your family die." That was one of the questions most of these bus conductors and drivers had to face: whether to continue to be a union member when it no longer "represented" them. Come to think of it, it was rather ironic if the only reason for remaining a union member was to "benefit" from the funeral contributions.

Somehow, without my asking, Ms. Chin then proceeded to tell me how much she respected Hong Hee Siaw and other old timers who had either retired or passed away. She told me that she once saw me talking with Lee at the Kuching wet market and said, "He was a good manager. It's not the same anymore. George, you know ... he has no *liau* [in Mandarin and Hakka: quality]." There is a certain pattern here: many SOC employees would tell me how they felt about Hong Hee Siaw and other former managers, all without my asking, in order to make a contrast with the precarious situation they now found themselves in. Ms. Chin also asked if I was aware of the SMH partnership, commenting: "*We will have more Malay managers from now onwards.*" She then glanced over at her passengers sitting across from us before lowering her voice, "Our CM [chief minister] has an interest in SMH! That family [meaning, the CM, his sons, and brothers] have their fingers on everything in Sarawak." Her remark about the chief minister and his family was pretty much a public secret.

To be sure, the existence of their union was currently more symbolic than practical. Even though there had not been a lot of conflicts between the union and the management in the past, the union had been involved in some negotiations of employee salaries. There had even been a half-day strike to reinstate an employee who was fired in the early 1970s when he was caught failing to issue a single bus ticket. But the working atmosphere had changed and so had the idea of the union. There was another issue. In the past, a union member was entitled to fifty-one days of bonuses each year as opposed to forty-nine days for a non-union employee. Since 1998 the number of days was reduced to forty-one for union employees and thirty-nine for non-union employees. That was a ten-day reduction. However, the reduction felt like a non-issue as the company had not handed out any bonuses since 1998. The insignificance of the union was also reflected by the decline in membership over the years. Most recent hires were non-union employees. Of the current labour force of approximately 650 employees, only around 50 per cent of them were union members. Indeed the comment, "*Buang masa saja*" (in Malay: Waste of time) was their usual response.[6]

One afternoon a bus driver, Mr. Fan Pan Chor, upon hearing my conversation with Zuariah and Tonlin about their union, drew a parallel between the union and the YBs (*Yang Berhormat*) of Sarawak that I thought was a rather apt description of the changing political scenario in Sarawak, and in retrospect, about the changes at SOC:

> The union representatives of the SOC are like the YBs. In the past, the YBs were outspoken and responsive in carrying out their duties to represent and protect the interests of their people. For instance, Stephen Yong was relentless in protecting the interest of the people. Then you have the second batch of YBs who were not as courageous as their predecessors. Take Sim Kheng Hong [another former secretary general of the SUPP]. He did not do much for his constituency. It's the same with the union representatives at the SOC.

He walked away as if satisfied with his analogy. I heard a similar comparison from another bus conductor, B.B. Chin who had discontinued his union membership after more than thirty-five years. He made this remark after he found out that I had just paid a visit to a YB, Datuk Sim Kheng Hui:[7] "The YB you saw this morning ... is a third generation SUPP leader." I was somewhat puzzled by what he meant by "third generation." He smiled before elaborating:

> The first generation SUPP leaders had to fight ... had to be arrested. Indeed, some of them were sent "back" to China. The second-generation SUPP leaders were slightly different. Some were arrested but they eventually became YBs; they obtained titles and became [part of] the government. Some of the second generations had to fight, but not a lot. But the third generations have it easy: they don't have to fight or get arrested. *They only need to be YBs.* [He grinned at his sarcasm before continuing] The foundation had already been laid down for them. It's the same with union representatives. They sit at the office, *goyang kaki,* and draw their salaries. They are like the civil servants, *gaji buta.*

I have already mentioned *goyang kaki* in reference to the good fortunes of the pepper farmers at the *new villages. Gaji buta* (in Malay: blind salary) means drawing a salary without doing any work. Both references are usually made to civil servants and government ministers.[8] Others at the station office were grinning, agreeing with Chin's assessment, but their grins were not without ironies since it did invoke the general feelings of inequalities in the social, political, and economic relations they had experienced for the most part of their lives. They worked hard to survive whereas the third-generation YBs and their union representatives (and most civil servants) had had it easy.

Most of them felt that it was a waste of their energy to talk about their union. Besides there were more urgent matters, their bonuses for one. Echoing the feelings of the majority of the bus conductors and drivers, Ms. Chin said: "We are very angry at the moment. Not a word from the company. In the past we were getting fifty-one days as our bonus. Sometimes, every six months of work, you get one extra month of salary. In the past when the company had financial difficulties, we would forgo our salaries." She felt that they deserved some respect and consideration. And then recalling something that really made her angry, she raised her voice: "Not only have we not received our bonuses, the company even tried to cheat us. They did not pay their shares of our EPF [Employee Providence Fund] in 1999. How low was that?" shaking her head in disbelief. "That was illegal," she continued. "They did not pay for April, May, and June [of 1999]."

Ms. Chin and others were not sure if the company eventually repaid the EPF contributions after some of her colleagues lodged a complaint to the EPF agency. Others said the company was fined but they were not entirely sure either. Still some were not worried at all, like Faizal, a Malay bus driver, who said one morning, "Even if the company hasn't repaid their shares of our EPF, they can't run away." He puts it quite simply: *"Itu law, company tidak dapat lari. Tidak! Nanti kena bayar bunga lagi"* (In Malay: That's the law! The company can't run away. No way! They will have to pay interest as well).

The next time I saw Ms. Chin on *her* bus, she reiterated her feelings towards her company, saying, "Right now, they have more managers, supervisors, ticket inspectors than *us* … and you have those whom the company liked and those they don't. Recently, do you know that George even hired a former army officer from Penang as our chief security officer?"[9] Again she contrasted it with the past:

> Unlike before, when everybody worked for the company, we did not have so many managers. The company was generous. But nowadays even our salaries are late. We used to get paid every first and sixteenth of the month, but not anymore. This is horrible for those who have children. They need to buy new uniforms, books, shoes, and tuition. Just last week, school started on the seventeenth but we got paid on the eighteenth. Many of my colleagues were really upset.

Like many of Ms. Chin's colleagues, she would only perform the minimum requirement of what was needed of her as a bus conductor. She showed up for work on time (meaning, in her case, getting on *her* bus at six in the morning), made the necessary bus runs each day, maintained the necessary minimal fare collections each week, and nothing more. That seemed to be the general attitude. Some of them even said: "We now work for ourselves." They could care less about the company.

Earlier I mentioned a certain bus driver, Keong Wen, who was complaining about his company in front of his colleagues. Keong Wen was in his early fifties and he lived with his wife and three young daughters in a rented room on the outskirts of Kuching. Over the months Keong Wen and I became quite close, but there were moments when he could be quite disruptive while I was talking with his colleagues. He was also extremely loud and had the knack of making others uncomfortable. But there was something interesting about him: he knew when to stop, where his limits were. My guess is that otherwise he would have been fired.

A few old timers conveyed to me they felt uneasy with Keong Wen's presence not so much because of his loudness but because his remarks made them consciously aware of their own precarious positions. For instance, Keong Wen once went on a tirade about the company to the point that even the supervisors, Mr. Fong and Ah Pin, pretended to look away. But there was this sympathetic look in their faces, as if agreeing with what they heard. Peter Kwong, the new station manager, was also present during this incident. He was whispering to Geok Bee, a ticketing employee whom all her colleagues called the biggest "brownnoser" at the SOC.

I sensed that there was something peculiar about the scene, as if the episode was revealing some structural division at the station office that in a sense was a microcosm of the SOC. It turned out I was right. There were two distinct divisions at the station: the old versus the new generation of supervisors and managers. Mr. Fong and Ah Pin represented the old generation, and Peter Kwong and a Mr. Poh – who visited the station office from time to time – represented the new. Apparently the new generation was chiselling away at the old power structure. This division also directly affected the general staff at the station office. Besides a few "brownnosers" who sided with Peter Kwong and Mr. Poh, the rest were with Mr. Fong and Ah Pin. Perhaps it was out of loyalty or out of empathy. But every employee at the station was fast succumbing to the rising influence of the new managers. After all, their sick leaves, annual leaves, assignment of shifts, overtime shifts, and the kind of buses they were assigned were determined by these new managers.

I have mentioned brownnosers because they were a crucial part of the experience at SOC. In Sarawak, brownnoser is called *saa kar*. It is also interesting to note that sometime *saa kar* was synonymous with *choo kuo* (running-dog, traitor). In fact, the terms were often used interchangeably. This interchangeability of terms is worth noting since it had to do with a certain history, or should I say a certain "scandal," in the making of their history. My usage of "scandal" here is influenced by a Nietzschean reading of the notion of "promise" in the "progression" of history. As opposed to Descartes's notion of humans as the thinking animals, Nietzsche suggests that it would be more accurate if we consider ourselves as "promising animals," essentially how history can be seen as a series of broken promises (Nietzsche [1874] 1983).[10] I prefer such a reading when it comes to the writing of history or the critiquing of history since it clearly incorporates the performative aspect of language that takes into consideration the notion of felicities and infelicities – of misfire, miscue, and broken promises. In such reading of history, history no longer proceeds, as it did for Marx, from a logic of contradiction (of contradictions between classes or contradictions inherent in the discourse of the dominant class), but rather from a logic of scandal – resulting from the scandalous promises made by leaders of nation states, the management of companies, and even that made by individuals.

Considering the experiences the bus drivers and conductors had gone through, in particular, the old timers, it would not be an exaggeration to say that the sense of comradeship between employees and the management had dissipated. The same could be said about how they felt towards SUPP who had not only given up their oppositional roles of bringing about changes in Sarawak, but had in essence become part of the status quo and had "forgotten" about these bus drivers and conductors as their past supporters. Wouldn't this then amount to a scandal in the sense that what they had believed in turned out to be a lie, a broken promise? Consider this history and the changes that occurred with the management reorganization in 1998, when all sorts of restrictions or conditions were institutionalized[11] and new positions were created,[12] generating an atmosphere of compartmentalization and distrust at the workplace. In so many ways it reminded many of them of the *new villages*.

Besides these new conditions, the working atmosphere had also become less personalized. Midway through my fieldwork, a fax machine was installed at the accounting office across from the bus station office. Obviously a fax machine served many functions but one of the primary purposes of installing the machine was to relay memos or directives from the head office to the station supervisors, thus replacing the face-to-face interactions between the office managers and station supervisors who in the past would visit each other to discuss company matters. Some of the staff at the station office conveyed to me that the idea behind this new channel of communication was to install a sense of distance between them, not to mention reinforcing a new hierarchy. A bus driver put it this way: "Since they installed the machine, orders and penalties are delivered to us via fax. They don't even have to see us anymore." *They see without being seen.*

Kuan Tar

In my discussion of employee relations or actions with each other as well as with their management, I treat this vast miscellany of actions and relations as refractory manoeuvres or refractory tropes as they zigzagged through the bureaucratic hierarchy instituted by the new management. By refractory I am referring to their tactical actions as seen by the building of alliances congregating at various anti-company spaces and their attitudes of indifference as well as their preference for minimal contact with the new management. Those who had to go to the head office for gasoline would leave in a hurry. And those who had to stick around for tickets or stationery preferred to hang out at the canteen.

The production of such attitudes of indifference reminds me of a study of a homeless shelter in Boston by Robert Desjarlais (1997). In his study, Desjarlais finds out that the shelter staff's effort to obscure the visibility of the homeless in the shelters is one of the factors that promote differences between the homeless and the staff. I found this to be true with these bus drivers and conductors. For instance, when asked how they felt towards the management, I often received the dismissive *kuan tar* (in Hakka or Mandarin: I could care less or why bother or who cares) or *"tar chor tar te, wor chor wor te"* (in Hakka or Mandarin: they work their ways, we work ours), as if saying, "Out of sight, out of mind." Part of these attitudes, as I have suggested, can be interpreted as their reaction towards the disrespect shown by the current management, which they counteract by being just as indifferent. A Chinese bus driver had this to say: "The managers at the head office often refer to us as dogs. I often hear them saying *nar ke koo, che ke koo* [in Mandarin:

that dog, this dog] when they talk about us. Now tell me, how can we respect them? In many ways, it unites us."

But I should point out that the formation of the different cliques was neither formal nor intentional, in the sense that it was not a political formation with clear purposes. Rather, they materialized partly as a function of the different anti-company spaces. It was at the *Warong Muhibah* and other coffee shops where the shaping of consensus feelings, sensations, and sensibilities were solicited amidst their teases, curses, and laughter as they drank their beverages, and tried to stay awake for the rest of their shifts. It was here that I witnessed their laughter over the installation of the fax machine and its purported intention and their gossip about the Sibu fiasco. But the determining factors behind the formation of these cliques and/or alliances was their reactions towards events that were most immediate to them, such as anger and sympathy over Kee Sey's termination, the current state of their union, their bonuses, or their anger when they found out that the company had tried to cheat them on their Employee Providence Fund.

To be sure, there were some who strategically sought some sort of vertical alliances for more favourable working hours, overtime shifts, nicer buses, and the permission for taking leaves. But I suspect that the true sentiments these employees had for the management would not go beyond mere "disinterested liking."[13] Also, there were some who brownnosed the management even though their feelings and sensations were not listened to, acknowledged, or acted upon by the management – similarly treated with an air of indifference by the management, homogenized like the rest of their colleagues as subordinates. Not forgetting, there were those who preferred to be alone, by staying out of the picture: the remaining few old timers who had been through a great deal with the company but were now disappointed with a management that had shown no sympathy, gratitude, and respect for their many years of service. Moreover, some preferred to keep their dissatisfaction to themselves, in part because of their respect for the former general manager and because they wanted to hold on to some fond memories of the company.

I should state that by paying attention to the bus conductors' and drivers' attitude of indifference to the management, I am recognizing their voices or agency without romanticizing them. As Talal Asad (2000, 29) has argued, there are "assumptions of self-empowerment, responsibility, and constructivism" among most contemporary anthropologists when they talk about agency that, intentionally or not, introduce "a triumphalist vision of history." They, according to Asad, "are not only inherently questionable, they also distract our attention away from the need to understand how different traditions articulate the idea of living sanely in a world that is inevitably painful" (2000, 1). Because of a lack of political capabilities, the employees tended to rely on tactics to get things done, to act and interpret rationales or reasons not in terms of future possibilities but more so in the present, the here and now. Much like the Japanese day labourers (*hiyatoi rōdōsha*) living at the margins of urban Japan described by Tom Gill (1999), my subjects orientation to "living in the present is an active, not passive, response to conditions of marginalization and social exclusion, and that at times it constitutes an effective cultural and political critique" (Day, Papataxiarchis, and Stewart 1999, 7). For the most part, through their tactical action towards the immediacies of their lives and the pragmatic, social, political, economic, cultural, and psychological elements of those immediacies, they became hardened individuals with an air of indifference towards the new divisions, regulations, and restrictions instituted by the new management that in many ways reminded them of the hot and chaotic Cold War, one quite similar to that of state-inscribed *new villages* spatiality from which some of them had escaped.

Even as most of these bus conductors and drivers lacked any political leverage, their adoption of an attitude of indifference generated a certain strength, a mental logic if I may, in dealing with the distancing and obscuring discourses they faced in their daily lives. It should be obvious by now that the notion of being indifferent was practised by both the employees and the management. Seen in this way, the notion of dependency would at least appear to be reciprocal to some degree. The employees needed to work and the company was having a difficult time hiring new bus drivers. Theirs was not like the patron–client relationships that describe the dependency linkages suffered by powerless clients at the hands of powerful patrons in their descriptions of vertical and top-down asymmetrical power relations.

Considering their common history, or the "scandal" in the making of their history, I believe their present self-interested attitude was a departure from what they used to feel in terms of their self-existence and their self-referentiality. In the past, they were part of a bigger family, as the employees of a bus company that was not just another business entity but also supported a political life. But they had since changed. These individuals had become ostensibly inassimilable to any current register outside of their naked self-interest. Some of them seemed to say, although sarcastically and remorsefully, that the only thing that interested them in the present was the pursuit of wealth, however little, as captured by the phrase *sui pe yao chien* (in Mandarin: who doesn't want money).

From the stories I collected from the bus conductors and drivers, the way they would talk about their dispositions gave voice to a social being situated within the hierarchies of power that were most immediate to them – the context of their working life. As much as they might want to think of the future, it was "the present" that underscored much of their coevality. They had to contend with a gamut of pressing concerns at their workplace and most of their energies were devoted to getting by on a daily basis. In short, their experience of exploitation, competition, alliance, brownnosing, and so on, did not take on that abstract form we call resistance or social change, but were embedded in the context of their daily working lives.

I also suspect the distance between the management and the employees will only widen with the SMH partnership. Whether one chose to form cliques and/or alliances, or chose to remain alone were all just tactical practices that on one level allowed them to buy time but on another level also served to reinforce and legitimate their subordination. Once again, I come back Michel de Certeau (1984, xii–xiii): "they escape it without leaving it." Their history had taught them, even if it may seem ironic from our point of view, to view resistance as something unworthy of their time and effort, since they had been dislocated and were now subordinated by a management that had shown little respect for them.

If one were to accept the "scandalous" nature of the writing of history, it would seem that their sense of history was one of constant promises and the breaking of these promises. Seen in this light, it is reasonable to suggest that the recourse available to them was to be indifferent, to remain obscure, to refract as much as possible from the discourse that subordinated them. As bad as it may sound, I prefer to be true to what I had observed as opposed to creating some form of illusion. By treating their actions as refractions, even refractory tropes, I hope to avoid the illusion of social change that so much scholarship seems to allude to when our interlocutors clearly lack such a luxury. On another level, as naïve as it may seem, this also proves to show that it is extremely rare that a common oppression necessarily leads to the formation of a common front.

A week after Kee Sey was fired, I ran into a Chinese bus conductor reading the afternoon edition of the *Nanyang Siang Pau* (a Chinese daily) in the passengers' waiting area. When asked what the news was that day, I thought his response expressively reflected the situation in Malaysia as well as the conditions at his workplace. He said: "The news? Oh, it is all about West Malaysia … Nothing about Sarawak! Here in Sarawak, we get no attention from the media. It's like SOC." "What do you mean it's like SOC?" I asked. He gave me a look, lifting his eyebrow, for not getting his coded message before saying, "What do I mean? Look at the station lately. Has anyone talked about Kee Sey? Thirty something years and just like that. Without a trace, without any news! It is as if everyone has forgotten him."

I felt compelled at that moment to speak with Mr. Fong or Ah Pin, to find out if there was anything we could do. But first I asked the conductor if Mr. Fong had already "represented" Kee Sey before the management. He lifted his eyebrow ever so slightly and shrugging his shoulders, "What can Tar Su [in Mandarin, uncle, referring here to Mr. Fong] do?" His response aptly described the general sentiments of most of his colleagues towards Kee Sey's termination. That evening as Ah Pin was leaving I decided to walk with him to the end of the station where he normally took the bus home. He knew exactly what my motive was. Walking side by side, he brought up Kee Sey's track record, telling me how he felt about the whole thing. He added: "He asked for it. He had been caught in the past and should have been more careful." I detected a sense of powerlessness when Ah Pin mentioned that both he and Tar Su (Mr. Fong) had been told to steer clear of the matter. I couldn't help but feel that all the old timers were now being phased out and the only recourse available to them was to try and ignore the new reality, by acting as indifferently or nonchalantly towards it. This was captured best by Ah Pin's speech: "*Kuan tar che yang-tor?*" (in Mandarin: Why bother so much about it?). He smiled and added after we had taken a few more paces: "After all I can retire anytime I want to. My children are married. I can spend time with my grandchildren." There is something implicit here: Ah Pin could afford to be indifferent to the new management and he could retire if he wanted to. In a way there was a sense of personal honour in Ah Pin's seeking to obtain satisfaction at least through speech. However, there was also a taint of bitterness in it, even before he followed up with this remark: "But it's still a shame. I never imagined this could happen, feeling unwanted after all these years." As he was getting on the bus, he turned around and said, "Sarawak has a history of running dogs." The synthesis between his current and past situations was obvious, if not incredibly touching.

When his bus left the station and as I turned back towards the station office, I felt I had had an incredible emotional experience to reflect upon that I could hand over to my readers. Perhaps this is the basis of many theories of ethnography, personal no less than worldly. For a brief moment I stood in the middle of the road staring at the station, feeling sad for the old timers who felt that they were no longer appreciated by the company they have spent their entire life with, that they were now taking up space. I also became aware at that moment that I had not heard Ah Pin speak more than one sentence to me during my stay there since he was usually glued to his table overseeing the daily schedules of all the buses coming and leaving the station. I was deeply touched by what he said, not by his pragmatic stance, not so much because he wanted to act and feel in a certain way, but because he had to in order to maintain a sense of pride and sensibility in an unjust situation, in an unjust world.

Having said that, the process of being indifferent towards the latest developments at SOC was double-edged, for while it involved the tactic of ignoring the institutionalization of various new arrangements that were encroaching on his authority, it also left behind a bitter sense of being disrespected, if not displaced, after years of hard work and loyalty to the company that took up most of his life. It seems to me that Ah Pin, like many old timers, was surviving only inertly, without getting involved in the dialectics of the prevailing conditions. If anything else, they were undermining the legitimacy of their continued existence. The firing of Kee Sey, supposedly over a forty-cent ticket, awakened an air of uncertainty and impermanence at the station, especially among these old timers. Up to the end of my fieldwork, Kee Sey never engaged a lawyer and he remained unemployed. I also thought of how the bus station, the old buildings across from it and the entire area would look like once the Kuching waterfront redevelopment project started. With it, what would happen to the lives and livelihoods of the people I had come to know?

I did mention to some bus drivers and conductors that I approached a lawyer friend who told me about Key Sey's chances of winning the case. Naturally, many of them were curious as to what their longtime colleague might do or was able to do. A few of them asked me in a joking manner if I would be writing about this episode and when I told them I probably would, some of them thought I was pulling their legs. A few shook my hand because I was concerned with their politics. Tonlin said, "Good, tell the world about this lousy company." I wanted to tell them I did not have such authority but I thought I should let them enjoy the moment, even if it was deceitful on my part. In fact, less than an hour later, a few bus drivers that normally frequented other Chinese coffee shops stopped by the *Warong Muhibah* to ask if I was serious about writing up this episode. I told them I might, together with many other topics I felt were important, for instance, their experiences during the Cold War. It was perhaps out of this episode that some of these bus drivers and conductors took my curiosity for a sincere interest in their welfare to heart, and became interested in talking with me. But still, there were others who wanted nothing to do with me.

Chapter Eight

Facing the Artefact

During the past decade there have been a growing number of countries in Africa, South America, and Southeast Asia that have witnessed a shift from repressive regime to more democratic governance with some sort of transitional justice initiatives to confront their haunting past. As a consequence, there has been a trend in the outpouring of oral histories from the subjugated populations and this has attracted great interest from the academy, human rights NGOs, governments, and multilateral institutions. This interest, in turn, has led to some impressive results: the arrests of Chile's Pinochet and Yugoslav's Milošević, the invalidation of amnesty laws in several countries, the setting up of Truth and Reconciliation Commissions (TRC), and the establishment of the International Criminal Court in 2002 for prosecuting international human rights crimes. To be sure, the degree of success these State- and international-instituted tribunals have in dealing with human rights abuse in each of these nation-states remains an empirical question and there remains an urgent need for other forms of public expression that speak truth to power.[1]

Closer to Sarawak, the endemic violence of the New Order period (1965–98) continues to haunt Indonesia, and it is perhaps for this reason that the current government called for the establishment of a TRC to facilitate reconciliation. Similarly, a Commission for Truth, Reception, and Reconciliation was established in East Timor in order to come up with some sort of historical accountability of patterns of abuse under Indonesia's occupation (van Zyl 2005). In my opinion, regardless of the problems, controversies, and complacency that these *truth commissions* are generating, it is a first step in dealing with systematic past abuses. Unfortunately, Sarawak, or Malaysia, has not even reached this first step and, ironically, the Malayan Emergency is still considered a success story. The same could be said about the *new villages* in Sarawak.

As such, it is no surprise that in my effort to *rescue* a certain past in Sarawak, I was confronted with a conundrum. I wanted to tell a story that was contrary to the wishes of the people I worked with. Most of them found it so difficult, for a variety of reasons, to share their feelings about the past with me. Almost half a century has passed since Sarawak became part of the Federal States of Malaysia but it has not produced a set of new perspectives and questions that would encourage its citizens to remember the past. What Margaret Steedly (1993) has written about self-censorship in the public memory of the 1965 bloodshed in Indonesia – that is, prior to 1998 – could be applied to Sarawak, "The monument unbuilt, the story unspoken, is no more than an invisible inscription along history's silent edge, marking an official limit placed upon the past by the present" (238). What is happening in Sarawak not only challenges us to think of more inclusive ways of melding the experience of human memory and forgetting, but also it forces us to think of them within their particular socio-economic, political, and spatial frame of reference. This raises some important, if not resonant, questions about remembering, forgetting, and history and its silences. Fundamentally, if the degree of forced self-censorship signifies how history has "conquered" memory, then following Nora's argument, it also leads to the question of whether government-directed ethnic mob attacks can indeed be placed and understood in a historical sequence when history is now nothing less than archetypal myths, a national memory as it were.

When most of the subjects chose to talk to me about the past or, in essence, how they chose to talk about it, they did not follow a strict constructionist view of memory as socio-politically embedded and interest-determined.[2] Indeed, when they spoke about their past, the meaning and significance of the past changed and they spoke of it with much detachment, reminding us, as Maurice Bloch (1998) once did, that narratives of the past and memories of the past are not the same. Indeed, we can remember our history, but we cannot freely choose the circumstances and conditions of our remembering. In short, collective memory is the complete stock of memories a society of each epoch can reconstruct within its present frame of reference (Halbwachs [1950] 1980). For most of my subjects, the regime they once fought against remained the ruling government and their experience in the jungles of Borneo remained outside of national consciousness. But episodes of communism, however much they chose to forget, silently structured their present. What this means is that practices of forgetting were one of many mechanisms through which they negotiate the lived culture of their contemporaneity.

As I have shown, my subjects' unwillingness to recall their past had to do with the degree of specificity in their history, a specificity shaped by the practices of the colonial and postcolonial regimes, especially in their construction of majority and minorities.[3] In addition, there were also the long-established divisions that existed between the different sectors of the Chinese population in Sarawak along the contours of speech groups, classes, occupations, political persuasions, religions, regions, and so on. It was precisely because of this specificity of history that many of the people I worked with seemed to ask about the use of talking when there were no audiences to acknowledge the dislocation they went through during that violent episode. In a sense their specificity seems to resemble the suffering of women during the Partition of India and Pakistan that Veena Das (1997) has eloquently pointed out: "In the register of the imaginary, the pain of the other not only asks for a home in language but also seeks a home in the body" (88).

It would not be inappropriate to stress that the conditions that allow for any social analysis must also take into account not only the specificity of a particular place but also its references to other sites that are of significance to our subjects' existence. To state it differently, when we talk about the specificity of history, memory, and forgetting in a place, we also need to consider our subjects' awareness of the history and events of other modern-state inscribed spatiality. Here I am alluding to the constant comparisons many of my subjects made in equating their perilous predicaments to situations in Indonesia, situations that were, in their opinions, far worse than their own. It would seem to me that it was within this understanding of the situations of many Indonesian Chinese in particular and other Indonesians in general that affected the ways they viewed themselves and thus how they acted accordingly in their own environment.

I bring up all of the above because I want to emphasize the multiple perspectives and ambiguities of our protagonists' motives and behaviour and point towards the unstable relationship between memory and history, a much greater factor than we care to acknowledge. If anything else, all these issues serve to put the relationship between memory and history under the sign of a question mark. Indeed, some of these Hakkas seemed to offer a few perspectives about memory and history: that it did not matter to their lives; that it was not crucial; that it could be a burden; or that memory and history continued to haunt them. For close to half a century, these memories of resistance in a postcolonial Sarawak have become blurred, even suppressed, by the imperatives of living as a permanent minority in a triumphalist "Malay" Malaysian state.

But as I have shown throughout the book, if we were to listen to the tangled exchange of noisy silences and their innuendos, we would find that the violence most of my subjects experienced had become part of their *structure of feeling*, still living in its aftermath. Their reluctant narratives, forgetfulness, and silences are the residual and denied historical fragments that are irreconcilable with the linearity of history. In the tradition of historical materialism, this book takes these denied and historical fragments "to blast open the continuum of history ... to blast a specific era out of the homogenous course of history (Benjamin 1968, 263).

Rather than treating silences and forgetting as outside of memory, my attempt is to understand and explain any features, both phenomenological and causal, of remembering, forgetting, confabulating, misremembering, and silencing (and its innuendos) as a legitimate part of the overall enquiry into memory and history. I have also addressed the kinds of political and moral predicaments that shaped how their past was narrated (and silenced) in everyday life. The approach to silences and forgetting here not only focuses on the contestation of personal memory in quotidian practices (Cole 1998), and in the presence of the ethnographer, but it also takes into account the contending or contradictory consciousness inherent in any memory community. Each and every story, and the accompanying silences and its innuendos, is given equal status, equal weight so as not to obscure the divisions between the individual and the collective, so as to bear witness to the structural relationality of violence (Feldman 2009).

Such a discursive recourse to memory allows us to account for how certain personal memories get displaced within the grand scheme of collective memories: how they might be attributed to individual ambiguities to past structures of beliefs, and to class, race, speech groups, and so on. It allowed us to account for why those who were directly victimized claimed most vociferously to have forgotten or to be unfamiliar with it. In essence, we are exploring the issue of silences and forgetting in order to provide answers to questions about just how, or how often, one remembers the past (Connerton 1989; Hacking 1990), or even cares to remember at all. I have also shown how new experience and revised expectation continually reshape our memories, revealing a past that is constantly being altered to conform to present expectation.

In addition to the filtering of memories, I have alluded to the need to consider the role of rumours, exaggeration, and fabrication of past events in the act of recalling or retelling events. How would these events play themselves out in the different facets and characteristics of *lieux de memoire* described by Pierre Nora (1996) and his colleagues? In other words, if *lieux de memoire* were external props that act to stimulate recollection, should we not also consider who is doing the recollecting and retelling, and hence, the degree of exaggeration and fabrication involved in such recollecting and retelling? Clearly these are very complex tasks that might prove to be methodologically daunting, but they are not impossible.

The Quotidian

In this book I talked about the miscellany of everyday actions of my interlocutors as actions that came about from their understanding of a certain common history, a collective memory, and their reactions to their current positioning. In essence, these were actions that were deployed to allow them, presumably, to live sanely in an insane and unjust world. I have drawn out a list of situations, contexts, and circumstances to help achieve an understanding of their actions as tactics of indifference, refraction, distancing, refusals to engage, or working the official discourses to its minimum disadvantages (Hobsbawm 1973). In this regard, what I was trying to do was to achieve an effect with their narratives (our conversations) and to do things with what was said – by showing that their tactical actions were reactions that came out of a set of cultivated sensibilities (Mauss 1973) and, for many of the bus drivers and conductors, as a result of a history of dislocation and an increasing and accelerating compartmentalization instituted at their workplace by the new management.

I have shown in their reactions a mix of dispositions: a muteness, perhaps denial, surely a bit of resignation, a bit of cunning among those who capitalized on their experience, but also a kind of stubbornness with respect to the longstanding relations of comradeship on the part of others. I have also talked about the pain and victimization that lingers in their everyday actions. Most of them find it so difficult, for a variety of reasons, to share their feelings about the past with me. In fact, most of them make their involvement in past struggles a non-subject, just something that happened, while others fabricate glories where none probably existed. To be sure, none of them are easy with this past. This is what the politics and economics of the Cold War meant to them. These Hakkas have been sacrificed and must live with the overriding image of sacrifice that gives it cause.

The subjects discussed in this book are characterized as conscripts of modernity – one that has less to do with individuals' exercise of free will or self-determination but more with their participating in a process of subjugation. If I portrayed, albeit unintentionally, their actions with a vocabulary of resistance, I am not suggesting these were actions that could amount to social change. To use a few military terms, these were actions that did not stockpile their winnings but were mainly tactical ploys that capitalized on time, as opposed to strategies, in a de Certeau sense. Some of these could be a refusal to participate through the relationship of silences to speech, or their famous tactical responses such as "I don't know" (*pu-chee-tao*) or "who cares" (*kuan-tar*) that had the force to forestall a query at a particular moment and end a conversation. Their silences and tactical responses can be seen as providing them with some sort of shield, "mental protection from attacks, by shifting themselves off from their injunctions" (de Certeau 1997, ix).

The Seduction of Theories

In my attempt to *rescue* the history of a certain population of Sarawak and of their contemporary conditions, I have also inevitably touched on the fecundity of certain theories concerning, to name only three, the performative aspect of language, historiography, and ethnography. In essence, this book is an exercise, in an Austinian fashion, in putting words to work, so to speak, of stories that are not without prejudice or feelings. By extension, I am also engaging my interpretations with certain theories that have seemed to capture the imagination of so many scholars. By using the narratives of my interlocutors (as well as my own), I sought to ask if there are ways in which people's stories, notwithstanding all the problems, can somehow expand and stretch the definitions and boundaries of history, and bring the messiness of the past back into the fore of history and public consciousness, even if it is only half the truth.

As I have stated at the outset of this book, it is also obvious that I am writing this manuscript through a political – and personal – engagement with history, contemporary nationalist discourses, and the popular discussion of the Cold War. The ethnographic writing I present here is pregnant with a multifaceted reflexivity in which there is an overlapping of voices and exchanging status, of subject and object. Such a mode of production requires that we expand the domain of the empirical considerably to include in our analysis the complex relation between subjection and subjectivity, specifically, the anthropologist's relation to the objects and subjects of analysis. To claim otherwise, to exempt oneself from the analysis is, in the words of Michael Taussig (1992), "an authoritarian deceit" (10).

By emphasizing the intersubjective process of the researcher with his/her interlocutors, it should be clear how I have read into the data collected and consequently what I have considered as significant and worthwhile to write about, to *represent*, keeping in mind, of course, who my potential readers are. It is this experience that comes before representation that takes up most of this book. This is not to suggest that "representation" is secondary in our ethnographic enterprise. As Taussig (2004) put it, it is "the writer's [read here: the anthropologist, storyteller, and translator] responsibility to the reader to try all means and modes to make that experience as full and as obvious as possible … [In short, to] show the means of its production" (313).

Since much of my research dealt not only with the investigation of memory and history but also with the memories of violence, there were times when I found myself facing situations in which I simply did not have the stomach or the courage to pursue certain queries, and I felt that certain things were better left unasked, unsaid, and left within the realm of silence. In my fieldwork, these queries referred to issues of alleged collaboration or betrayals that some of my subjects were involved in, whether intentionally or otherwise. Besides, there was also the danger that if I were to be too insistent, it might sever an existing relationship, a trust that took much time and effort to cultivate. I also need to address the ethical dimension of my work since what I chose to write may inexorably affect the welfare and safety of my interlocutors.

Furthermore, there is also the question of the roles we can or should play as researchers when excavating history in repressive regimes in which people are "discouraged" from remembering. In such cases, should we look at forgetting as a loss of openness and integrity, in a sense, a destruction of memory by history? Or, to bring up an important question raised by the Holocaust historian Lawrence Langer (1991; 1995): should we hope to cure or to right a wrong? I agree with Langer that the worst thing to do is to minimize human misfortune by celebrating the success of survivors or treating them as a discourse of resistance that replaces the one of meaningless suffering. He argues instead that we must accord all possible dignity to our subjects and be honest about the nature of the violence and injustice, which means, in the case of Sarawak, that the memories of dislocation and the violent experiences at the *new villages*, other controlled areas, the detentions and imprisonments, the torture and so on are not an illnesses from which they could be cured by our writing.

In my effort to write about the history of ordinary people, of their feelings and emotions, I hope to thrust life into history itself, to deconstruct the authoritarian construct and myth of an aesthetic nationalist history, providing a means for a transformation of the social meaning of history. But I want to stress that it is one thing to develop close and personal ties to subjects and acknowledge our subjectivity. It is, however, quite another to wonder if such an undertaking would raise the level of consciousness of the overall population, or if it has any political usefulness to the Hakkas in Sarawak. After all, the history of Sarawak (if not elsewhere) is still written as part of the State's project, and this with increasing vigour in the era of neoliberal imperialism (Cheah 1999) and, lately, "terrorism."

The last point is especially important when we consider the asymmetrical relations in the enterprise we call "fieldwork" and its resulting ethnography. In the majority of cases, as Taussig (2004), Klima (2002), and others have mentioned, fieldwork is a kind of gift exchange, albeit an unequal one between the ethnographer and the strangers he/she met. We received the gifts from the strangers we worked with: in the form of shelter, food, hospitality, information, knowledge, connections to other people, history, and so on. Besides the usual giving of gifts and/or monetary compensation, how could we truly reciprocate with interest when we are the ones who are getting the academic mileage out of this encounter? Indeed, how do we reciprocate without feeling awkward and guilty about the gifts we receive? In a sense, *we* are also inscribed with the burden of debts. This awkwardness becomes even more apparent when some of our subjects are not interested in or are even irritated with the stories we have to tell? These are indeed *our* silences; silences we need to address.

It is with such guilt that I hope the approach I have chosen to write about the lives and livelihoods of these displaced subjects in Sarawak will encourage others to raise important questions about ethnographies of memories in situations that remained unchanged, to strive to understand the conditions under which silences and forgetfulness are produced, and to see the contradictions, misrecognitions, and innuendos within the realm of seething absences and muted presences. These are the complexities, multiple perspectives, and ambiguities of our subjects' motives and behaviour, as well as the unstable relationship between memory and history that we need to consider. It is also my hope that this book (and others) will serve in some minor way of what will become part of a vast archive of dossiers, records after records that are not yet available to those most concerned to read them, and that these Hakkas' recountabilities, no matter how reluctant and fragmented, are conceived as repositories for future accountability, for the time that will surely come for some to think radically and confront the meaning of "communism" and "not-communism" in Sarawak and beyond in the era of "after communism." More importantly, it is to remind us that the spectrality of social life and the silences produced in the midst of unchanging social, economic, and political conditions are more common than we thought, if not a central feature of modernity itself.

If my descriptions of their actions seem to lack something or have the feeling of incompleteness, it would then be an infelicity or a mistake on my part, begging for alternative interpretations, a new beginning. Perhaps it is only proper that I quote a passage by Shoshana Felman (1983) in the closing section of this book:

> Perhaps I have only spoken the seduction exercised on me by certain texts, certain theories, certain languages; perhaps I have in turn, in this book, only perpetrated scandal, only articulated my own promise. Perhaps I have spoken here only the unknown of my own pleasure. (12)

I want to end this book with an episode. During the last two weeks of my fieldwork, I went to say goodbye to the old-timers Poh and Lee. At some point during our meeting, I looked straight into their eyes and asked: "Were you once communists?" This time I was hoping they would be more straightforward with me since we had been working with each other for almost a year. They looked at each other and started to smile. While still smiling, all they said was that the past was past and it was not worth talking and writing about. They also said that they had forgotten about the past and thus, their moral imperative to *forgive*, albeit paradoxical, before *justice* arrived.[4] I believe it was their way of saying that *forgiving* allows them to claim a moral victory that seems to put oppression in the past, or that *forgiving* provides an illusion of victory and moral repudiation of those whose power remain unchanged.

Lee assured me, as both he and Poh had done in the past, somewhat strategically ignoring my query, by saying, "The SOC is a business entity for making profit. We were good at running a bus operation and that was all we did." Once again, Poh's son signalled to me that I was on the right track by nodding his head. When Poh realized that his son had once again given away the answer to my question, he smiled, first facing his son and then turning to me, saying, "Please do not write it down. That was the past." His son added by mentioning that his dad once had an encounter with a police constable who accused him of being a communist, to which Poh laughed and said, "I looked straight into the constable's eyes and I said: If I am a communist, you must be Mao Zedong."

Notes

Introduction

1 Except for political and public figures, I have substituted pseudonyms for all my subjects as well as for the names of businesses used throughout this book.

2 The Hokkiens are one of the main Chinese speech groups in Sarawak. Historically, they were the most powerful economic group in Kuching. The other main Chinese language groups in Sarawak are the Teochiu, Hakka, and Foochow (or the Fukinese). In this book I use the term "Chinese speech group" instead of dialect even though the regional languages of China have often been described as "dialects." As Robert Ramsey (1987, 16) points out, these dialects "are as different from each other as French from Italian and, when taken together, are probably more complex than the whole Romance family." In linguistic parlance, they are mutually unintelligible in spoken forms.

3 The Ibans are the largest indigenous group in Sarawak. The Bidayuhs are the biggest indigenous group in northwest Sarawak.

4 The Hakkas are the largest Chinese speech group in Sarawak, and one that once resided predominantly in the rural areas. They are also called Khek, which means "guest people," a historical designation that was used for them in southern China and signified their foreignness to the region. To this day the Hakka populations in Fukien and Amoy provinces are predominantly found in the highlands, areas that are supposedly less fertile compared to the lowlands occupied by the Hokkiens and Teochius. There are numerous interpretations as to the origin and history of the Hakkas in China. For a review of these interpretations of the Hakka people in China and elsewhere, see the collection of essays in *Guest People: Hakka Identity in China and Abroad*, edited by Nicole Constable (1996).

5 The concept "context statements" is taken from Allen Feldman (2004) on the performed narratives of the South African Truth and Reconciliation Commission (TRC). Obviously my subjects' context statements were devoid of the "memory theatre" that existed during the TRC.

6 As will become clear in this book, I have my reservations with the term "collective memory." Communities that have experienced a violent past do not necessarily establish solidarity or collective memory.

7 This is not to suggest that face-to-face interactions are no longer important in producing collective memories in both capitalist centres and in the peripheries. See Pandey (2005) for a similar observation.

8 See Anderson (1966), Reid (1980), and Friend (1988).

9 This would explain why the post-war European propaganda against Japan used such racist language to describe the "yellow savages."

10 The Rape of Nanjing, also known as the Nanjing Massacre, was a massacre and war rape that occurred during the six-week period following the Japanese Imperial Army's siege on Nanjing, the former capital of the Republic of China, on December 1937. During this period, hundreds of thousands of Chinese civilians and disarmed soldiers were murdered and the Imperial soldiers reportedly raped 20,000 to 80,000 women. An accurate estimation of the number of casualties has never been achieved since most military records of the killings were deliberately destroyed or kept secret after Japan's surrender in 1945. To this day, the massacre remains one of the obstacles to positive Sino-Japanese relations (see Chang 1997; Fogel 2000). Incidentally, I have never come across a single entry about the Rape of Nanking in the Chinese newspapers I examined from the period of my investigation. I have a feeling that it was/is a traumatic, even shameful event that most Chinese, including those in the diaspora, find hard to talk about. Similarly, I never heard anything about it from the people I worked with.

11 See the excellent dissertation by Hui (2007, chapter 3) for a discussion of the atrocities against the Chinese in West Borneo. Mary Somers Heidhues argues that the large-scale massacre of the Chinese in West Kalimantan made them imagine their fate to be conjoined with that of the other Chinese in the region (Heidhues 2003, 208). Heidhues also argues that the scale of the killings of Chinese in West Kalimantan probably represents Japan's worst war crimes in the Malay Archipelago (2005).

12 It is important to note that Singapore was expelled not by members of the original Alliance government but by leaders of UMNO. The Alliance Party was formed in the 1950s before Malaya achieved its independence in 1957. At that time, it consisted of the United Malay National Organization

(UMNO), the Malayan Chinese Association (MCA), and the Malayan Indian Congress. From its inception, this was an alliance formed under communal (i.e., racial) politics. Like most political parties in Malaysia, UMNO remains a race-based party. I mention "remains" because the founding father of UMNO, Dato Onn Jaafar, wanted to get rid of its race-based politics by inviting non-Malays to be associate members of the organization and to enjoy its rights and privileges. Having failed to do so, Dato Onn eventually resigned from the party.

13 This area is home to many souvenir, handicraft, and antique shops, as well as businesses like grocery stores and coffee shops. At the western end of the Main Bazaar is where the SOC bus station is located, one of my primary field sites.

14 For economic accounts of the Cold War, see also Mamdani (2004), Simpson (2008), and Khalidi (2009).

15 As Haugerud and Edelman noted, contrary to public knowledge, the Marshall Plan on Europe was fairly inexpensive, less than 3 per cent of the United States' GDP.

16 As Lefebvre points out, an "appearance" of homogeneity and not its actualization is key in masking differences, and the state figures centrally in producing this effect.

17 See, for example, Andre Gunder Frank (1966), Immanuel Wallenstein (1974), and Arturo Escobar (1995).

18 For a more informative discussion of various twentieth-century accounts of gift and gift giving, see Alan Schrift (1997) and Rosalyn Diprose (2002).

19 Derrida frequently draws attention to the gift as *pharmakon*, especially in *Given Time*.

20 Sanjay Krishnan offers an interesting take on Adam Smith's *The Wealth of Nations* ([1776] 2003). In Sanjay's reading, *The Wealth of Nations* is a text that pioneered the global, albeit a Western global, as a perspective for the realization of the project of a good and just imperialism. Sanjay points out that the book was written in the context of financial instability at home, territorial expansion in Asia, military rivalry in Europe, and the imminent revolt in the colonies in North America. Smith's accounts of world history is crucially dependent upon a conceit: a model of material progress guided by nature, by which he meant this natural "human propensity to truck, barter and exchange" the world over. It is in such rhetoric of free trade that the global was configured as a single, interconnected, and united entity, serving writers such as Adam Smith and those that followed in his wake a way of making the newly acquired heterogeneous spaces and non-white subjects "legible" (Krishnan 2007, 25–57).

21 Sanjay Krishnan (2007) points out that Adam Smith emphatically identified the Malay Archipelago as a central focus of the Western imperial project, a geopolitical and commercial zone defined by the sea route between
two great imperial prizes of Asia: India and China.

22 As John Hutnyk (2004) puts it so eloquently, "Rio Tinto is hardly known
for its desire to redistribute the global share of surplus expenditure for the
welfare of all" (179). On the national context, as recent as October 2009, the
current prime minister Najib Razak said in the capital, Kuala Lumpur that
he was not in favor of using coal as a source of energy, calling it "dirty, not
environmentally friendly." However, less than a month later, on November
2009, speaking at the state capital of Sabah, Kota Kinabalu, he said that for
the state to achieve *development*, some sacrifices had to be made. He said
he had made the decision to go ahead with the proposed coal-fired power
plant at the Sahabat Felda scheme in Lahad Datu (November 8, 2009,
http://www.dailyexpress.com.my/news.cfm?NewsID=68713).

23 On both field trips I was working as a research assistant for Professor
Nancy Peluso, first when she was a professor at Yale University and later
at the University of California, Berkeley.

24 I use the term "working relations" to denote my interactions with my subjects. It has several connotations. It could be an ongoing working relation,
sometimes even a confidential one. It could be sporadic conversations or
only greetings. It also stresses the unequal footing between the researcher
and his/her interlocutors.

25 Experience here is both a verb, as in experiencing something, as well as a
noun, as in something one has. This double-barrelled connotation for experience, noted by William James (1912), included both what men did and
suffered as well as how they acted or were acted upon, cited in Desjarlais
(1997, 12).

26 Literally, *bumiputra* means the "sons of the soil." Symbolically, it refers to
the Malays and the indigenous, but in reality it applies only to the Malays
or, more accurately, to the elites within UMNO.

27 The rhetorical predisposition of the current regime would make an interesting study in the history of rhetoric and its links to imperialism and
colonialism.

28 It was not until 2006 that the law draughtsman of the ISA, Professor Regi-
nald Hugh Hicking, called for its abolishment. Many people have perished
under this infamous law.

29 Malaysia is currently ranked fifty-sixth out of 178 countries by Transparency International in its latest Corruption Perception Index for 2010. This
is the lowest rating ever for Malaysia.

30 The Singapore Census of Population 2010 revealed that 25 per cent of Singaporeans and permanent residents were not born in Singapore. Of that group, 23 per cent were from Malaysia.

31 Some scholars have argued that the Cold War is not over. As Rashid Khalidi (2009) points out, the defense budget and spending by the United States (and Russia) continues to reflect a Cold War mentality. Incidentally, it was not until February 24, 2009 that, for the first time, an American leader (President Obama) categorically stated in his address to congress that the U.S. defense budget should no longer reflect the kind of spending based on the Cold War era.

32 In the Moroccan case, at least some of the victims of political persecution have spoken out and had their grievances attract the attention of Amnesty International and other NGOs. This is not the case with the community represented here in Sarawak.

33 Credit goes to Professor Virginia Dominiguez, then executive editor of the *American Ethnologist*, for pointing this out to me.

34 Nietzsche wrote in the second essay of *On the Genealogy of Morals*: "Now this animal which needs to forget, in which forgetting represents a force, a form of *robust* health, has bread in itself an opposing faculty, a memory, with the aid of which forgetfulness is abrogated in certain cases – namely in those cases where promises are made" ([1967] 1989, 58, emphasis in original).

35 As Arturo Escobar (1995) has so eloquently argued, the emphasis on *development* in the Third World is not only couched in terms of progress but also as a moralizing attitude. Development as a discourse probably would not have existed without the persistent Cold War–based geography of fear.

1. Overseas Chinese

1 The term "overseas Chinese" has certain connotations, among them "China-centredness" and "sojourning," a highly inaccurate depiction since many of the Chinese living in Southeast Asia and beyond had no plans to "return." It is vital to stress that the "cultures" of Chinese living outside of mainland China grew out of particular social circumstances and are not a mere approximation of the culture of their "homeland."

2 My thanks to Talal Asad for pointing this out.

3 The vocabularies used for anti-Sino discourse were borrowed from available anti-Semitic terms and concepts. For example, terms like "middlemen," "shrewd businessmen," "unpatriotic" subjects towards the countries

they settled in," "wanderers," "strangers," and so on were commonly
applied to Chinese communities throughout Southeast Asia.

4 *Kongsi* were Chinese business enterprises that were larger than small,
family-run businesses. *Kapitan* was the term for a Chinese leader who was
elected by the colonial government to collect tax revenues and manage the
internal affairs of his particular Chinese community.

5 Three recent essays in an edited volume called for more attention to as-
pects of intra-ethnic-group life among the different Chinese populations in
Malaya/Malaysia and southern Thailand. See Wong (2008); Teo (2008); and
Montesano (2008).

6 As Mbembe (2001, 27) points out, the white man's burden may be called
the Bergsonian tradition of colonialism. It rested on the idea that the colonizer could, as with a domesticated animal, *sympathize* or *love* the colonized
but only up to a point. The dominant tropes here were domestication
and servitude, and like a domestic animal, the colonized was an object of
experimentation, a game played by the colonizer whereby the colonized is
forever denied any sense of coevality, forever enclosed in the virtual and
the contingent (cf. Fabian 1983).

7 One important element about this period that has received little treatment is the degree of collaboration between the Japanese military and
the indigenous, the Malays, and (to a degree) some Chinese merchants.
According to anthropologist T'ien ([1953] 1997), there were many Chinese
collaborators in Sarawak who were not only permitted to retain most of
their property but who in many cases added to their possessions during
the Japanese Occupation.

8 Most of my Chinese subjects conceded that the Chinese newspapers – or,
for that matter, the many mainstream newspapers in Malaysia – no longer
played an important role in terms of disseminating news and viewpoints.
Rimbunan Hijau, a company owned by Sarawak tycoon Tan Sri Tiong Hiew
King, now controls all the major Chinese newspapers in Malaysia, effect-
ing a monopoly of the Malaysian Chinese newspaper industry. These include the *Sin Chew Daily, Guang Ming, Nanyang Siang Pau,* and *China Press.*

9 See Nietzsche's *On the Genealogy of Morals* ([1967] 1989).

10 Events like these became "sites of memory" that were often invoked by
some of my Chinese subjects when they reminisced about the SUPP's
once-radical past. They often seemed to ask, with melancholia and even
resentment, "What happened to the SUPP?"

11 For example, the *See Hua Daily News* reported that "China needs [a] great
quantity of rubber. To trade with China will improve the livelihood of
Sarawakians in the country" (March 1, 1968). Other countries that were
importing rubber from Sarawak include the former Soviet Union and

Yugoslavia, both of which were communist regimes. A headline on the *Chinese Daily News* read, "Good news for rubber trade – China, the Soviet Union, and Yugoslavia to buy rubber from Sarawak" (January 27, 1968).

12 The following discussion of the May 13 Incident is taken from Kua Kia Soong's recent book, *May 13: Declassified Documents on the Malaysian Riots of 1969* (2007).

13 Some of these institutions and agencies servicing the rural sector included Bank Pertanian (Agriculture Development Bank), Lembaga Padi Nasional (National Padi Authority), Food Industries of Malaysia (FIMA), MAJUI-KAN (Fisheries Development Authority), MAJUTERNAK (Livestock Development Authority), RISDA (Rubber Industry Smallholders Development Authority), FOA (Farmers Organisation Authority), and MARDI (Malaysian Agricultural Research and Development Institute).

14 Part of Soeharto's speech reads, "Our intention is to build a greater Maphilindo, which means we would like to unite with the Malay race and other friendly neighbouring countries" (*Newsweek*, September 5, 1966, 43). It is important to stress that the term "Malayness" is a modern construction that has the tendency to obscure its diverse source of identities. See, for example, Reid (2010, 295–313) and Kahn (2006).

15 Criticism of the Green Revolution is beyond the scope of this book but it is important to note that instead of eradicating rural poverty, it in fact accentuated class differentiation. See Scott (1985).

16 A Ministry of Land Development was set up to coordinate the activities of the various land development agencies, such as the Federal Land Development Authority (FELDA) schemes. Other agencies included the Urban Development Authority, Lembaga Padi Negara (National Padi Authority), Council of the People's Trust (MARA), Amanah Rakyat, State Economic Development Corporations, Perbadanan Nasional (National Corporation), and so on.

17 There are some who would go so far to argue that the more Chinese are discriminated against in Malaysia, the better the community performs. This is a theory explored by two professors from Yale University and the University of British Columbia who postulate that the NEP could actually be the reason for, rather than an obstacle to, the Chinese's economic success in Malaysia. See Fang and Norman (2006). While Fang and Norman's theory may be applicable to a certain segment of the Chinese, and only during the 1980s, it doesn't cover the working class, wage earners, and their children, who have been shut out by the NEP.

18 I owe my usage of the "holy trinity" concept to Achille Mbembe (2001), who uses it to illuminate similar systems of inequality and domination in postcolonial Africa.

19 Forty years after the implementation of the NEP, the current regime still refuses to admit the real reasons for the brain-drain phenomenon. In his recent calling for "Malaysian talents" to come home for the country to have a real "knowledge-based and innovation economy" – never mind the buzzword – Prime Minister Najib Razak attributes the reason for the brain drain to the global neoliberal economy and the mobility of Malaysian skilled workers (see "PM vows to bring home talented Malaysian diaspora," *Malaysiankini*, November 14, 2009, http://www.malaysiakini.com/news/117430).

20 The concept "political identities" is taken from Mahmood Mamdani's (2001a; 2001b) account of the organization of power and state formation that led to the Rwanda genocide.

21 PEMANDU is the latest government think-tank that is said to have come at a whopping price tag of RM 66 million even before it got down to work, with most of the money going to foreign consultants. Several documents obtained by the electronic portal *Malaysiakini* reveal that, before PEMANDU was even launched, a huge sum of the money went to the American consultancy firm McKinsey and Co., which took the lion's share of RM 36 million; most of the rest went to salaries for its *bumiputra* directors. See "McKinsey Paid RM36 Mil to Set Up Pemandu," *Malaysiakini*, December 3, 2010, http://www.malaysiakini.com/news/149861.

22 Hegel's (1953) position on this continues to be influential: "History is the charting of Freedom and Freedom is only possible in the State" (74–5 and *passim*, cited by Pandey 2005).

23 For an excellent ethnographic account of people who share an effort to live in the present, with little interest in the past and little thought for the future, see the edited volume by Sophie Day et al. (1999), *Lilies of the Field: Marginal People Who Live for the Moment.*

2. The Greater Malaysia Plan

1 Using the pretext of the revolt, Lee Kuan Yew of Singapore arrested scores of his political opponents – much to the delight of Tunku, who had demanded the elimination of leftist elements as part of his conditions for admission to Malaysia. See Jones (2002).

2 The political parties in Sarawak that joined the Alliance Parties of Malaya in 1963 consisted of Persaka Bumiputra Bersatu, Sarawak National Party, Parti Negara Sarawak, and Sarawak Chinese Association.

3 The estimation of 2,500 communist members comes from Justus van der Kroef (1966b). According to government estimates, by the mid-1960s the

communist movement in Sarawak possessed a combat-ready force of 3,500 strong, backed by 25,000 civilians (Staar 1969, 390).

4 Following the Brunei Revolt, Indonesian President Soekarno publicly declared his support for Azahari and within months, in January 1963, the Indonesian Foreign Minister announced the initiation of a policy known as *Konfrontasi* that would involve political, economic, and military struggles against the neocolonial, pro-British Malaya. Besides Brunei, the CIA reported that Indonesian intelligence, local army units, and left-wing parties were assisting anti-Malaysia opponents in Kalimantan. See Simpson (2008, 115).

5 To be sure, diplomatic efforts were undertaken to settle the Malaysian issue. Soekarno and Tunku met in Tokyo in May 1963 and a Foreign Ministers' conference was held in Manila. In the spirit of solidarity among ethnic Malays (which was called "Maphilindo"), the Manila Accord was signed. It also called for a UN commission headed by Secretary-General U Thant to ascertain the views of North Borneans concerning Malaysia. However, prior to the UN team's arrival in Sarawak, Britain and Malayan leaders decided that Malaysia would be officially proclaimed on August 31, 1963, something that infuriated Soekarno. Consequently, the first of a series of *Gangang Malaysia* demonstrations was held at the British embassy in Jakarta. Soekarno also rejected the eventual findings of the UN team that North Borneans supported the Greater Malaysian Plan. Tunku responded by severing all diplomatic ties with Indonesia. Within days, anti-British demonstrations rocked Jakarta, culminating in the destruction of the British embassy and the looting of dozens of British homes throughout Jakarta (Mackie 1974). In July 1964, ethnic riots hit Singapore and a small group of Indonesia raiders infiltrated the southern tip of the Malay Peninsula (Davidson 2008).

6 The United Nations team who assessed the situation in Sarawak on the Malaysian Plan stated that one-third of Sarawakians were pro-Malaysia, another one-third undecided, with the remaining one-third anti-Malaysia (Porrit 2004). This was contrary to the evidence on the ground. For starters, there were several thousand anti-"Malaysia" demonstrators "welcoming" the United Nations team when it arrived in Sarawak to ascertain the views of the people on "Malaysia." This information was even reported in the Sarawak Information Service's monitoring of Chinese newspapers (33/63), which stated that anti-"Malaysia" demonstrators were waiting at the Kuching airport as well as in the towns of Sibu and Miri to "welcome" the UN team. When news of the UN's pro-"Malaysia" report became public, several anti-Malaysia riots broke out in Sibu, Miri, and several other towns

(SIS, 35/63). See also Leigh (1974). Similarly, the United Nations also supported Indonesia's integration of Papua in 1969 in what was then called an "act of free choice," despite a rising separatist movement, demonstrations, and riots. See Jamie Davidson (2008, 5).

7 *Konfrontasi*, together with Soekarno's somewhat leftist expansionist ambitions, would transform the regional strategies of the U.S. and the UK, each inseparable from the downward spiralling effect of the war in Vietnam. As *Konfrontasi* accelerated in tandem with the Vietnam War, the Johnson administration was forced to gradually abandon its "accommodationist" strategy for a covert strategy aimed at ousting Soekarno. See Simpson (2008, 114).

8 This also explains why the U.S. was the principle *donor* to the Colombo Plan, a plan designed to achieve *security* and so-called *development* in the region.

9 The Special Branch was established as part of the Malayan Police during the Malayan Emergency (1948–60). It was recognized by the British colonial government as the supreme intelligence organization in providing political and security intelligence to the Malayan Police, the government, and the army – information on which counterinsurgency operations could be carried out against the communist insurgency.

10 Similar assertions were made by Dutch historian van der Kroef (1966a) and sociologist B.G. Grijpstra (1976).

11 According to Special Branch assessment, there were about 6,000–7,000 armed communist guerillas in the jungle at the outset of the Emergency. The Special Branch also believed that these guerillas were getting material assistance (including food) and information about the movement of government forces from Chinese squatters living on the jungle fringes (Comber 2008, 67).

12 In 1948, Malaya exported 371,000 tonnes of rubber and 155,000 tonnes of tin to the USA, earning Britain U.S. $170 million at a time when the sterling had an overall deficit of U.S. $1,800 million. The Soviet Union was also not averse when it came to trading with Malaya and Singapore – so much for the Cold War being an ideological war (Comber 2008, 14).

13 Since the end of the Second World War, the British army has spent more time in "low-intensity" warfare – also called counterinsurgency operations – than in conventional warfare. The term "low-intensity" is defined as conflict between contending forces that occurs below the level of conventional war involving large military formations. Some of Britain's major operations were at Palestine (1943–8), Malaya (1948–60), Kenya (1952–6), Cyprus (1955–9), and Aden (1964–7). These were by no means

cheaper endeavours. According to Comber (2008), at the beginning of the
Emergency, there were two battalions of British troops, one battalion of
the Malay Regiment, 2,500 Gurkhas, and 72,000 Malayan police (including
the SB) to counter the communist insurgency. By 1949, they were further
reinforced by four British infantry battalions, one regiment of British Royal
Artillery, two battalions of the Malay Regiment, a squadron of the Royal
Air Force Regiment, and many additional Gurkhas. Further reinforcements
were on their way that included the 4th Hussar (armoured car unit) from
the British army commander for the Far East, as well as three battalions
of the Scots Guards. Later in the Emergency, military and air forces were
made available and committed from Britain, Australia, New Zealand,
Africa, and Fiji. Over the period of the Emergency, the security forces committed were often between five to twelve times larger than the communist
guerilla forces. See Short (1975) for a discussion of accessing the correct,
if not inflated, estimates. Regardless, according to Colonel John Cross
(1989), one of the characteristics of guerrilla warfare is the large number of
government forces needed to take on the offensive against much smaller
insurgent forces. For example, "in Central America in 1957 a strike force of
no fewer than 43,000 of Guatemala's soldiers was required to contain 3,000
guerillas; in El Salvador 49,000 government troops against 4,000 guerillas;
in Honduras 22,000 against 2,000; and in Nicaragua 75,000 against 18,000"
(cited in Comber 2008, 78).
14 See Mao Zedong's "Primer on Guerrilla War" (1962), 5–11.
15 It is interesting to note that besides race, there was a spatial element in
determining who among the Chinese were to be dispossessed and relocated. In the case of the Malayan Emergency, it was the proximity of the
Hokkiens and Teochius to the jungles. As we shall see later, in the case of
Sarawak, the Hakkas were chosen because they were mainly farmers living in rural areas.
16 Interestingly enough, as Comber (2008, 150) points out, Briggs's resettlement plan bears a close resemblance to the Japanese Protection Village
program in Manchuria and China in the 1930s.
17 Up to this date, the only source of acknowledgement of these excessive
strong-arm measures to extract information came from a little-known
booklet on the Emergency written by a former head of the Federal Special
Branch, Richard Craig. According to Comber (2008), Craig probably wrote
it after he retired from the Malayan Special Branch to join MI6 in 1964. It is
worth quoting the passage:

Officers on the ground were left to collect information in whatever manner they saw fit. The employment of excessive strong-arm measures to

extract information was common, and much use was made of the highly
vaunted truth drug [emphasis in original] ... Fortunately, the police soon
realized that such measures were proving to be counterproductive because in a guerrilla situation it is of fundamental importance that at least
part of the civil population is won over. (RJW Craig, "A Short Account
of the Malayan Emergency," cited in Comber 2008, 83)

Though Craig felt that torture was symptomatic of the times, albeit
unjustifiable, his account was clearly at odds with the generally accepted
"British" standards for fair treatment of prisoners and detainees under the
Geneva Convention.

18 The index number for this report with the U.S. Information Agency is
R-118-63 [AF], June 17, 1963. I focus on this document not because it is
an accurate guide to the so-called Dayak oppositions against the Greater
Malaysia Plan, but because it arguably has been the single most important
"official" revelation of Dayak anti-Malaysia sentiments that have otherwise been obscured or denied by the Malaysia authorities in their coordi-
nated strategy of ideological legitimation that the communist problem in
Sarawak was a Chinese problem.

19 Incidentally, according to Davidson (2008), this is the same Oeray who together with his military band of Dayaks (known as the Laskar Pangsuma)
collaborated with the ABRI (Angkatan Bersenjata Republik Indonesia,
Armed Forces of the Republic of Indonesia) in one of Indonesia's most
hideous massacres and forced relocation of its Chinese subjects in West Kalimantan. A year after Oeray was dismissed from his governorship in 1966,
he saw the opportunity to work with ABRI to relocate the rural Chinese in
West Kalimantan as his chance not only to disprove the leftist accusations
against him but also to prove his nationalism with the new Soeharto regime. Oeray was also driven by economic interests. He figured the Dayak
would dominate the economy in the Anjungan-Mador-Menjalin triangle in
West Kalimantan once the Chinese were driven out, even massacred.

20 According to the 1947 Census, 83 per cent of the Chinese in Serian District
and 89 per cent in Bau District were of Hakka origin (cited by Porrit 1991).

21 For the literature that contextualizes the territorialization of modern state
power as a historically specific form of politico-spatial organization, see
Lefebvre (1991), Arrighi (1995), and Escobar (2003).

22 A political observer based in Hong Kong wrote that it seemed highly
unlikely these settlements would win over Chinese loyalty as they had the
appearance of penal stockades (Van der Kroef 1966a).

23 I owe this piece of information to a certain *penghulu* (chief) who confided
to me that he was once a communist.

24 For example, the Chinese Newspaper *The Sarawak Vanguard* reported that under the White Terror Operation, more than thirty Dayaks were arrested in a jungle-based military/police operation in the Second Division – in the Engkilili/Lubok Antu area. Nineteen of them were *Tuai Rumahs*. These arrested Dayaks were said to be strong supporters of SUPP; some were Executive Committee members of SUPP's Engkilili Branch (*Sarawak Vanguard*, August 17, 1968).

25 Funnily enough, it was widely rumoured among the Hakka, Hokkien, and Teochiu I met in Kuching that the tremendous wealth and influence of one of the richest Chinese families in Sarawak, the Ong family (Hokkiens), came about because they had harboured James Brooke (the White Rajah) in their house when the Hakka miners were burning Kuching to the ground during the Bau Revolt. The Hakkas I met at Bau gave an even more insidious description, insisting that James Brooke was hiding underneath Ong Eng Lai's bed during the Bau revolt and that this particular bed was later given as a *gift* to the Sarawak Museum. It is true that there is a traditional Chinese bed on display at the museum but there is no indication that it belongs to the Ong family or that James Brooke hid underneath it.

26 There are plenty of reports of skirmishes and clashes between the Sarawak Malays and the Malay soldiers from West Malaysia in the local newspapers, even in the Malay newspaper *Utusan Sarawak (Sarawak Information Service*, December 26, 1965). Incidentally, most of the newspaper reports about the fighting claim that it had to do with jealousy over women.

27 "Ngayau" is an Iban word, specially designed to describe waging war against an enemy. "Ngayau" is almost a synonym to "headhunting." So, when used in an Iban context, "ngayau" often refers to the taking of heads. There is something quite presumptuous about adopting the word "ngayau" for an anti-communist operation. It not only gives the impression that such an operation is synonymous with the "warlike" campaign of the Ibans, but also that the Ibans, being the largest indigenous group in Sarawak, were pro-Malaysia and anti-communist during the Cold War. I would like to thank Kelvin Egay for pointing this out to me (personal communication, March 12, 2006).

28 Of course, it would be an error to assume that such a phantom justice system exists only in Sarawak – or, for that matter, only in Third World countries. See Arendt (1951).

29 At a conference organized by the Institute of Southeast Asia Studies and the Singapore Heritage Society in the summer of 2010, there were three papers presented by Malaysian participants that touched on various aspects of communism in Malaysia. From an academic perspective, there

was nothing sensitive about these papers. But the Malaysian government did not share this perspective, as all three presenters were called up for an interview at different hotel rooms by the Malaysian Special Branch. I bring out this episode to illustrate how the authority would prefer academics (and the public) to abstain from talking about communism or the history of communism in Malaysia, especially if it might shed some light on some of the pioneers who fought for Malaysian independence, something that has been erased from Malaysian history textbooks.

30 A different version of this section is published as "The Politics and Aesthetics of Place-Names in Sarawak," *Anthropological Quarterly* 80 (1): 65–91 (Yong 2007b).

31 All italicized place-names refer to the translated Hakka versions of the state-inscribed Malay place-names. Names of individuals, places, and Chinese expressions are left in their original dialect forms as they were narrated to me instead of in the standardized, romanized pinyin. I understand this is against convention but I feel compelled to retain the local flavour and, at least, that this is my obligation to return the gift of their conversation (if that is even possible), which they were willing to share with me (however reluctantly), and to accommodate the possibility that their children or grandchildren might get the chance to read it.

32 Earlier, I had recorded a list of all the operations. Incidentally, the controlled settlements that came out of Operation Freedom were called the Islands of Freedom.

3. The Sri Aman Treaty

1 Following Trouillot's thesis on history (1995), every move and non-move in the construction of history is a reflection of conscious choice, even the very act of determining what gets reported and what gets archived. And the very selections of sources for an archive predetermine a whole range of "silences." The flip side is that history is the story of what is not silenced, of what is broadcasted and generally accepted as history. In short, "broadcasts" and "silences" are dialectical counterparts of which history is the synthesis.

2 Deconstructing the notion that the archival labour be seen mainly as an extractive enterprise, Derrida, in his discussion of the archive as double silencing, looked at archival production as a consequence of governance – even one with violent effects in producing and/or reinforcing the friend/enemy schema that Carl Schmitt (1996) theorized. For Derrida's various discussions on the archive, see *Specters of Marx* (1994), *The Politics of Friendship* (1997), and *Archive Fever* (1998). See also Ann Stoler (2010).

3 As Robert Desjarlais (1997, 28) put it, we need to develop the habit of critically examining "the plurality of forces that occasion diverse ways of being at any moment within a society ... How patterns of sensation, forms of agency, or a sense of personhood came about in specific social interactions."

4 The communist movements in Sarawak were by no means a unified movement. For example, the Sarawak Communist Organization had a militant wing called *Pasukan Gerilya Rakyat Sarawak* (PGRS or Sarawak People's Guerilla Force), a wing said to liaise with *Partai Komunis Indonesia*. This was prior to 1965 when the *Partai Komunis Indonesia* had much political clout under the Sukarneo regime. Similarly, the Sarawak Liberation League was closer to the *Tentera Nasional Kalimantan Utara* (TNKU), an armed group led by Azahari in Brunei, than it was to groups in Indonesia. To show its solidarity with TNKU, SLL changed its name to the North Kalimantan Liberation League. Different members from this organization split off to form the United National Revolutionary Front of North Kalimantan in 1965 to represent a concerted effort to unify a common cause with all the guerilla forces from Brunei, Sabah, and Sarawak, irrespective of their differing political ideologies. Similarly, in an effort to attract international recognition, on similar lines to the *Partai Komunis Indonesia* and the Communist Party of Malaya, the Sarawak Communist Organization decided to form a second wing, the *Pasukan Rakyat Kalimantan Utara* (PARAKU or North Kalimantan People's Army) in 1965. Again, following the policy of adopting names reflecting the communist aim of establishing a unitary state of North Kalimantan, the Sarawak Advanced Youths' Association was renamed the North Kalimantan Communist Youth League.

5 See Yong (2007a).

6 According to official estimates, there were more than seven battalions of Allied soldiers against less than 700 guerillas in Sarawak (The Sri Aman Treaty, 1974). According to my own source, there were close to 2,000 card-carrying communists.

7 For our purpose, it seems important to warn against any suggestion that collective memory stimulates and determines individual memory, or that memories are backwards constructions after the fact. Halbwachs was indeed critical of the individualism of the psychological theory of his time. In his book *On Collective Memory* (1992, 37–40), what he called "social frameworks of memory" are not the simple product of isolated individual memories, constructed after the fact by combinations of separate reminiscences, but are rather, in part, their source: the instruments used in particular acts of recall. "Social frameworks of memory" are best seen as public scaffolding of various forms that can trigger the specific content of

individual memory, and imbued in these forms is the embedded nature of memory and the selective or self-conscious qualities of remembering and forgetting.

8 I heard similar stories from some former guerrillas in the townships of Bau, Lundu, and Serian.

9 From my several experiences doing fieldwork in Sarawak, beginning in the summer of 1996, there seemed to exist two different layers of interaction among the different ethnic groups or the general public in Sarawak: one based on relatively amicable interactions without involving entanglements with the law, and the other informed by the politics of race that constantly remind its population of the racial and political divide. In other words, from one perspective, Malaysia is a shining example of racial harmony in the postcolonial age. However, seen another way, the social construct of race pervades the national consciousness at every turn. The way most of the lower working class Chinese population had been categorized and displaced in Sarawak and their cynicism towards the State (and this applies to the general public as well) contributed to a fortified separation between the general public and those in office.

10 Besides Lefebvre, for a discussion of the modern state project of nationalizing territorial spaces under socialism, see Poulantzas (1978). On India, see Goswami (2004).

11 The alleged rumor about Bong's complicity with the State is understandable considering the gifts he received upon "persuading" his comrades to "come out." As Marcel Mauss ([1950] 1990) pointed out long ago, the social character of any gift enjoins not only reciprocity but also complicity as well (Boyer 2006).

12 The fact that these former guerillas were given this gift was not without its ironies. Their acceptance of the gift signified their acceptance of a certain risk, the possibility of enforced alliance, and made them easier to monitor within a single complex – that of the Hawker Centre. As I mentioned earlier, I believe this was what Bataille and Deleuze took from Nietzsche about the risk of accepting a *gift* in their discussions about the problems of inscription, of coding, of marking the bodies of those who receive the debts of gifts.

13 I was told that there had been more Malay vendors ten years ago but, due to the lack of business, they had either given up or moved to more "modern" retail venues. One of the Chinese vendors told me it was easier for the Malays to relocate because they could secure small business loans from the government, something that is not available to non-Malays.

14 When asked to describe their living conditions, some of my interlocutors would tell me they owned the house they lived in as opposed to others who rented theirs, including those who could only afford a room: "They are quite poor, five to a room."

15 The collective memories of a society, especially on issues of violence, differ in focus and intensity depending on the prevailing social and historical context. For example, in repressive societies, when the population does not want to remember a certain past, we talk about not only a loss of social continuity, characterized by the language of loss – "rupture," "fissure," and "fracture" – but also a loss of openness and integrity. Seen in a different light, one might say that it is something people in those societies have forgotten to remember. Drawing on Nietzsche's ([1874] 1983) essay, "On the Uses and Disadvantages of History for Life," Edward Casey (1987, 1–4) suggests that, like the bovine, people are capable of "forgetting what it is to remember," even to the point of having "forgotten [their] own forgetting."

16 Gunung Gading is located in the northwest of Sarawak. Part of this mountain's range falls on the Indonesian side of Borneo.

17 Once, Chao Kui Ho asked me if the Ghurkas were aware that they were colonized subjects of the British Empire. Similarly, on two different field projects with the Selakos in northwest Sarawak, I heard some of them talking about the bravery of the Ghurkas when it came to jungle warfare, noting that they were always sent to the front line of the conflict before the Allied forces.

18 I am using "ideology" here in a generalized sense; some details or descriptions of communist ideologies will come up in this chapter and beyond, thus giving a local flavour to the idea of what communism was in Sarawak.

19 As E.P. Thompson's (1980) classic study points out, bread riots and food protests are not mere rebellions of the belly but are best viewed as a highly complex form of direct popular action, disciplined and with clear objectives. Thompson's formulation about the eighteenth-century English crowd offers one description of Sarawak in the 1960s and 1970s as an area where antigovernment revolts play out his concept of a "moral economy of protest."

20 According to Porrit (2004), the government filled up the land because the waterways were thought to work as a convenient network of escape routes for the communists.

21 As Carolyn Nordstrom and Antonius Robben (1995) note, rumours are a common problem for ethnographers investigating issues on past violence, and the important thing is to explicate the secrecy behind these rumors. As

far as mass graves at *Hai Wai* are concerned, I am not aware if anyone has investigated the truth behind such rumours.

22 For a discussion of linguistic phenomena and political economy, see Irvine (1989) and Gal (1989). Again, for a discussion of the use of modern state power to spatialize national landscape, see Lefebvre (1991).

23 What is significant for understanding these narratives is the way in which gender and societal position define what is considered to be authoritative discourse. Indeed, Bakhtin (1981) shows that hierarchies are intrinsic to language.

4. Any Other Day at the Bus Station

1 "Old timers" refers to the original partners that helped set up the company, as well as employees who had worked at SOC for more than thirty or forty years.

2 Some anthropologists and other advocates of "conversation analysis" are sensitive to the difference between dialogue and conversation. To them, "conversation" is preferred over "dialogue" in order to stress the unequal power relations in any communication (see Goodwin and Heritage 1990; M. Goodwin 1990; Desjarlais 1997). For the purpose of my research, I am using the terms interchangeably, in part because my interlocutors described our verbal interactions or socializing with the Chinese term *"Tan-Hua"* or *"Cerita"* in Malay. *"Tan-Hua"* can mean a dialogue, a conversation, or multiple conversations. *"Cerita"* literally means stories but here it refers to conversations or a dialogue. I use "conversations" since, most of the time, not only was I having a dialogue with both of them but there was also concurrent dialogue between the two of them. In short, there were concurrent, if not simultaneous, dialogues happening at certain points of our meeting.

3 Throughout my fieldwork, most if not all of my working relations would have been impossible had I insisted on taping our conversations. Some of them would only talk to me on condition that I did not ask for their names and addresses.

4 As Robert Desjarlais (1997) points out, the Bakhtinian focus on intertextuality that underscores the role of others in shaping the self and personhood in people's lives (and thus getting away from the idea of human beings as autonomous, monadic, monologic, and self-constituting), is unfortunately geared towards a tendency that pays more attention to the discourse of speaking than to active reception in listening. See also Don Ihde (1976) and Gemma Corradi Fiumara (1990) for a similar critique of ideas of discourse and talking over those of listening.

5 For the most part, the lingua franca in rural Sarawak is Hopo Khek.
6 Incidentally, considering Hopo and Taipu as Hakka dialects would fit awkwardly within the usual linguistic definitions of dialect and language. In Western linguistic terms, speakers of different dialects should understand each other as long as the dialects they speak are from the same language. Hopo and Taipu are quite different and they are not necessarily fully comprehensible for speakers from each dialect group. For that reason, some of my interlocutors could not understand my Taipu Khek and would subsequently converse with me in Mandarin, Hokkien, or Teochiu, depending on the language with which we felt most comfortable.
7 Since being in North America, I have not had any opportunity to converse in the Chinese languages with which I am familiar. As such, it took me more than a month of living in Sarawak to "recover" the languages I used during my fieldwork.
8 Sometimes I leave phrases in the original language(s) before attempting to translate them into English, in part because a translation loses the original feeling or meaning and also because certain words, phrases, or expressions are difficult, if not impossible, to translate directly into English.
9 John Brewer's (1990) *Sinews of Power* provides a brilliant insight into Britain's emergence as a major international power in the eighteenth century. It shows how the drastic increase in Britain's military involvement in Europe and elsewhere, and the development of her commercial and imperial interests, would not have happened without a concurrent radical increase in taxation along with a substantial public administration.
10 See especially the introduction chapter of *Questions of Modernity* (Mitchell 2000).
11 I would constantly hear from many Sarawakians about the devaluation of their currencies. Since the 1997 financial and economic crisis, the Malaysian ringgit has been pegged at 1 U.S. dollar for 3.8 Malaysian ringgits. Prior to that, it was 1 U.S. dollar for 2.1 Malaysian ringgits.
12 In 1999, the tax was 60 ringgits per passenger per annum. As such, for a bus with a carrying capacity of fifty passengers, the tax will be $60 \times 50 = 3,000$ ringgits per year. With the SOC owning 200 buses, it cost the company quite a lot of taxes per year.
13 For example, the minivans I mentioned earlier that serve the Malay villages in the coastal area (*Hai Wai*).
14 This was the main news for over a week. It concerned a group of heavily armed men who attempted to rob guns and artillery from a military installation. According to all the local newspapers, the government claimed that the entire affair was masterminded by the PAS, one of the opposition

parties, to disrupt the so-called peace and prosperity of the country. Of course, this proved to be untrue.

15 Subjects that were once taught in English were switched to Malay at national schools following the implementation of the NEP. Consequently, many non-Malay families who could afford to send their children abroad to receive an English education, especially to England, did so in the 1970s. According to Foreign Minister A. Kohilan Pillay, in 2007, the number of Malaysians who had migrated overseas was 139,696. As of August 2009, the figure had jumped to 304,358. This was incidentally reported by the government official news agency, *Bernama* (November 30, 2009, http://www.bernama.com/bernama/v5/newsindex.php?id=458777).

16 A few bus drivers and conductors at another bus company, the Kuching Transport Company (KTC), had mentioned these anti-government pamphlets as well.

17 A red identification card was issued to convicts regardless of whether one was ever charged while being detained in prison. The colour red, obviously, is not without any indexical intention. Once one was released from prison, one received a brown identity card, forever marking the subject as an ex-convict. The "normal" identity card is blue in colour.

18 To be sure, William Skinner, the leading scholar on the Chinese in Southeast Asia during the Cold War period, also compared the Chinese in Thailand with the Chinese in Indonesia.

19 In early 1967, the Indonesian authorities forced thousands of Chinese in West Kalimantan into labour programs. Thousands were forced to work on road construction, in rice fields, and on the construction of army barracks. In late 1967, in an effort to wipe out local communist rebellion, Soeharto's military officers together with Dayak "warriors" massacred thousands and expunged close to 450,000 ethnic Chinese, the majority of which were Hakkas from inland Sambas area of West Kalimantan. The massacres of late 1967 and early 1968 were accompanied by the massive relocation of ethnic Chinese into hundreds of camps at Pontianak, Singkawang, Mempawah, and Pemangkat where overcrowding, food rations, scant medical supplies, assault by guards, malaria, and incidents of suicide were common (Davidson 2008; see also Peluso 2006; Hui 2007; Heidhues 2005). Incidentally, it is quite ironic that only the Indonesian Chinese are referred to as "citizens of Indonesia" (*warga negara* Indonesia) where everyone else, meaning non-Indonesian Chinese, are either sons or daughters of the soil. I should also mention that it was not until the year 2000 that the "citizens" of Indonesia were allowed to celebrate their Chinese New Year.

20 In the aftermath of the 1997 Asian Financial Crisis and Soeharto's resignation, anti-Chinese riots broke out in Jakarta and Solo. Reports of rapes of

Chinese Indonesian women occurred on a widespread scale on May 13, 14, and 15, 1998. See, for example Sai (2006); Tay (2006) for the racial riots in Jakarta; Purdey (2006) for another anti-Chinese riot in Solo.

5. What's There to Tell?

1 Even though the Special Branch was once tasked with the mission to gather information from the public as part of its strategy to fight the communist insurgency during the Malayan Emergency and beyond, after the end of the Cold War, it turned its attention towards repressing dissent at all levels, essentially becoming one of the eyes and ears of the ruling regime.

2 Only as recently as 2009 has there been "whispers" about possible mass graves located in so-called communist sensitive areas in Sarawak. I hadn't heard of it during my fieldwork from 1999 to 2000. In 2009, the Friendship Associations were set up by former communists in Kuching, Sibu, and Miri in an effort to present their oral version of the struggles against colonialism. It is important to note that there is no mention of their struggles against the current government.

3 Interestingly, when I asked one of these pepper farmers when the fences were taken down, all I got was an approximated answer, sometime during the mid-1970s. When I asked him again, a few weeks later, he said, after some hesitation, that it must have been sometime in the 1980s. Such is memory and such is the anxiety of the anthropologist to get the facts right. According to historian Vernon Porrit (2004), it was not until 1976 that the government decided to shorten the curfew at these new villages by two hours, from 7:00 p.m. to 4:00 a.m. to allow residents to leave the settlements early if they needed to attend to their gardens. It would take another four years, not until March 5, 1980, that all restrictions were finally lifted in the entire Operation Hammer area. For fifteen years these residents lived through a dusk-to-dawn curfew with its corresponding restrictions and trauma.

4 *Goyang kaki* (shaking one's leg) denotes that one's life is so free that it allows one a lot of time to sit around and shake one's leg. Similarly, *Senang* (easy) means one is having an easy life.

5 These agreements were informal because there was no written documentation. Legally, only the indigenous can have titles to NCR lands in Sarawak.

6 Once I helped Huah Li move into a low-cost apartment she would be sharing with her cousins. This was the bus conductor I mentioned earlier whose father and brother were killed in Siburan. As if Huah Li was aware that I might be thinking how tiny her two-bedroom apartment was, she assured me it was far better than Siburan. As she put it, "At least

I now have my own bedroom. Back then, we were crammed up, all seven of us!"

7   The normal way of taking a shower is to use a plastic cup to scoop water from a plastic or ceramic container.

8   I heard from some drivers that the soldiers would confiscate these "weapons" as proof of one's complicity with the communists and would then use these confiscated "weapons" as propitious tools by which they surveyed and controlled the *new villages'* populations.

9   As Michael Taussig (1999) points out, truth often comes in the form of a public secret; something that *one knows but ought not to know*. I might add: it is something that *one knows but ought not to talk about*.

10 There are no official records of such an ice-slab torture technique as a means to extract information. As such, who is going to believe these stories?

11 Veena Das (2007) argues that the abduction and rape of women during the Partition ironically opened up the way in which the state could be institutes as a social contract between men, in essence as men in charge of keeping violence against women. In all of these, women were not allowed to speak. As Das (2007) points out, "Thus, the story about abduction and recovery acts as a foundation story that authorizes a particular relation between social contract and sexual contract – the former being a contract between men to institute the political and the latter the agreement to place women within the home under the authority of the husband/father figure" (21).

12 The bus companies in Sarawak issued employee's identification numbers and the employees at the KTC had the habit of addressing each other by the employee's ID numbers as opposed to their names or nicknames. In the case of Mrs. Pang, her number was C61. "C" stood for conductor and "D" for driver. This was not the case at SOC.

13 Recall the three heroes at the opening of this book.

14 Depending on the routes, on an average twelve-hour workday (from 6 a.m. to 6 p.m.), a bus has to make between twenty to thirty-two runs. Each run begins at the bus station and goes on a predetermined route. There is a maximum break of only five minutes between each run and this was when most bus conductors and drivers took their quick lunch or coffee break. Most drivers would speed up during certain runs to make up more time for lunch. The bottom line is that they had to make the number of assigned bus runs. I have seen bus conductors having their lunch on the bus while they were working. Some bus drivers would eat snacks while driving as part of their lunch.

15 This reminds me of something Trinh Minh-ha T. (1989) once wrote: "Silence as a refusal to take part in the story does sometimes provide us with
a means to gain a hearing. It is a voice, a mode of uttering, and a response
in its own right. Without other silences, however, my silence goes unheard,
unnoticed; it is simply one voice less, (one) more point given to the silenc-
ers" (83). To remain indifferent to the gossip in this case, is to not give in
and to not participate, since speaking up might intensify the gossip and
losing one's temper would mean having to see the satisfied grins and the
mean pleasure of having gotten a reaction. Speech for the sake of speech
only worked to keep Huah Li tied to those who would assume her silence.
Perhaps Huah Li was aware of that.

16 *Maggie Mee* is a popular brand of instant noodles. It is a common practice
in Malaysia for politicians from the ruling regime to promise development
projects, even money (read sarcastically as "instant noodles" goodies) as a
tool in this carrot-and-stick game to garner votes days before an election.
This is especially true for the rural constituents that were without or lack-
ing in modern amenities.

17 False consciousness in this sense usually denotes a degree of passivity, if
not a fatalistic acceptance and personal complicity on the part of the subordinates of their social order. In the Marxist tradition, this is usually associated with the arguments made by Gramsci (1971) that emphasize more
the level of ideas than behaviour. However, many have argued that even
a close reading of Gramsci does not tell you how voluntary and complete
hegemony is in any setting (for an excellent discussion of hegemony and
consciousness, see Joseph Femia (1975). Similarly, Perry Anderson (1976)
has pointed out that "hegemony" was first used by the Bolsheviks to refer
to the domination of the peasantry by the proletariat, which implies more
political control rather than consent (for a convincing elucidation that
there was dominance without hegemony during British Colonial India, see
Guha 1997).

6. Virtuous Subjects

1 Following the work of Lefebvre in theorizing space, or more specifically,
on the state mode of production of state space or state territory, there has
been an intensification of scholarly interest in the geographies of state
space (see, for example, Soja 2000; Escobar 2003; Goswami 2004; Agnew
2005; Sassen 2006).

2 See Purdey (2006) for an analysis of the complicity of ethnic brokers in the
context of Indonesia.

3 I use the concept "hegemony" with reservation since I am not entirely
   convinced it is an appropriate concept for the (post)colonial given that
   most subjectivities were born out of conscriptions instead of acceptance
   or compliance (for a similar argument, see, Guha 1997; Mbembe 2001;
   Comaroff 1991).

4 See especially *On the Old Saw: That May Be Right in Theory but It Won't Work
   in Practice* (1974).

5 See also Jameson (1981), especially chap. 1.

6 In Mandarin, egg (*chee-tan*) also stands for zero or nothingness.

7 See Tanya Li's (1999) discussion of similar phenomenon in Indonesia.

8 Obviously, it is not just surveys and statistics that should concern us but
   the actual processes, the inscription of subject-making of these technologies that allow us to explicate the links between State scientific power and
   statistics for they are steeped in political, economic, and technological imperatives. As Eduardo Galeano (1992) has written so eloquently, statistics
   see only what it wants to see, citing a few "successful" examples and obscuring others. Statistics admits but does not repent. The ways it has been
   used usually ends up sacrificing the poor as the "social cost" of progress.

9 *Pakatan Rakyat* (PR) is a coalition of opposition parties formed in April 2008
   as a counterweight to the ruling *Barisan Nasional* regime. PR is comprised
   of the People Justice Party (PKR), the Democratic Action Party (DAP), and
   the Pan-Malaysian Islamic Party (PAS). In the 2008 Twelve Malaysian general elections, PR managed to capture the state of Selangor, Penang, Kelantan, Kedah, and Perak. However, the BN has since recaptured the state of
   Perak due to the jumping-over of some PR state parliament representatives
   to either BN component parties or as pro-BN independent representatives.

10 As I have noted earlier, this was a moot point, since the 1969 Sarawak state
   elections were suspended by the federal government after the May 13 riots
   in West Malaysia.

11 Within a span of a few minutes, Hong had twice compared the situation in
   Sarawak against Indonesia. He was, after all, a representative of the State.

12 Pay had a few years of medium-level Chinese education. He was also one
   of the old timers.

13 In contrast, the Malay bus conductors and drivers I got to know were
   quite vocal when it came to the *Reformasi* movement taking root in various
   Malay villages around Kuching. There were many *Reformasi* flags flying on
   long bamboo poles in the Malay villages across the Sarawak River.

14 In Malaysia, the term "Very Important Person" is no longer trendy.
   Anyone who can afford philanthropy can have some sort of *pangkat* (title)
   bestowed on them by the sultans or the king. As such, you now have the

term, "VVIP" for "Very, Very, Important Person." However, I should add that because of the facility with which one could acquire titles in Malaysia, many of my subjects considered them as meaningless, although still in use, the same way one may be an atheist and still say "Thank God."

15 Stephen Yong was the former chairman and the secretary general of the SUPP.

16 A bus driver also confided in me that he suspected Hong was told to shut up "or else." Or perhaps Hong might have seen the bigger picture; that it was pointless to oppose the coalition government when all the SUPP possessed during the 1960s was diplomacy without firepower. The odds were stacked too heavily against them – they had to deal with the federal government in Kuala Lumpur and the Alliance Government in Sarawak and, on top of that, the powerful external forces that were subsidizing the War on Communism. The manoeuvres available to the leaders of the SUPP were simply ploys to buy time, not positions they could secure or improve upon.

17 This split-voting trend is not unique to the Chinese populations in Sarawak but is also common among the minorities across Malaysia.

18 See Duranti (1993, 1994) for a similar argument from the participants in a politico-judiciary meeting in a Western Samoa village.

19 See Asad (1991) for a discussion of postcolonial subjects as conscripts of modernity.

7. Sites of Impermanence

1 This cashier used to be a bus conductor. She told me she missed chatting with her former colleagues.

2 The policy of rewarding ticket inspectors for catching employees "stealing" on the job had the effect of encouraging them to fabricate cases. During my fieldwork, upon mounting complaints by the employees, the management was forced to fire a ticket inspector because he was fabricating all sorts of questionable "cheating incidents." In fact, this ticket inspector often boasted about his feats to me.

3 It is worth emphasizing here that the restructuring and transformation of space is not a recent phenomenon. Lefebvre's point that space must never be viewed as having a static character anticipates recent works that emphasize the contemporary reconstitution of territory rather than its erosion or dissolution (see Scholte 2000).

4 I mention "if and when the development happened" because that was how most of these individuals at the bus station talked about it. In Sarawak,

such a project usually takes a long time to materialize. But it did happen. The bus station, wet market, and the Ban Hock Hawker Centre were demolished in 2009 and the SOC is now operating at a new bus station in the outskirts of Kuching. Meanwhile, it is anyone's guess as to who the new tenants were once the "modern" retail arcades were built.

5 These were funeral expenses for a union member or a member of his/her immediate family.

6 According to the old timer, Pay Lai En, before the 1980s, 70 to 80 per cent of the SOC employees were union members and the company had around 800 employees. Considering that, the actual percentage of union members was not a mere drop of 20 to 30 per cent but significantly higher.

7 YB Datuk Sim Kheng Hui, was the secretary general of the SUPP as well as a State Assemblyman. There is no blood relation with YB Sim Kheng Hong. He was one of the few YBs I spoke to about my research. As I mentioned earlier, this was my strategy to get the story to George Hong's uncle, the mayor of Kuching South, especially about me being escorted out of the SUPP headquarters by this security guard under the directive of the new management.

8 From an economic standpoint, since the implementation of the NEP, Malaysia's systems of inequality and domination could be credited with a degree of effectiveness in the allocation of utilities and privileges. I am referring here to the salaries of the massive number of civil servants. It is important to bring out the relations that existed between the salary and the constitution of political subjects. In theory, a salary is a remuneration obtained for work done or services and duties performed. "Work" is understood as the time and the effort devoted to the production of what is "useful." It would not be a stretch to state that within the government and semi-government bureaucracies in Malaysia, there was no automatic relationship either between work (its quantity and its value) and salary, or between the salary earned, the utilities produced, and the resulting general wealth. One could get "rich" without much "effort," devoting time to the production of things that were perfectly useless or, at any event, contributed nothing to the formation of the common wealth. In these contexts, the prime purpose of the salary was not to remunerative productivity but rather, an essential cog in the dynamic of relations between state and society. It acted as a resource the state could use to buy obedience and gratitude and to break the population to habits of discipline. The salary was what legitimated not only subjection but also the constitution of a type of political exchange based not on the principle of political equality and equal representation but on the existence of *claims through which the state created*

debts on society. By transforming the salary into a claim, the state granted a means of livelihood to all it had put under obligation. This, moreover, is why, in some public speeches, these claims were treated if not as favours, then at least as privileges (see Mbembe 2001).

9 This was the same security officer who interrupted my conversation with a bus driver.

10 It was Nietzsche's explication on *promises* that Austin uses to formulate his theorization of speech act, especially on the notion of felicity/infelicity (see Shoshana Felman 1983).

11 For example, the difficulties in getting paid leaves or sick leaves, a three-day limit to receiving an answer to a memo from head office, a guarantor and deposit to work at the SOC, the difficulty of meeting face to face with their colleagues at head office, and so on.

12 For example, new station managers, office managers at the head office, security officers, and more ticket inspectors.

13 The concept "disinterested liking" is taken from Kant, *Critique of Judgment* ([1952] 1964).

8. Facing the Artefact

1 I could think of South Africa's TRC that was considered a success by the international community in allowing the country to transcend apartheid, to be *born again* so to speak, and move towards the building of a new nation-state. But other social critics have argued that the TRC was nothing but a theatre that sidestepped the true violence of the apartheid regime (Mamdani 2000; Feldman 2004). Similarly, the degree of selectivity in the appointment of judges and other officials to the Cambodian TRC gives one pause over the national and international politics behind the commission. The refusal of the *mothers* in Argentina to participate in the yearly government-sponsored day of forgiveness also speaks volumes not only to such orchestrated theatres of reconciliation but also to the refusal on the part of these *mothers* to find *closure* that the *romantic* scrip of the state is demanding (Gordon 1997). The list of problems with the TRCs, not to mention issues in defining *rights*, is well documented and to rehash these problems would be unnecessary.

2 Views of memory as embedded or embodied is nothing new. Frederic Bartlett (1932) once argued that the memories that we are allowed "to speak of are interest-determined, interest-carried traces" (211–12). Halbwachs (1980) was among the first to point out the connection between memory and identity. (See also Casey 1987.) Many critics have pointed

out its functionalist legacy and suggest that the relationship between past and present cannot be reduced to an interest-based model (Hamilton 1998; Cole 2001). Others have also pointed out how such a view of memory has the tendency to emphasize the political aspect of memory at the expense of the moral (Cole 1998; Lambek 1998; Werbner 1995).

3 One easily forgets that the category majority and minority share a similar characteristic to the age-old equation of master/slave. One came into existence in tandem with the other. But unlike master/slave, majority/minority is a recent creation in Southeast Asia. There is no word or concept for it in any of the Southeast Asian indigenous languages. As Benedict Anderson (1998) points out, the construction of majority and minorities "were born out of the political and cultural revolution brought about by the maturing of the colonial state and by the rise against it of popular nationalism. The former fundamentally changed the structures and aims of governance, the latter its legitimacy" (318).

4 According to Arendt (2005, 58-9), there is always the paradoxical and ethical tension with *forgiveness* in that forgivers can be deservedly criticized for failing to remember the injustices they had endured – and remembrance implies, if not vengeance, at least an unwillingness to let go of the desire for vengeance. See also Agamben (2005).

Bibliography

Ackerman, Susan E., and Raymond L.M. Lee. 1988. *Heaven in Transition: Non-Muslim Religious Innovation and Ethnic Identity in Malaysia*. Honolulu: University of Hawaii Press.

Agamben, Giorgio. 2005. *The Time that Remains: A Commentary on the Letter to the Romans*. Translated by Patricia Dailey. Stanford, CA: Stanford University Press.

Agha, Asif. 2005. "Introduction." *Journal of Linguistic Anthropology* 15 (1): 1–5. http://dx.doi.org/10.1525/jlin.2005.15.1.1.

Agnew, John. 2005. "Sovereignty Regimes: Territoriality and State Authority in Contemporary World Politics." *Annals of the Association of American Geographers. Association of American Geographers* 95 (2): 437–61. http://dx.doi.org/10.1111/j.1467-8306.2005.00468.x.

Alatas, Syed Hussein. 1977. *The Myth of the Lazy Native: A Study of the Image of the Malays, Filipinos and Javanese from the 16th to the 20th Century and Its Function in the Ideology of Colonial Capitalism*. London: Frank Cass.

Amadiume, Ifi, and Abdullahi An-Na'im, eds. 2000. *The Politics of Memory: Truth, Healing and Social Justice*. London: Zed Books.

Anderson, Benedict. 1966. "Japan: The Light of Asia." In *Southeast Asia in World War II: Four Essays*. Edited by Josef Silverstein, 13–50. New Haven: Yale University Southeast Asian Studies.

Anderson, Benedict. 1991. *Imagined Communities: Reflections on the Origin and Spread of Nationalism*. Rev. ed. London: Verso.

Anderson, Benedict. 1998. *Spectre of Comparisons: Nationalism, Southeast Asia and the World*. London: Verso.

Anderson, Perry. 1976. "The Antinomies of Antonio Gramsci." *New Left Review* 100: 6.

Antze, Paul, and Michael Lambeck, eds. 1996. *Tense Past: Cultural Essays in Trauma and Memory.* New York: Routledge.

Arendt, Hannah. 1951. *The Origin of Totalitarianism.* New York: Harcourt Brace Jovanovich.

Arendt, Hannah. 2005. "The Tradition of Political Thought." In *Arendt, The Promise of Politics.* Edited by Jerome Kohn, New York: Schocken.

Arrighi, Giovanni. 1995. *The Long Twentieth Century: Money, Power and the Origins of Our Times.* London: Verso.

Asad, Talal. 1987. "Are There Histories of Peoples Without Europe?" *Comparative Studies in Society and History* 29 (3): 594–607. http://dx.doi.org/10.1017/S0010417500014742.

Asad, Talal. 1991. "Conscripts of Western Civilization." In *Dialectical Anthropology: Essays in Honor of Stanley Diamond.* Vol. 1, *Civilization in Crisis.* Edited by Christine Gailey, 335–51. Gainesville, FL: University Press of Florida.

Asad, Talal. 1993. *Genealogies of Religion: Discipline and Reasons of Power in Christianity and Islam.* Baltimore, MD: Johns Hopkins University Press.

Asad, Talal. 2000. "Agency and Pain: An Exploration." *Culture and Religion* 1 (1): 29–60. http://dx.doi.org/10.1080/01438300008567139.

Asli, Mohd Reduan Hj. 1993. *Pemberontakan Bersenjata Komunis diMalaysia* (Armed communist rebellion in Malaysia). Kuala Lumpur: Dewan Bahasa dan Pustaka.

Austin, J.L. 1962. *How to Do Things with Words.* Cambridge, MA: Harvard University Press.

Bahloul, Joelle. 1996. *The Architecture of Memory: A Jewish-Muslim Household in Colonial Algeria, 1937–1962.* New York: Cambridge University Press.

Bakhtin, Mikhail. 1981. *The Dialogic Imagination: Four Essays.* Michael Holquist. Edited and translated by Caryl Emerson and Michael Holquist. Austin: University of Texas Press.

Bakhtin, Mikhail. [1965] 1984. *Rabelais and His World.* Translated by H. Iswolsky. Bloomington: Indiana University Press.

Barthes, Roland. [1957] 1972. *Mythologies.* Translated by Annette Lavers. New York: Hill and Wang.

Bartlett, Frederic. 1932. *Remembering: A Study in Experimental and Social Psychology.* Cambridge: Cambridge University Press. http://dx.doi.org/10.1111/j.2044-8279.1933.tb02913.x

Bassett, David. 1980. "British Attitudes to Indigenous States in Southeast Asia in the Nineteenth Century." Centre for South-East Studies Occasional Papers, No.1. University of Hull, Yorkshire, UK.

Basso, Keith. 1983. "'Stalking with Stories': Names, Places, and Moral Narratives among the Western Apache." In *Text, Play, and Story: The Construction and Reconstruction of Self and Society, Proceedings of the American Ethnological Society.* Edited by Edward M. Bruner, 19–55. Long Grove, IL: Waveland Press.

Basso, Keith. 1996. "Wisdom Sits in Places: Notes on a Western Apache Landscape." In *Senses of Place.* Edited by Steven Feld and Keith Basso, 53–90. Santa Fe, NM: School of American Research Press.

Bataille, Georges. 1991. *The Accursed Share. An Essay on General Economy.* Vol. 1. *Consumption.* New York: Zone Books.

Benda, Harry J. 1972. "The Structure of Southeast Asian History: Some Preliminary Observations." In *Continuity and Change in Southeast Asia,* 121–53. New Haven: Yale University Southeast Asian Studies. http://dx.doi.org/10.1017/S0217781100000582

Benjamin, Walter. 1968. "Theses on the Philosophy of History." In *Illuminations. Hannah Arendt.* Edited and translated by Harry Zohn, 253–64. New York: Schocken.

Benjamin, Walter. 1978. "A Berlin Chronicle." In *Reflections.* Edited by Peter Demetz. Translated by Edmund Jephcott, 3–62. New York: Schocken.

Benjamin, Walter. 1999. *Selected Writings.* Vol. 2, *1927–1934.* Edited by Michael W. Jennings, Howard Eiland, and Gary Smith. Translated by Rodney Livingstone et al. Cambridge, MA: Belknap Press.

Berger, John. 1972. *Ways of Seeing.* London: British Broadcasting Corporation, with Penguin Books.

Berger, Peter, and Hsin-Huang Hsiao, eds. 1988. *In Search of an East Asian Development Model.* New Brunswick, NJ: Transaction.

Blanc, Cristina Szanton. 1997. "The Thoroughly Modern 'Asian': Capital, Culture, and Nation in Thailand and the Philippines.' In *Ungrounded Empire: The Cultural Politics of Modern Chinese Transnationalism.* Edited by Aihwa Ong and Donald Nonini, 261–86. New York: Routledge.

Blanchot, Maurice. [1980] 1995. *The Writing of the Disaster.* Translated by Ann Smock. Lincoln: University of Nebraska Press.

Bloch, Maurice. 1998. *How We Think They Think.* Boulder, CO: Westview Press.

Boyer, Dominique. 2006. "Ostalgie and the Politics of the Future." *Public Culture* 18 (2): 361–81. http://dx.doi.org/10.1215/08992363-2006-008.

Breman, Jan. 1989. *Taming the Coolie Beast: Plantation Society and the Colonial Order in Southeast Asia.* Delhi: Oxford University Press.

Brenner, Neil, and Stuart Elden. 2009. "Henry Lefebvre on State, Space, Territory." *International Political Sociology* 3 (4): 353–77. http://dx.doi.org/10.1111/j.1749-5687.2009.00081.x.

Brewer, John. 1990. *The Sinews of Power: War, Money and the English State.* Boston: Harvard University Press.

Buruma, Ian. 1995. *Wages of Guilt: Memories of War in Germany and Japan*. New York: Farrar, Straus, and Giroux.

Buse, Peter, Ken Hirschkop, Scott McCracken, and Bertrand Taithe. 2005. *Benjamin's Arcades: An Unguided Tour*. Manchester: Manchester University Press.

Butalia, Urvashi. 2000. *The Other Side of Silence: Voices from the Partition of India*. Durham, NC: Duke University Press.

Campbell, Persia Crawford. 1971. *Chinese Coolie Emigration to Countries within the British Empire*. 2nd ed. London: Frank Cass.

Carroll, John. 1981. "Toward a Functional Theory of Names and Naming." *Linguistics* 21: 341–71.

Casey, Edward S. 1987. *Remembering: A Phenomenology Study*. Bloomington: Indiana University Press.

Castells, Manuel. 1996. *The Rise of the Network Society*. Malden, MA: Blackwell Publishers.

Chang, Iris. 1997. *The Rape of Nanking: The Forgotten Holocaust of World War II*. New York: Basic Books.

Cheah, Pheng. 1999. "Grounds of Comparison." *Diacritics* 29 (4): 3–18. http://dx.doi.org/10.1353/dia.1999.0026.

Chew, Daniel. 1990. *Chinese Pioneers on the Sarawak Frontier, 1845–1941*. Singapore: Oxford University Press.

Chin, C.C., and Karl Hack. 2004. *Dialogues with Chin Peng: New Light on the Malayan Communist Party*. Singapore: Singapore University Press.

Chirot, Daniel, and Anthony Reid. 1997. *Essential Outsiders: Chinese and Jews in the Modern Transformation of Southeast Asia and Central Europe*. Seattle: University of Washington Press.

Clark, Katerina, and Michael Holquist. 1984. *Mikhail Bakhtin*. Cambridge, MA: Harvard University Press.

Clifford, James. 1988. *The Predicament of Culture: Twentieth-Century Ethnography, Literature, and Art*. Cambridge, MA: Harvard University Press.

Cole, Jennifer. 1998. "The Uses of Defeat: Memory and Political Morality in East Madagascar." In *Memory and the Postcolony: African Anthropology and the Critique of Power*. Edited by Richard Werbner, 102–25. London: Zed Books.

Cole, Jennifer. 2001. *Forget Colonialism? Sacrifice and the Art of Memory in Madagascar*. Berkeley: University of California Press.

Comaroff, Jean, and John Comaroff. 1991. *Of Revelation and Revolution*. Vol. 1, *Christianity, Colonialism, and Consciousness in South Africa*. Chicago: University of Chicago Press.

Comber, Leon. 2008. *Malaya's Secret Police 1945–60: The Role of the Special Branch in the Malayan Emergency*. Singapore: Institute of Southeast Asian Studies.

Connerton, Paul. 1989. *How Societies Remember*. Cambridge: Cambridge University Press. http://dx.doi.org/10.1017/CBO9780511628061.

Constable, Nicole, ed. 1996. *Guest People: Hakka Identity in China and Abroad*. Seattle: University of Washington Press.

Coppel, Charles. 1983. *Indonesia's Chinese in Crisis*. Kuala Lumpur: Oxford University Press.

Corrigan, Philip, and Derek Sayer. 1985. *The Great Arch: English State Formation as Cultural Revolution*. New York: Basil Blackwell.

Crapanzano, Vincent. 1984. "Life-Histories." *American Anthropologist* 86 (4): 953–60. http://dx.doi.org/10.1525/aa.1984.86.4.02a00080.

Crapanzano, Vincent. 2004. *Imaginative Horizons: An Essay in Literary Philosophical Anthropology*. Chicago: University of Chicago Press.

Cross, John. 1989. *Jungle Warfare: Experiences and Encounters*. London: Guild Publishing.

Cushman, Jennifer, and Gungwu Wang. 1988. *Changing Identities of the Southeast Asian Chinese Since World War II*. Hong Kong: Hong Kong University Press.

Daniel, E. Valentine. 1996. *Charred Lullabies: Chapters in an Anthropography of Violence*. Princeton, NJ: Princeton University Press.

Das, Veena. 1997. "Language and Body: Transaction in the Construction of Pain." In *Social Suffering*. Edited by A. Kleinman, V. Das, and M. Lock, 67–92. Berkeley: California University Press.

Das, Veena. 2000. "The Act of Witnessing: Violence, Poisonous Knowledge, and Subjectivity." In *Violence and Subjectivity*. Edited by Veena Das, Arthur Kleinman, Mamphela Ramphele, and Pamela Reynolds, 205–25. Berkeley: University of California Press.

Das, Veena. 2007. *Life and Words: Violence and the Descent into the Ordinary*. Berkeley: University of California Press.

Davidson, Jamie. 2008. *From Rebellion to Riots: Collective Violence on Indonesian Borneo*. Madison: University of Wisconsin Press.

Davis, Mike. 1984. "The Political Economy of Late-Imperial America." *New Left Review* (1) 143: 6–38.

Daws, Gavan. 1994. *Prisoners of the Japanese: POWs of World War II in the Pacific*. New York: William Morrow.

Day, Sophie, Evthymios Papataxiarchis, and Michael Stewart. 1999. "Consider the Lilies of the Field." In *Lilies of the Field: Marginal People Who Live for the Moment*. Edited by Sophia Day, Evthymios Papataxiarchis, and Michael Stewart, 1–26. Boulder, CO: Westview Press.

de Certeau, Michel. 1984. *The Practice of Everyday Life*. Berkeley: University of California Press.

de Certeau, Michel. 1997. *The Capture of Speech and Other Political Writings*. Edited by Luce Giard. Translated by Tom Conley. Minneapolis: University of Minnesota Press.

Deleuze, Gilles, and Felix Guattari. [1972] 1983. *Anti-Oedipus: Capitalism and Schizophrenia*. Minneapolis: University of Minnesota Press.

Derrida, Jacques. 1992. *Given Time: 1. Counterfeit Money*. Chicago: Chicago University Press.

Derrida, Jacques. 1994. *Specters of Marx: The State of the Debt, the Work of Mourning, and the New International*. Translated by Peggy Kamuf. New York: Routledge.

Derrida, Jacques. 1997. *The Politics of Friendship*. Translated by George Collins. New York: Verso.

Derrida, Jacques. 1998. *Archive Fever: A Freudian Impression*. Translated by Eric Prenowitz. Chicago: University of Chicago Press.

Desjarlais, Robert. 1997. *Shelter Blues: Sanity and Selfhood among the Homeless*. Philadelphia: University of Pennsylvania Press.

de Senarclens, Pierre. 1997. "How the United Nations Promote Development through Technical Assistance." In *The Post-Development Reader*. Edited by Majid Rahnema and Victoria Bawtree, 190–201. London: Zed Books.

Diner, Dan. 1992. "Historical Understanding and Counterrationality: The Judenrat as Epistemological Vantage." In *Probing the Limits of Representation. Nazism and the "Final Solution."* Edited by Saul Friedlander, 128–43. Cambridge, MA: Cambridge University Press.

Diprose, Rosalyn. 2002. *Corporeal Generosity: On Giving with Nietzsche, Merleau-Ponty, and Levinas*. Albany: State University of New York Press.

Dirlik, Arif. 1993. "Introducing the Pacific." In *What Is in a Rim? Critical Perspectives on the Pacific Region Idea*. Edited by A. Dirlik, 3–12. Boulder, CO: Westview.

Dostoyevsky, Fyodor. [1834] 1980. *Notes from Underground; White Nights; The Dream of a Ridiculous Man; and Selections from The House of the Dead*. Translated by Andrew R. MacAndrew. New York: New American Library.

Duby, Georges. [1974] 1985. "Ideologies in Social History." In *Constructing the Past: Essays in Historical Methodology. Jacques Le Goff and Pierre Nora*. Edited and translated by David Denby, 151–65. Cambridge: Cambridge University Press.

Duranti, Alessandro. 1993. "Intentions, Self, and Responsibility: An Essay in Samoan Ethnopragmatics." In *Responsibility and Evidence in Oral Discourse*. Edited by Jane Hill and Judith Irvine, 24–47. New York: Cambridge University Press.

Duranti, Alessandro. 1994. *From Grammar to Politics: Linguistic Anthropology in a Western Samoan Village*. Berkeley: University of California Press.

Dwyer, Leslie. 2009. "A Politics of Silences: Violence, Memory, and Treacherous Speech in Post-1965 Bali." In *Genocide: Truth, Memory, and Representation*. Edited by Alexander Laban Hinton and Kevin Lewis O'Neill, 113–46. Durham, NC: Duke University Press.

Easter, David. 2004. *Britain and the Confrontation with Indonesia, 1960–1966*. London: Tauris.

Elias, Norbert. [1969] 1983. *The Court Society*. Translated by Edmund Jephcott. New York: Pantheon Books.

Escobar, Arturo. 1995. *Encountering Development, The Making and Unmaking of the Third World*. Princeton, NJ: Princeton University Press.

Escobar, Marcelo. 2003. "Exploration, Cartography and the Modernization of State Power." In *State/Space: A Reader*. Edited by N. Brenner, B. Jessop, M. Jones, and G. MacLeod, 29–52. Cambridge, MA: Blackwell.

Evans, Gareth. [1973] 1990. "The Causal Theory of Names." In *The Philosophy of Language*, 2nd ed. Edited by Aloysius P. Martinich, 295–307. New York: Oxford University Press.

Fabian, Johannes. 1983. *Time and the Other: How Anthropology Makes Its Object*. New York: Columbia University Press.

Fang, Han-ming, and Peter Norman. 2006. "Government-Mandated Discriminatory Policies: Theory and Evidence." *International Economic Review* 47 (2): 361–89. http://dx.doi.org/10.1111/j.1468-2354.2006.00382.x.

Fanon, Frantz. 1963. *The Wretched of the Earth*. New York: Verso.

Far Eastern Economic Review. 1965. Editorial. *Far Eastern Economic Review*, July 15: 12.

Feldman, Allen. 2004. "Memory Theaters, Visual Witnessing, and the Trauma-Aesthetic." *Biography* 27 (1): 163–202. http://dx.doi.org/10.1353/bio.2004.0030.

Feldman, Allen. 2009. "The Structuring Enemy and Archival War." *Modern Language Association* 124 (4): 1240–9.

Felman, Shoshana. 1983. *The Literary Speech Act: Don Juan with J.L. Austin, or Seduction in Two Languages*. Translated by Catherine Porter. Ithaca, NY: Cornell University Press.

Femia, Joseph. 1975. "Hegemony and Consciousness in the Thoughts of Antonio Gramsci." *Political Studies* 23 (1): 29–48. http://dx.doi.org/10.1111/j.1467-9248.1975.tb00044.x.

Fidler, Richard C. 1972. "Kanowit: A Bazaar Town in Borneo." PhD diss., University of Pennsylvania.

Fiumara, Gemma Corradi. 1990. *The Other Side of Language: A Philosophy of Listening*. New York: Routledge.

Foucault, Michel. 1977. *Discipline and Punish: The Birth of the Prison*. Translated by A.M. Sheridan Smith. New York: Vintage.

Frank, Andre Gunder. 1966. "The Development of Underdevelopment." *Monthly Review (New York, N.Y.)* 18: 17–31.

Franklin, Cynthia, and Laura Lyons. 2004. "Bodies of Evidence and the Intricate Machines of Untruth." *Biography* 27 (1): v–xxii. http://dx.doi.org/10.1353/bio.2004.0031.

Freedman, Maurice. 1975. "An Epicycle of Cathay or the Southward Expansion of the Sinologists." In *Social Organization and the Applications of Anthropology*. Edited by R.J. Smith, 302–32. Ithaca, NY: Cornell University Press.

Freedman, Maurice. 1979. "The Chinese in Southeast Asia: A Longer View." In *The Study of Chinese Society*. Edited by Maurice Freedman and G. William Skinner, 39-60. Stanford, CA: Stanford University Press.

Frege, Gottlob. 1960. "On Sense and Reference." In *Translations from the Philosophical Writings of Gottlob Frege*, 2nd ed. Edited by Peter Geach and Max Black, 58–85. Oxford: Blackwell.

Friend, Theodore. 1988. *The Blue-Eyed Enemy: Japan against the West in Java and Luzon, 1942–1945*. Princeton, NJ: Princeton University Press.

Furnivall, John S. 1948. *Colonial Policy and Practice: A Comparative Study of Burma and Netherlands India*. Cambridge: Cambridge University Press.

Furnivall, John S. [1939] 1967. *Netherlands India: A Study of Plural Economy*. Cambridge, MA: Cambridge University Press.

Gal, Susan. 1989. "Language and Political Economy." *Annual Review of Anthropology* 18 (1): 345–67. http://dx.doi.org/10.1146/annurev.an.18.100189.002021.

Galeano, Eduardo. 1992. *We Say No: Chronicles of 1963–1991*. Translated by Mark Fried. New York: W.W. Norton.

Geertz, Clifford. 1963. *Peddlers and Princes: Social Change and Economic Modernization in Two Indonesian Towns*. Chicago: University of Chicago Press.

Ghosh, Amitav. 2001. *The Glass Palace*. New York: Random House.

Gill, Tom. 1999. "Wage Hunting at the Margins of Urban Japan." In *Lilies of the Field: Marginal People Who Live for the Moment*. Edited by Sophie Day, Evthymios Papataxiarchis, and Michael Stewart, 119–36. Boulder, CO: Westview Press.

Gillis, John. 1994. "Memory and Identity: The History of a Relationship." In *Commemorations: The Politics of National Identity*. Edited by John Gillis, 3–24. Princeton: Princeton University Press.

Goldberg, Michael. 1985. *The Chinese Connection: Getting Plugged in to Pacific Rim Real Estate, Trade, and Capital Markets*. Vancouver: University of British Columbia Press.

Gomez, Edmund T., and Jomo K.S. 1997. *Malaysia's Political Economy: Politics, Patronage and Profits*. New York: Cambridge University Press.

Goodwin, Charles, and John Heritage. 1990. "Conversation Analysis." *Annual Review of Anthropology* 19 (1): 286–307. http://dx.doi.org/10.1146/annurev.an.19.100190.001435.

Goodwin, Majorie Harness. 1990. *He-Said-She-Said: Talk as Social Organization among Black Children*. Bloomington: Indiana University Press.

Gordon, Avery. 1997. *Ghostly Matters: Haunting and the Sociological Imagination*. Minneapolis: University of Minnesota Press.

Goswami, Manu. 2004. *Producing India: From Colonial Space to National Economy*. Chicago: University of Chicago Press.

Gramsci, Antonio. 1971. *Selections from the Prison Notebooks*. Edited and translated by Quinten Hoare and Geoffrey Novell Smith. London: Lawrence and Wishart.

Grijpstra, B.G. 1976. *Common Efforts in the Development of Rural Sarawak, Malaysia*. Amsterdam, the Netherlands: Van Gorcum, Assen.

Guha, Ranajit. 1997. *Dominance without Hegemony: History and Power in Colonial India*. Cambridge, MA: Harvard University Press.

Hacking, Ian. 1990. *The Taming of Chance*. New York: Cambridge University Press.

Halbwachs, Maurice. [1950] 1980. *The Collective Memory*. Translated by Francis J. Ditter and Vidayazdi Ditter. New York: Harper and Row.

Halbwachs, Maurice. 1992. *On Collective Memory*. Edited and translated by Lewis A. Coser. Chicago: University of Chicago Press.

Hamilton, Carolyn. 1998. *Terrific Majesty: The Power of Shaka Zulu and the Limits of Historical Invention*. Cambridge, MA: Harvard University Press.

Hardy, Tim. 1963. *The Danger Within: A History of the Clandestine Communist Organization in Sarawak*. Kuching: Information Ministry of Sarawak.

Haugerud, Angelique, and Marc Edelman, eds. 2004. *The Anthropology of Development and Globalization: From Classical Political Economy to Contemporary Neoliberalism*. London: Blackwell.

Hegel, G.W.F. 1953. *Reason in History: A General Introduction to the Philosophy of History*. Translated by *Robert S. Hartman*. Indianapolis: Bobbs-Merrill Co.

Heidhues, Mary Somers. 1974. *Southeast Asia's Chinese Minorities*. Melbourne: Longman Australia..

Heidhues, Mary Somers. 1996. "Chinese Settlements in Rural Southeast Asia: Unwritten Histories." In *Sojourners and Settlers: Histories of Southeast Asia and the Chinese*. Edited by Anthony Reid, 164–82. Sydney, Australia: Allen and Unwin.

Heidhues, Mary Somers. 2003. *Golddiggers, Farmers, and Traders in Pontianak and the "Chinese Districts of West Kalimantan, Indonesia*. Ithaca, NY: Southeast Asia Publication Program, Cornell University.

Heidhues, Mary Somers. 2005. "The Makam Juang Mandor Monument: Re-
membering and Distorting the History of the Chinese in West Kalimantan."
In *Chinese Indonesians: Remembering, Distorting, Forgetting*. Edited by Tim
Lindsey and Helen Pausacker, 105–29. Singapore: Institute of Southeast
Asian Studies, and Australia: Monash Asia Institute.

Hobsbawm, Eric J. 1973. "Peasants and Politics." *Journal of Peasant Studies*
1 (1): 3–22. http://dx.doi.org/10.1080/03066157308437870.

Ho Tai, Hue-Tam, ed. 2001. *Country of Memory: Remaking the Past in Late Socialist Vietnam*. Berkeley: University of California Press.

Hsu, C.Y. 1983. *The Rise of Modern China*. Hong Kong: Oxford University Press.

Hui, Yew Foong. 2007. "Strangers at Home: History and Subjectivity among
the Chinese Communities of West Kalimantan, Indonesia." PhD diss., Cornell University.

Hutnyk, John. 2004. *Bad Marxism: Capitalism and Cultural Studies*. London:
Pluto Press.

Idhe, Don. 1976. *Listening and Voice: A Phenomenology of Sound*. Athens, OH:
Ohio University Press.

Irvine, Judith T. 1989. "When Talk Isn't Cheap: Language and Political
Economy." *American Ethnologist* 16 (2): 248–67. http://dx.doi.org/10.1525/
ae.1989.16.2.02a00040.

James, William. 1912. *Essays in Radical Empiricism*. New York: Longmans,
Green.

Jameson, Fredric. 1981. *The Political Unconscious: Narratives as a Symbolic Act*.
Ithaca, NY: Cornell University Press.

Jesudason, James. 1989. *Ethnicity and the Economy: The State, Chinese Business
and Multinationals in Malaysia*. Singapore: Oxford University Press.

Jing, Jun. 1996. *The Temple of Memories: History, Power, and Morality in a Chinese
Village*. Stanford, CA: Stanford University Press.

Jomo, K.S. 1986. *A Question of Class: Capital, the State, and Uneven Development
in Malaya*. Singapore: Oxford University Press.

Jones, Mathew. 2002. *Conflict and Confrontation in Southeast Asia, 1961–1965:
Britain, the United States, Indonesia, and the Creation of Malaysia*. Cambridge:
Cambridge University Press.

Fogel, Joshua, ed. 2000. *The Nanjing Massacre in History and Historiography*.
Berkeley: University of California Press. http://dx.doi.org/10.1525/
california/9780520220065.001.0001.

Kahn, Joel. 2006. *Other Malays: Nationalism and Cosmopolitanism in the Modern
Malay World*. Singapore: National University of Singapore Press.

Kant, Immanuel. [1952] 1964. *The Critique of Judgment*. Translated by James
Creed Meredity. Oxford: Clarendon Press.

Kant, Immanuel. 1974. *On the Old Saw: That May Be Right in Theory but It Won't Work in Practice*. Introduction by G. Miller. Translated by E.B. Ashton. Philadelphia: University of Pennsylvania Press.

Khalidi, Rashid. 2009. *Sowing Crisis: The Cold War and American Dominance in the Middle East*. Boston: Beacon Press.

Klima, Alan. 2002. *The Funeral Casino: Meditation, Massacre, and Exchange with the Dead in Thailand*. Princeton, NJ: Princeton University Press.

Kracauer, Siegfried. [1929] 1998. *The Salaried Masses: Duty and Distraction in Weimar Germany*. Translated by Quinten Hoare. New York: Verso.

Krishnan, Sanjay. 2007. *Reading the Global: Troubling Perspectives on Britain's Empire in Asia*. New York: Columbia University Press.

Kua, Kia Soong. 2007. *May 13: Declassified Documents on the Malaysian Riots of 1969*. Petaling Jaya, Selangor: Suaram Komunikasi.

Laidlaw, James. 2000. "A Free Gift Makes No Friends." *Journal of the Royal Anthropological Institute* 6 (4): 617–34. http://dx.doi.org/10.1111/1467-9655.00036.

Lambek, Michael. 1998. "The Sakalava Poiesis of History: Realizing the Past through Spirit Possessions in Madagascar." *American Ethnologist* 25 (2): 106–27. http://dx.doi.org/10.1525/ae.1998.25.2.106.

LaCapra, Dominick. 1994. *Representing the Holocaust: History, Theory, and Trauma*. Ithaca, NY: Cornell University Press.

Langer, Lawrence L. 1991. *Holocaust Testimonies: The Ruins of Memory*. New Haven: Yale University Press.

Langer, Lawrence L. 1995. *Admitting the Holocaust*. Oxford: Oxford University Press.

Lee, Yong Leng. 1970. *Population and Resettlement in Sarawak*. Singapore: Asia Pacific Press.

Lefebvre, Henri. 1976. *The Survival of Capitalism: Reproduction of the Relations of Production*. Translated by Frank Bryant. New York: St. Martin's Press.

Lefebvre, Henri. 1991. *The Production of Space*. Translated by Donald Nicolson-Smith. Oxford: Blackwell.

Legge, James. 1971. *Confucian Analects: The Great Learning, and the Doctrine of the Mean*. Translated by James Legge. New York: Dover Publications.

Leigh, Michael. 1974. *The Rising Moon: Political Change in Sarawak*. Sydney, Australia: Sydney University Press.

Li, Tania Murray. 1999. "Compromising Power: Development, Culture, and Rule in Indonesia." *Cultural Anthropology* 14 (3): 295–322. http://dx.doi.org/10.1525/can.1999.14.3.295.

Liew, Yung Tzu. 1956. *Ri Ben Zhi Xa de Sha Lao Yue* (Sarawak under the Japanese). Sibu, Sarawak: Hua Ping Press.

Lim, Pui Huen. 1970. "Newspapers Published in the Malaysian Area." Institute of Southeast Asian Studies, Occasional Paper #2. Singapore.

Lockard, Craig. 1973. "The Southeast Asian Town in Historical Perspective: A Social History of Kuching, Malaysia 1820–1970." PhD diss., University of Wisconsin.

Lowenthal, David. 1996. *The Heritage Crusade and the Spoils of History*. London: Viking. http://dx.doi.org/10.1017/CBO9780511523809.

Luhmann, Niklas. 1982. "The Autonomy of the Legal System." In *The Differentiation of Society*. Translated by Stephen Holmes and Charles Larmore, 122–37. New York: Columbia University Press.

Mackie, Jamie. 1974. *Konfrontasi: The Indonesian-Malaysia disputes, 1963–1966*. Kuala Lumpur: Oxford University Press.

Mackie, Jamie. 1996. "Introduction." In *Sojourners and Settlers: Histories of Southeast Asia and the Chinese*. Edited by Anthony Reid, xii–xxx. Sydney, Australia: Allen and Unwin.

Mahmud, E. 1993. "Kesan Perletakan Senjata Parti Komunis Malaya (PKM) dan Parti Komunis Kalimantan Utara (PKKU) Terhadap Masa Depan Tentera Darat" (The effects of arms surrendering by the Communist Party of Malaya and the North Kalimantan Communist Party towards the future of the armed forces of Malaysia). Debate held at the University Kebangsaan Malaysia.

Malkki, Liisa. 1995. *Purity and Exile*. Chicago: University of Chicago Press.

Malinowski, Bronislaw. 1922. *Argonauts of the Western Pacific: An Account of Native Enterprise and Adventure in the Archipelagos of Melanesian New Guinea*. London: Routledge.

Mamdani, Mahmood. 2000. "The Truth According to the TRC." In *The Politics of Memory: Truth, Healing and Social Justice*. Edited by Ifi Amadiume and Abdullah An-Na', 176–83. London: Zed Books.

Mamdani, Mahmood. 2001a. *When Victims Become Killers: Colonialism, Nativism and the Genocide in Rwanda*. Princeton: Princeton University Press.

Mamdani, Mahmood. 2001b. "Beyond Settler and Native as Political Identities: Overcoming the Political Legacy of Colonialism." *Society for Comparative Study of Society and History* 43: 651–64.

Mamdani, Mahmood. 2004. *Good Muslim, Bad Muslim: America, the Cold War, and the Roots of Terror*. New York: Three Leaves Press.

Mao Zedong. 1962. "Primer on Guerrilla War." In *The Guerrilla and How to Fight Him*. Edited by T.N. Greene and translated by S.B. Griffith II. New York: Frederick A Praeger.

Mauss, Marcel. [1950] 1990. *The Gift: The Form and Reason for Exchange in Archaic Societies*. Translated by W.D. Halls. New York: W.W. Norton.

Mauss, Marcel. 1973. "Techniques of the Body." In *Economy and Society* 2(1): 70-88.

Mbembe, Achille. 2001. *On the Postcolony*. Berkeley: University of California Press.

Mehmet, Ozay. 1986. *Development in Malaysia: Poverty, Wealth and Trusteeship*. London: Croom Helm.

Meister, Robert. 2011. *After Evil: A Politics of Human Rights*. New York: Columbia University Press.

Milner, Anthony. 1986. "Colonial Records History: British Malaya." *Kajian Malaysia* 4 (2): 1–8.

Mitchell, Timothy. 2000. *Questions of Modernity*. Minneapolis: University of Minnesota Press.

Montesano, Michael J. 2008. "Capital, State, and Society in the History of Chinese-Sponsored Education in Trang." In *Thai South and Malay North Ethnic Interactions on a Plural Peninsula*. Edited by Michael J. Montesano and Patrick Jory, 231–72. Singapore: National University of Singapore Press.

Moore, Sally Falk. 1998. "Systematic Judicial and Extra-Judicial Injustice: Preparation for Future Accountability." In *Memory and the Postcolony: African Anthropology and the Critique of Power*. Edited by Richard Werbner, 126–51. London: Zed Books.

Mrazek, Rudolf. 2010. *A Certain Age: Colonial Jakarta through the Memories of Its Intellectuals*. Durham, NC: Duke University Press.

Nietzsche, Friedrich. 1969. *On the Genealogy of Morals and Ecce Homo*. Translated by *Walter Kaufmann*. New York: Random House.

Nietzsche, Friedrich. 1978. *Thus Spoke Zarathustra: A Book for All and None*. Translated by Walter Kaufmann. Harmondsworth: Penguin.

Nietzsche, Friedrich. [1874] 1983. "On the Uses and Disadvantages of History for Life." In *Untimely Meditations*. Translated by R.J. Hollingdale, 57–123. Cambridge: Cambridge University Press. http://dx.doi.org/10.1017/CBO9780511812101.007.

Nietzsche, Friedrich. 1984. *Human, All Too Human: A Book for Free Spirits*. Translated by Marion Faber, with Stephen Lehmann. Lincoln: University of Nebraska Press.

Nonini, Donald M. 1997. "Shifting Identities, Position Imagineries: Transnational Traversals and Reversals by Malaysian Chinese." In *Ungrounded Empire: The Cultural Politics of Modern Chinese Transnationalism*. Edited by Aihwa Ong and Donald Nonini, 203–27. New York: Routledge.

Nonini, Donald M., and Aihwa Ong. 1997. "Introduction." In *Ungrounded Empire: The Cultural Politics of Modern Chinese Transnationalism*. Edited by Aihwa Ong and Donald Nonini, 3–33. New York: Routledge.

Nora, Pierre. 1996. *Conflicts and Divisions*. Vol. 1, *Realms of Memory: Rethinking the French Past*. Translated by Arthur Goldhammer. New York: Columbia University Press.

Nordstrom, Carolyn, and Antonius Robben. 1995. *Fieldwork Under Fire: Contemporary Studies of Violence and Culture*. Berkeley: University of California Press.

Ooi, Keat Gin. 1997. *Of Free Trade and Native Interests: The Brookes and the Economic Development of Sarawak, 1841–1941*. Kuala Lumpur: Oxford University Press.

Osman-Rani, Hassan. 1990. "Economic Development and Ethnic Integration: The Malaysian Experience." *Sojourn (Singapore)* 5 (1): 1–34. http://dx.doi.org/10.1355/SJ5-1A.

Pandey, Gyanendra. 1999. *Remembering Partition: Violence, Nationalism, and History in India*. Cambridge: Cambridge University Press.

Pandey, Gyanendra. 2005. *Routine Violence: Nations, Fragments, Histories*. Stanford, CA: Stanford University Press.

Peluso, Nancy Lee. 2006. "Passing the Red Bowl: Creating Community Identity through Violence in West Kalimantan, 1967–1997." In *Violent Conflicts in Indonesia: Analysis, Representation, Resolution*. Edited by Charles Coppel, 106–28. New York: Routledge.

Porrit, Vernon Leslie. 1991. "The Dynamics of the Politics of Enforced Resettlement in Sarawak in 1965." BA thesis, Murdoch University, West Australia.

Porrit, Vernon Leslie. 2004. *The Rise and Fall of Communism in Sarawak*. Victoria, Australia: Monash University Press.

Poulantzas, Nicos. 1978. *State, Power, Socialism*. Translated by Patrick Camiller. London: New Left Books.

Poulgrain, Greg. 1998. *The Genesis of Konfrontasi: Malaysia, Brunei, Indonesia, 1945–1965*. Bathurst, Australia: Crawford House Publishing.

Purcell, Victor. [1951] 1965. *The Chinese in Southeast Asia*. London: Oxford University Press.

Purdey, Jemma. 2006. "The 'Other' May Riots: Anti-Chinese Violence in Solo, May 1998." In *Violent Conflicts in Indonesia: Analysis, Representation, Resolution*. Edited by Charles Coppel, 72–89. New York: Routledge.

Pusat Arakib Negara (National Archives). 1994. *Counter Insurgency in Sarawak 1963–74*. Sarawak: Sarawak Branch.

Radtke, Kurt. 1999. "Remembering and Forgetting in China and Japan." In *Remembering and Forgetting*. Lund, Sweden, 15–17 April 1999. Nordic Institute of Asian Studies and the Centre for East and Southeast Asian Studies at the University of Lund.

Ramsey, Robert S. 1987. *The Languages of China*. Princeton, NJ: Princeton University Press.

Redfield, Marc. 1999. "Imagi-Nation: The Imagined Community and the Aesthetics of Mourning." *Diacritics* 29 (4): 58–83. http://dx.doi.org/10.1353/dia.1999.0033.

Reid, Anthony. 1980. "Indonesia: From Briefcase to Samurai Sword." In *Southeast Asia under Japanese Occupation*. Edited by A.W. McCoy, 16–32. New Haven: Yale University Southeast Asian Studies.

Reid, Anthony. 2005. "Remembering and Forgetting War and Revolution." In *Beginning to Remember: The Past in the Indonesian Present*. Edited by Mary S. Zurbuchen, 168–91. Singapore: Singapore University Press.

Reid, Anthony. 2010. *Imperial Alchemy: Nationalism and Political Identity in Southeast Asia*. New York: Cambridge University Press.

Rizal, Josè. 1997. *Noli Me Tangere* (Touch me not). Translated by Ma. Soledad Lacson-Locsin. Honolulu: University of Hawai'i Press.

Runciman, Steven. 1960. *The White Rajahs: A History of Sarawak from 1841 to 1946*. Cambridge: Cambridge University Press.

Sai, Siew Min. 2006. "'Eventing' the May 1998 Affair: Problematic Representations of Violence in Contemporary Indonesia." *Violent Conficts in Indonesia: Analysis, Representation, Resolution*. Edited by Charles Coppel, 39–57. New York: Routledge.

Said, Sanid. 1976. *Anti-Cession Movement, 1946-51: The Birth of Nationalism in Sarawak*. BA Thesis, University of Malaya.

Sarawak Gazette. 1965. Editorial. *Sarawak Gazette*. July 17: 1.

Sassen, Saskia. 2006. *Territory, Authority, Rights: From Medieval to Global Assemblages*. Princeton, NJ: Princeton University Press.

Schmitt, Carl. [1932] 1996. *The Concept of the Political*. Chicago: University of Chicago Press.

Scholte, Jan. 2000. *Globalisation: A Critical Introduction*. Basingstoke, UK: Macmillan.

Schrift, Alan. 1997. "Introduction: Why Gift?" In *The Logic of the Gift: Toward an Ethic of Generosity*. Edited by Alan Schrift, 1–22. New York: Routledge.

Scott, James. 1985. *Weapons of the Weak: Everyday Forms of Peasant Resistance*. New Haven: Yale University Press.

Searle, John R. 1958. "Proper Names." *Mind* 67 (266): 166–73. http://dx.doi.org/10.1093/mind/LXVII.266.166.

Short, Anthony. 1975. *The Communist Insurrection in Malaya 1948-60*. London: Frederick Muller.

Simpson, Bradley R. 2008. *Economists with Guns: Authoritarian Development and U.S.–Indonesian Relations, 1960–1968*. Stanford, CA: Stanford University Press.

Skinner, William G. 1957. *Chinese Society in Thailand: An Analytical History*. Ithaca, NY: Cornell University Press.

Skinner, William G. 1996. "Creolized Chinese Societies in Southeast Asia." In
    Sojourners and Settlers: Histories of Southeast Asia and the Chinese. Edited by
    Anthony Reid, 51–93. Sydney, Australia: Allen and Unwin.
Slyomovics, Susan. 2005. *The Performance of Human Rights in Morocco.* Phila-
    delphia: University of Pennsylvania Press. http://dx.doi.org/10.1525/
    an.2005.46.5.23.2.
Smith, Adam. [1776] 2003. *The Wealth of Nations.* New York: Bantam Book.
Sodhy, Pamela. 1988. "Malaysian–American Relations During Indonesia's
    Confrontation against Malaysia, 1963–1966." *Journal of Southeast Asian Stud-
    ies* 19 (01): 111–36. http://dx.doi.org/10.1017/S0022463400000369.xxx.
Soja, Edward. 2000. *Postmetropolis: Critical Studies of Cities and Regions.* Oxford:
    Blackwell.
Soon, Alice Tay Erh. 1962. "Chinese in Southeast Asia." *Race* 4 (1): 34–48.
    http://dx.doi.org/10.1177/030639686200400104.
Sri Aman: Peace Restored in Sarawak. 1974. Compiled and published by the
    Malaysian Information Services, Sarawak.
Staar, Richard F., ed. 1969. "Malaysia." In *Yearbook on International Affairs, 1968,*
    383–91. Palo Alto, CA: Hoover Institute Publications.
Steedly, Margaret. 1993. *Hanging Without a Rope: Narrative Experience in Colo-
    nial and Postcolonial Karoland.* Princeton, NJ: Princeton University Press.
Stoler, Ann. 2010. *Along the Archival Grain: Epistemic Anxieties and Colonial Com-
    mon Sense.* Princeton, NJ: Princeton University Press.
Strauch, Judith. 1981. *Chinese Village Politics in the Malaysian State.* Cambridge,
    MA: Harvard University Press.
Subritzky, John. 1999. *Confronting Sukarno: British, American, Australian and
    New Zealand Diplomacy in the Malaysian-Indonesian Confrontation, 1961–65.*
    New York: St. Martin's Press.
Tai, Hung-chao, ed. 1989. *Confucianism and Economic Development: An Oriental
    Alternative?* Washington, DC: Washington Institute for Values in Public Policy.
Tambiah, Stanley J. 1996. *Leveling Crowds: Ethnonationalist Conflicts and Collec-
    tive Violence in South Asia.* Berkeley: University of California Press.
Taussig, Michael. 1977. "The Genesis of Capitalism amongst a South Ameri-
    can Peasantry: Devil's Labor and the Baptism of Money." *Comparative
    Studies in Society and History* 19 (02): 130–55. http://dx.doi.org/10.1017/
    S0010417500008586.
Taussig, Michael. 1992. *Nervous System.* New York: Routledge.
Taussig, Michael. 1999. *Defacement: Public Secrecy and the Labor of the Negative.*
    Stanford, CA: Stanford University Press.
Taussig, Michael. 2004. *My Cocaine Museum.* Chicago: University of Chicago
    Press.

Tay, Elaine. 2006. "Discursive Violence on the Internet and the May 1968 Riots." In *Violent Conflicts in Indonesia: Analysis, Representation, Resolution.* Edited by Charles Coppel, 58–71. New York: Routledge.

Tejapira, Kasian. 1992. "Pigtail: A Prehistory of Chineseness in Siam." *Sojourn (Singapore)* 7 (1): 95–122. http://dx.doi.org/10.1355/SJ7-1D.

Teng, David L.C., and Daniel K.A. Ngieng. 1990. *The Challenges: SUPP in Focus.* Sibu, Sarawak: Think Management Consultants and Services Sendirian Berhad.

Teo, Kok Seong. 2008. "Chinese–Malay–Thai Interactions and the Making of Kelantan Peranakan Chinese Ethnicity." In *Thai South and Malay North Ethnic Interactions on a Plural Peninsula.* Edited by Michael J. Montesano and Patrick Jory, 214–30. Singapore: National University of Singapore Press.

Thant, U. 1963. "Mission to Sarawak and Sabah, Secretary-General's Conclusions." *United Nation Review* 10 (9): 1–15.

The Vanguard. 1965. Editorial. *The Vanguard.* July 7: 1.

Thompson, Edward Palmer. 1980. *The Making of the English Working Class.* London: V. Gollancz.

Thongchai, Winichakul. 1997. *Siam Mapped: The History of the Geo-Body of a Nation.* Honolulu: University of Hawai'i Press. http://dx.doi.org/10.1002/9780470979587.ch53.

Thongchai, Winichakul. 2002. "Remembering/Silencing the Traumatic Past: The Ambivalent Memories of the October 1976 Massacre in Bangkok." In *Cultural Crisis and Social Memory: Modernity and Identity in Thailand and Laos.* Edited by Shigeharo Tanabe and Charles F. Keyes, 243–83. Honolulu: University of Hawai'i Press.

T'ien, Ju-Kang. [1953] 1997. *The Chinese of Sarawak.* Kuching: Research and Resource Centre Committee, SUPP Headquarters.

Todorov, Tzvetan. 1984. *Mikhail Bakhtin: The Dialogic Principle.* Minneapolis: University of Minnesota Press.

Toer, Pramoedya Ananta. 1996. *This Earth of Mankind.* Translated by Max Lane. New York: Penguin.

Trinh, Min-ha T. 1989. *Woman, Native, Other: Writing Post-Coloniality and Feminism.* Bloomington: Indiana University Press.

Trouillot, Michel-Rolph. 1995. *Silencing the Past: Power and the Production of History.* Boston: Beacon Press.

Teubner, Gunther. 1989. "How the Law Thinks: Toward a Constructivist Epistemology of Law." *Law & Society Review* 23 (5): 727–58. http://dx.doi.org/10.2307/3053760.

Uehling, Greta Lynn. 2004. *Beyond Memory: The Crimean Tatars' Deportation and Return.* New York: Palgrave Macmillan.

United States Information Agency (USIA). 1963. "Sarawak and North Borneo Insurgency: Racial and Ethnic Factors." R-118–63 [AF], June 17. Washington, DC: USIA.

Van der Kroef, Justus M. 1966a. "Communism and Chinese Communalism in Sarawak." *China Quarterly* 20 (October–December): 38–66.

Van der Kroef, Justus M. 1966b. "Communism and the Guerilla War in Sarawak." *World Today* 20: 50–60.

van Zyl, Paul. 2005. "Dealing with the Past: Reflections on South Africa, East Timor and Indonesia." In *Beginning to Remember: The Past in the Indonesian Present*. Edited by Mary S. Zurbuchen, 324–42. Singapore: Singapore University Press.

Walker, John. 2002. *Power and Prowess: The Origins of Brooke Kingship in Sarawak*. Crows Nest, Australia: Allen and Unwin.

Wallenstein, Immanuel. 1974. *The Modern World-System: Capitalist Agriculture and the Origins of the European World-Economy in the Sixteenth Century*. New York: Academic Press.

Wang, Gungwu. 1981. *Community and Nation: Essays on Southeast Asia and the Chinese*. Sydney: Allen and Unwin.

Wang, Gungwu. 1996. Sojourning: The Chinese Experience in Southeast Asia. In *Sojourners and Settlers: Histories of Southeast Asia and the Chinese*. Edited by Anthony Reid, 1–14. Sydney: Allen and Unwin.

Werbner, Richard. 1995. "Human Rights and Moral Knowledge: Argument of Accountability in Zimbabwe." In *Shifting Contexts*. Edited by Marilyn Strathern, 99–116. London: Routledge. http://dx.doi.org/10.4324/9780203450901_chapter_5.

Wertheim, Wim F. 1964. *East–West Parallels: Sociological Approaches to Modern Asian*. The Hague: V. Van Hoeve.

Wertheim, Wim F. 1995. "The Contribution of Weberian Sociology to Studies of Southeast Asia." *Journal of Southeast Asian Studies* 26 (1): 17–29. http://dx.doi.org/10.1017/S0022463400010456.

Wickberg, Edgar. 1965. *The Chinese in Philippine Life, 1850–1898*. New Haven: Yale University Press.

Williams, Lea. 1960. *Overseas Chinese Nationalism*. Glencoe, IL: The Free Press.

Wong, Yee Tuan. 2008. "Penang's Big Five Families and Southern Siam during the Nineteenth Century." In *Thai South and Malay North Ethnic Interactions on a Plural Peninsula*. Edited by Michael J. Montesano and Patrick Jory, 201–13. Singapore: National University of Singapore Press.

Yen, Ching-hwang. 1970. "Ch'ing Sale of Honors and the Chinese Leadership in Singapore and Malaya (1877–1912)." *Journal of Southeast Asian Studies* 1 (2): 20–32. http://dx.doi.org/10.1017/S0022463400020221.

Yen, Ching-hwang. 1976. *The Overseas Chinese and the 1911 Revolution*. Kuala Lumpur: Oxford University Press.

Yoneyama, Lisa. 1994. "Taming the MemoryScape: Hiroshima's Urban Renewal." In *Remapping Memory: The Politics of TimeSpace*. Edited by Johathan Boyarin, 99–137. Minneapolis: University of Minnesota Press.

Yong, Kee Howe. 2007a. "Divergent Interpretations of Communism and Currents of Duplicity in Post-Cold War Sarawak." *Critique of Anthropology* 27 (1): 63–86. http://dx.doi.org/10.1177/0308275X07073819.

Yong, Kee Howe. 2007b. "The Politics and Aesthetics of Place-Names in Sarawak." *Anthropological Quarterly* 80 (1): 65–91.

Yong, Stephen. 1998. *A Life Twice Lived: A Memoir*. Kuching: Borneo Adventure.

Yoshihara, Kunio. 1988. *The Rise of Ersatz Capitalism in Southeast Asia*. Singapore: Oxford University Press.

Young, James E. 1990. *Writing and Rewriting the Holocaust: Narrative and the Consequences of Interpretations*. Bloomington: Indiana University Press.

Zizek, Slavoy. 2008. *Six Sideways Reflections*. London: Profile Press.

Zurbuchen, Mary S., ed. 2005. *Beginning to Remember: The Past in the Indonesian Present*. Singapore: Singapore University Press.

Index

role of, 19–20; workday routine of, 208n14

bus drivers: and communication with office staff, 155–6; indifference of, 171–3; relationship with management, 163–73; social role of, 19–20; workday routine of, 208n14

business partnerships: and race, 42–3

capitalism: and charity, 11–12; state capitalists in Malaysia, 40–2

Chao Kui Ho: after "coming out," 75–9; and the people's court, 81–3

Cheok, Bong Kee. See Bong Kee Cheok

Chinese (language): reading of, 102–3; speech groups, 35–6, 59, 187n2

Chinese (people): and communism, 37, 53; discrimination against, 30–1; and Eastern philosophy, 138–50; and ethnic labels, 135–6; history in Southeast Asia, 29–38; in Indonesia vs. Sarawak, 145; and Japanese Occupation, 6–7, 34–5; and politics, 145–6

Chinese-Malay relations: and business loans, 202n13; differing treatment of groups, 85–6; favouritism for Malays, 132–3; in government, 123–4; and *Zhong Yong*, 141–2

Chinese newspapers, 36, 37–8

Chung Hwa schools: and pan-dialect unity, 35–6; prevalence of, 102–3

citizenship: and race, 38–9

Clandestine Communist Organizations, 70

clothing vendors, 75–6, 78–80

Cold War, the, 9, 11–13, 18; continuation to present, 191n31; economy of, 16–17; and memory, 108–9,

126; and political economy, 11–12; relocation during, 115–16

collective memory, 4–5; and individual memory, 201–2n7; problems with term, 188n6; in repressive society, 203n15; and violence, 8–9

colonial government: and bus company operation, 94–7

colonialism, 5–6; Britain in Malaysia, 50–2; effects of, 32–3, 61–2, 192n6; and newspaper bias, 18–19

"coming out" as communist, 76–7; Bong Kee Cheok, 72–3; Chao Kui Ho, 75–9; gifts for, 72–3, 202n12

common enemy (term), 22

communism, 22; ability to discuss, 89–90, 199–200n29; as a Chinese problem, 53, 56, 59; current portrayal of, 69; end of in Sarawak, 68–9; and identity, 80–1; linked to SUPP, 51–2; local aid to, 128; official history vs. reality, 23–4, 68–9; organization of movements, 201n4; reasons for joining, 80; and Sarawak Omnibus Company (SOC) (*see* Sarawak Omnibus Company); statistics of, 194–5n3, 196n11

communist identity: allure of, 125–6; determination of, 108–10; difficulty of determining, 119–20

communist pamphlets: distribution by bus company, 101–3, 106

Communist Party of Malaya (CPM): and Malayan Emergency, 54–5

communist-influenced areas, 59–60

conductors. See bus conductors

Constitution of Malaysia: Article153, 38–9

conversation vs. dialogue, 204n2

coolies, recruitment of, 29–30

corruption: and Malaysian politics, 22–3

Malay-Chinese relations: and business loans, 202n13; differing treatment of groups, 85–6; favouritism for Malays, 132–3; in government, 123–4; and *Zhong Yong*, 141–2

Malayan Emergency, The, 54–5

Malayan People's Anti-Japanese Party (MPAJA): removal from history, 78

Malaysia: corruption in, 22–3; and democracy, 9; East vs. West, 7–8; economy of, 21; formation of, 50–2

marital status: as topic of gossip, 127

Marshall Plan, 9–10, 11; Georges Bataille on, 15

massacre of Chinese in Indonesia, 206n19

Mauss, Marcel: definition of *habitus*, 46; *The Gift*, 13–14

May 13 Incident, 39–40

memory, 8–9, 60, 62–3; burden of, 84; and the Cold War, 126; as embedded, 213–14n2; and forgetfulness, 203n15; and history, 178–81; and the Holocaust, 60–1; in repressive societies, 203n15; and silence, 24–6, 110; sites of, 4–5. *See also* collective memory

merchants at the Main Bazaar, 46–8

minivans: vs. bus companies, 95–6; use by Malays vs. Hakkas, 85–6

modernizing state projects, 135

molestation in *new villages*, 117–18

MPAJA. *See* Malayan People's Anti-Japanese Party (MPAJA)

narratives, performance of, 62–3

National Economic Policy (NEP): and Chinese achievement, 193n17; economic effects of, 212n8; hypocrisy of, 40–4

National Operations Council (NOC), 40

nationalism, 6–7, 21–2

new villages: conditions in, 57, 114–15, 128–30; employment in, 113–14; as *gift*, 57–8; invention of, 45; and Malayan Emergency, 54–5; and memory, 47, 112–13; names of, 63; and Operation Hammer, 57–8; violence in, 114–18, 122–4, 128

newspapers, 36, 37–8, 192n8; colonial bias in, 18–19

ngayau: definition, 199n27

Nietzsche, Friedrich: and the burden of debt, 15–16; on forgetfulness, 23; on history, 169

NOC. *See* National Operations Council (NOC)

Nora, Pierre, 4–5

North Kalimantan National Army. *See Tentera Nasional Kalimantan Utara* (TNKU)

nuclear power, 37–8

Ong Kee Hui, 3–4, 5

Operation Hammer, 57–60; acknowledgment of, 64–6; length of restrictions, 207n3

overseas Chinese (in Southeast Asia): as financial resource for China, 124; history of, 29–38; and integration theory, 31–2; use of term, 191n1

padi schemes, 41

Pakatan Rakyat (PR), 210n9

pamphlets, anti-government/ communist: distribution by bus company, 101–3, 106

pan-dialect unity, 35

PEMANDU, 43–4; cost of, 194n21

pembangunan (development): and the State, 136–7

People's Party of Brunei (PRB), 51

people's court, 81–3

Sarawak United People's Party
(SUPP): formation of, 20, 36–7;
and joining the coalition government, 146–7; linked to communism, 51–2; opposition to Greater
Malaysia Plan, 51–2; and Sarawak
Omnibus Company (SOC), 104,
105, 108–9, 110; and *Zhong Yong*,
142–3, 144, 148, 151–2
Schmitt, Carl, 12
school: Chung Hwa, 35–6, 102–3; for
non-Malay families, 206n15
Searle, John, 66–7
Second Imperial World War, 35–8
sexual assault in *new villages*, 117–18
Sibu: and Sarawak Omnibus
Company (SOC), 154–5
Siburan. *See new villages*
silence: and forgetfulness, 69–70;
and history, 200n1; meaning of in
work, 24–6, 180; and narratives,
62; as protection, 181–2
Simanggang, 71–5
Simpson, Bradley, 12–13
Sinophobia, 30–1
Slyomovics, Susan, 24
SMH. *See* Sarawak Multipurpose
Holdings (SMH)
Smith, Adam: *The Wealth of Nations*,
189n20
SOC. *See* Sarawak Omnibus Com-
pany (SOC)
soldiers: in *new villages*, 116–18,
123–4; soldiering as a job, 79
Special Branch: establishment of,
196n9; and Malayan Emergency,
54–5
speech group differences (Chinese),
35–6
speeches on development, 136–7
squatters, resettlement of, 131–2
Sri Aman, 71–5
Sri Aman Treaty, 68–72

state capitalist class, 40–2
state discourse, 136–8
statistics: of communism, 194–5n3,
196n11; as problematic, 210n8
stories, variations in, 122–3, 124–5
SUPP. *See* Sarawak United People's
Party (SUPP)
surveillance, fear of, 128–30
swa ngiau chee (jungle rat): vs. "good
mice," 76–7; boasts about, 125

tax, for bus company, 94–7
Tentera Nasional Kalimantan Utara
(TNKU), 51
Teochiu-Hakka relations, 47–8
three heroes, 3, 4
TNKU. *See Tentera Nasional Kaliman-
tan Utara* (TNKU)
torture, 147–8, 208n10
Transfer ID, 120–1, 206n17
Trobrianders, 13–14
truth and reconciliation commis-
sions: establishment of, 177–8;
problems with, 213n1
Tunku. *See* Rahman, Tunku Abdul

UMNO. *See* United Malays National
Organization (UMNO)
unfamiliarity, as tactic, 114
union for bus employees, 160–7
United Malays National Organization (UMNO): and elections/
democracy, 9; explusion of Singapore, 7; and the May 13 Incident,
39–40; and race/citizenship, 38–9,
188–9n12; and state capitalism,
40–2
United Nations Development
Program, 10–11
unsaid. *See* silence

violence, 4; "out there," 122–3;
expression of, 45; of the gift,

ANTHROPOLOGICAL HORIZONS

Editor: Michael Lambek, University of Toronto

Published to date:

The House of Difference: Cultural Politics and National Identity in Canada / Eva Mackey (2002)

Writing and Colonialism in Northern Ghana: The Encounter between the LoDagaa and the 'World on Paper,' 1892–1991 / Sean Hawkins (2002)

Guardians of the Transcendent: An Ethnography of a Jain Ascetic Community / Anne Vallely (2002)

The Hot and the Cold: Ills of Humans and Maize in Native Mexico / Jacques M. Chevalier and Andrés Sánchez Bain (2003)

Figured Worlds: Ontological Obstacles in Intercultural Relations / Edited by John Clammer, Sylvie Poirier, and Eric Schwimmer (2004)

Revenge of the Windigo: The Construction of the Mind and Mental Health of North American Aboriginal Peoples / James B. Waldram (2004)

The Cultural Politics of Markets: Economic Liberalization and Social Change in Nepal / Katherine Neilson Rankin (2004)

A World of Relationships: Itineraries, Dreams, and Events in the Australian Western Desert / Sylvie Poirier (2005)

The Politics of the Past in an Argentine Working-Class Neighbourhood / Lindsay DuBois (2005)

Youth and Identity Politics in South Africa, 1990-1994 / Sibusisiwe Nombuso Dlamini (2005)

Maps of Experience: The Anchoring of Land to Story in Secwepemc Discourse / Andie Diane Palmer (2005)

Beyond Bodies: Rain-Making and Sense-Making in Tanzania / Todd Sanders (2008)

We Are Now a Nation: Croats between 'Home' and 'Homeland' / Daphne N. Winland (2008)

Kaleidoscopic Odessa: History and Place in Post-Soviet Ukraine / Tanya Richardson (2008)

Invaders as Ancestors: On the Intercultural Making and Unmaking of Spanish Colonialism in the Andes / Peter Gose (2008)

From Equality to Inequality: Social Change among Newly Sedentary Lanoh Hunter-Gatherer Traders of Peninsular Malaysia / Csilla Dallos (2011)

Rural Nostalgias and Transnational Dreams: Identity and Modernity among Jat Sikhs / Nicola Mooney (2011)

Dimensions of Development: History, Community, and Change in Allpachico, Peru / Susan Vincent (2012)

People of Substance: An Ethnography of Morality in the Colombian Amazon / Carlos David Londoño Sulkin (2012)

'We Are Still Didene': Stories of Hunting and History from Northern British Columbia / Thomas McIlwraith (2012)

Being Māori in the City: Indigenous Everyday Life in Auckland / Natacha Gagné (2013)

The Hakkas of Sarawak: Sacrificial Gifts in Cold War Era Malaysia / Kee Howe Yong (2013)